OUTLINES OF THE
LIFE OF CHRIST

BY

W. SANDAY, D.D., LL.D., Litt.D.

LADY MARGARET PROFESSOR AND CANON OF CHRIST CHURCH, OXFORD
HON. FELLOW OF EXETER COLLEGE
FELLOW OF THE BRITISH ACADEMY
CHAPLAIN - IN - ORDINARY TO THE KING

SECOND EDITION
REVISED, WITH ADDITIONS

EDINBURGH: T. & T. CLARK, 38 GEORGE STREET
1906

J.P. Evans

Pencader

Flint

Blaenau

Garth

OUTLINES OF
THE LIFE OF CHRIST

PRINTED BY
MORRISON AND GIBB LIMITED,

FOR

T. & T. CLARK, EDINBURGH.

LONDON : SIMPKIN, MARSHALL, HAMILTON, KENT, AND CO. LIMITED.
NEW YORK: CHARLES SCRIBNER'S SONS.

PREFACE TO THE SECOND EDITION

———◆———

In preparing to issue a second edition of this little book, the writer has been very conscious that it represents, not only the general position but the position in his own mind of the years 1898–1899 rather than of 1905. It was explained in the Preface to the First Edition that he deliberately abstained from attempting to bring the book really up to date. His reasons for this abstention were two : partly because such advances as he is able to make proceed as a rule by steps, and it seemed better that the steps should be allowed to stand out distinctly than that they should be confused and obliterated ; and partly, it seemed, that the great amount of time that would have been taken up in re-casting and adapting the old work would be better employed upon the larger undertaking which is promised for the future. It seemed better to look forward than to look backward.

In the meantime, as some substitute for a more systematic treatment, the writer may be excused for referring to his own books and papers, written since 1899, which are really grouped round the central subject

v

and were intended to carry forward the study of it.
The list is as follows:

An Examination of Harnack's 'What is Christianity?'
London: Longmans, 1901. A pamphlet, out of
print.

Paper read at the Church Congress at Northampton on
'The Miracles and Supernatural Character of the
Gospels.' October 1902.
  This subject is taken up again in *The Criticism of the
Fourth Gospel*, pp. 169–184.

Sermon on 'The Virgin Birth of our Lord Jesus Christ,'
published in a volume entitled *Critical Questions*.
London: S. C. Brown, Langham & Co., 1903.

Sacred Sites of the Gospels. Oxford: Clarendon Press,
1903.

'The Site of Capernaum,' in *The Journal of Theological
Studies*, v. 42 ff. October 1903.
  The object of this article was to retract a view pre-
viously expressed and to give a definite preference to
the common identification of Capernaum with *Tell Ḥûm*.

Paper read at the Church Congress at Bristol on 'The
Interpretation of the Gospels as affected by the
Newer Historical Methods.' October 1903.

'The Injunctions of Silence in the Gospels,' an article
in *The Journal of Theological Studies*, v. 321 ff.
April 1904.
  This article contains a criticism of Wrede, *Das
Messiasgeheimnis in den Evangelien*. Göttingen, 1901.

The Criticism of the Fourth Gospel. Oxford : Clarendon
Press ; New York : Scribner's, 1905. Eight lectures on the Morse Foundation, delivered in
the Union Seminary, New York. October and
November 1904.

These lectures may be taken as justifying the use
that is made of the Fourth Gospel ; they also discuss
the principles of criticism, and the way in which criticism has been applied to the Gospel in recent years.

Paper read at the Diocesan Conferences at Chichester
and Taunton on ' The Gospels in the Light
of Recent Historical Criticism.' October and
November 1905.

In near proximity to some of the above papers will
be found others by well-known writers, dealing with
similar topics and in the same general spirit : *e.g.*, in
the Reports of the two Church Congresses at Northampton and Bristol, in the volume *Critical Questions*
(sermons by Dr. Swete and Dr. A. Robertson), and in
The Journal of Theol. Studies (especially an important
article by Dr. Chase on ' The Lord's Command to
Baptize,' St. Matt. xxviii. 19, which appeared in July
1905). Mention should be also made of papers on the
Incarnation by the Dean of Westminster, and on the
Virgin Birth by Dr. R.J. Knowling (both London, 1903),
and of three valuable essays on subjects connected with
the Gospels by Drs. J. O. F. Murray, F. H. Chase and
A. J. Mason, in the recently published *Cambridge
Theological Essays*.

Two of the papers in the list given above were
devoted to a survey of the critical situation relating to
the Gospels in the years 1903 and 1905 ; and it has been

thought that they might with advantage be reprinted as Appendices to the present volume. It is hoped that they may serve to give some account of the course of thought in the last six years. A few slight omissions and alterations have been made in the text, to avoid repetition. It may also be explained that the time allowed for the reading of the first paper was limited, while there was no limit in the case of the second.

A generous critic of the book on the Fourth Gospel, in *The Oxford Magazine*, reminded the writer of the obligation which he has assumed by the promise of a larger work on the Life of Christ, and seemed to think of these other publications as standing in the way of the fulfilment of that promise. The writer may, however, be allowed to say that he does not himself regard them in this light. He is most anxious to fulfil his promise; but he has permitted himself to engage in these apparent digressions, at once as a help towards digesting his materials, and also that he may by these means make his larger work more compact and concentrated when the time for it comes.

December 1905.

PREFACE TO THE FIRST EDITION

———◆———

THE Publishers are of opinion that the time has now come when it would be right to accede to a wish that has been expressed in various quarters, for a separate issue of the article JESUS CHRIST in volume ii. of Dr. Hastings' *Dictionary of the Bible*. This volume appeared in 1899; and it has been thought best to reprint the article much as it stood, with such amount of change as is necessary to carry out the principle of *mutatis mutandis*, and to convert it into a book. The writer is engaged upon a larger work on the same subject, which is not likely to appear for some years; and he thinks it better not to attempt to bring his first experiment more strictly up to date, but rather to leave it as an expression of his own mind and of such a view as he was able to form of the general position at the time when it was written, *i.e.* in the years preceding 1899. The principal addition to the present issue is the map, which has been carefully prepared by Messrs. W. & A. K. Johnston, on the basis mainly of the map in the writer's *Sacred Sites of the Gospels* (Oxford, 1903), with improvements and with some additions suggested by the map to illustrate the article ROADS AND TRAVEL by Professors Buhl and W. M. Ramsay, in the *Extra Volume of the Dictionary;* and also by the map accompanying an article on the 'Onomasticon' of Eusebius published in the *Zeitschrift d. Deutschen Palästina-Vereins*, vol. xxvi. part 4 (Leipzig, 1903). The map further embodies the writer's changed opinion as to the site of Capernaum, explained in the *Journal of Theological Studies* for October 1903. It will be understood that the purpose was to illustrate the state of Palestine in or near the time of our Lord, and in part to connect it with the Palestine of the present day. For this reason a few crusading or modern sites are given where there are still notable ruins. The free use that has been made of the map in *Sacred Sites* is with the kind permission of the Delegates of the Clarendon Press.

OXFORD, *January* 1905.

N.B.—The abbreviations in this book are those adopted in Hastings' *Dictionary of the Bible* (Edinburgh : T. & T. Clark).

CONTENTS

CONTENTS

APPENDIX I.

APPENDIX II.

OUTLINES OF
THE LIFE OF CHRIST

———◆———

CHAPTER I.

INTRODUCTORY.

§ **1.** *Method.*—What method is fittest for a Christian
writer to use in approaching the Life of Christ? There
is a tendency at the present moment, on the Continent
perhaps rather than in England, to approach it from
the side of the consciousness of Jesus as the Messiah.
A conspicuous instance of this would be Baldensperger's
Das Selbstbewusstsein Jesu (Strassburg, 1888; 2nd ed.
1892), a work which attracted considerable attention
when it first appeared. No doubt such a method has
its advantages. It places the inquirer at once at the
centre of the position, and enables him to look down
the various roads by which he will have to travel. The
advantage, however, is more apparent than real. It
would hold good only if we could be sure of obtain-
ing a far more adequate grasp of the consciousness

I

to be investigated than on any hypothesis is likely to be obtained.   On the Christian hypothesis, frankly held, any such grasp would seem to be excluded, and the attempt to reach it could hardly be made without irreverence.

It is on all grounds a safer and sounder, as well as a more promising method, to adopt a course which is the opposite of this—not to work from within outwards, but from without inwards; to begin with that aspect of the Life which is most external, and only when we have realized this as well as we may to seek to penetrate deeper, allowing the facts to suggest their own inner meaning.   We may then take in certain sidelights which our documents also afford us, which, because they come, as it were, from the side, are not therefore less valuable.   And we may finally strengthen our conclusions by following the history some little way into its sequel.   In other words, we shall begin by placing ourselves at the standpoint of an observer, one of those who saw the public ministry of Jesus in its early stages, in its development, and to its close.   When that has been fully unrolled before us, we can draw upon other data which are not of this public character; and we may further seek to argue backwards from effects to causes.

By pursuing this method we shall have the advantage of taking the facts in no imaginary order, but in the order of the history itself.   We shall have them disclosed to us in the same sort of sequence in which they were disclosed to the first generations of Christians— a method always advisable where it can be had, and in this instance peculiarly advisable, because both the origins and the immediate sequel to the origins are of extreme interest and importance.

We shall also have the incidental advantage of following, not only the historical order, but the critical order suggested by the documents. It was natural that what was transacted in public should have the fullest and the earliest attestation: it lay in the nature of the case that some of the details which were most significant, just because of their private and intimate character, should become known only by degrees. This state of things is reflected in the Gospels as we have them. The common matter of the Synoptic Gospels is also the most public matter. It by no means follows that what is peculiar to a single Gospel is by that fact stamped as less historical: no one would think (*e.g.*) of affirming this of some of the parables peculiar to St. Luke; but it is fair to suppose that in the first instance it was less widely diffused. To this class would belong the narratives of the Nativity and of the Infancy. It will be in some ways a gain not to begin with these, but to let them enter into the story as they entered into it with the first Christians. More than one point which might otherwise perplex us will in this way suggest its own explanation.

§ 2. Limits of space do not allow us to go elaborately into the question as to the trustworthiness of our materials. It may suffice to point to one undoubted fact which furnishes at least a considerable presumption in their favour. The apostolic age produced some strongly marked personalities, with well defined types of thought and phraseology. Now, broadly speaking, these types have left but little trace upon the Gospels. The special type characteristic of the Gospels themselves stands out conspicuously over-against them. We need hardly do more than refer to such very significant facts as that the Gospels alone contain specimens of teaching by parables; that the idea of the 'kingdom of heaven' (or 'of God'), which is quite central in the Gospels, recedes into the background in the writings of the apostles; that the same holds good of that most significant title 'Son of Man'; that, on the other hand, such a term as 'justify' is rare and hardly technical, while 'justification,' 'sanctification,' 'reconciliation' (or 'atonement'), and a number of others, are wholly absent. It may be said that the Fourth Gospel is an exception, that there we have a suspicious resemblance to the style and diction of the Epp. of St. John. Some resemblance there is, and we would not entirely reject the inference drawn from it. But even here the exception is but partial. It has often been noticed that the evangelist scrupulously confines his doctrine of the Logos to the prologue.

The writer of this may be allowed once more to express the conviction,* which he believes that continued investigation will confirm, that the great mass of the Synoptic Gospels had assumed its permanent shape not later than the decade 60–70 A.D., and that the changes which it underwent after the great catastrophe of the fall of Jerusalem were but small, and can without difficulty be recognized.

But the task on which we are at present engaged must in the main supply its own vindication. The

---

* See the *Bampton Lectures* for 1893, p. 286 ff.

picture which it is here attempted to draw will commend itself so far as it is consistent and coherent, and no further. No one, indeed, expects in these days the formal and external consistency aimed at in the older Harmonies; but the writer himself believes that in their inner essence the Gospels are consistent and coherent, and if he fails to convey the impression of this, the failure will be his own. He is conscious of something tentative in the way in which he has sought to work in data derived from the Fourth Gospel with those derived from the other three. But here, again, he is giving expression to the best opinion he can form, and the value of that opinion must be judged by the result. Where he is not satisfied with his own success, he has not hesitated to say so.

§ 3. To what has been said above it should be added, that if we assume the standpoint of a spectator, a brief preface will be needed to explain what that standpoint is. In other words, we shall have at the outset to take a rapid survey of the conditions under which the Life of Christ was lived, so that we may see to what His teaching had to attach itself, and what served for it as a foil, by way of contrast and antagonism.

The main divisions of our subject will thus be—

 I. SURVEY OF CONDITIONS.
 II. THE PUBLIC MINISTRY OF JESUS, preceded by that of the Baptist.
 III. SUPPLEMENTAL MATTER, not included in the Public Ministry, and derived from special sources.
 IV. THE VERDICT OF HISTORY.

CHAPTER II.

SURVEY OF CONDITIONS.

§ **4.** The picture which we form for ourselves of Palestine in the time of our Lord is apt to be wanting in play and variety. A few strong and simple colours are all that are used; we do not allow enough for their blending, or for the finer and subtler tones which mingle with them. We see the worldly ambition of the Sadducees, the self-seeking and formalism of the Pharisees; over both, the rough stern rule of the Roman; and under both, the chafing tide of popular passion, working itself up to its outburst of fury in the Great War. Perhaps we throw in somewhere in a corner the cloistered communities of the Essenes; but if so, it is rather as standing apart by themselves than as entering into the general life.

It is not so much that this picture is wrong as that it needs to be supplemented, and it needs a little toning down of the light and shade. This is the case especially with the internal conditions, the state of thought and of the religious life.

7

A. External Conditions: Government, Sects, and Parties.

§ 5. The external conditions are so comparatively simple and so well known that a rapid glance at them will suffice.

At the time of our Lord's public ministry, Judæa and Samaria were directly subject to the Romans, and were governed by a *procurator* (**Pontius Pilate,** A.D. 26–36), who was to some extent subordinate to the *legatus* of Syria. Pilate had a character for cruelty (cf. Lk 13[1]). And the Roman rule was no doubt as a whole harsh and unfeeling: we read of wholesale executions, which took the horrible form of crucifixion. But the people whom Rome had to govern were turbulent in the extreme; and so far as the Roman authorities come before us in NT, we cannot refuse them the credit of a desire to do a sort of rough justice.

The odious duty of collecting tolls and taxes for the Romans led to the employment of a class of underlings (τελῶναι, *publicani*), who were regarded almost as outcasts by their Jewish countrymen.

The north and east of Palestine were still in the hands of sons of Herod. **Antipas** (4 B.C. to 39 A.D.) held Galilee and Peræa; and his brother Philip (4 B.C. to 34 A.D.), Ituræa and Trachonitis. The name given to the former, 'that fox' (Lk 13[32]), will sufficiently describe him; he was living in open sin with Herodias, the wife of another brother, but was not wholly unvisited by remorse, and had at least curiosity in matters of religion (Mk 6[20]‖, Lk 23[8]). His capital was at Tiberias, on the Sea of Galilee, and he also held possession of the strong fortress of Machærus * E. of the Dead Sea. Herod Philip governed his dominions quietly, and was the best and most popular of his father's sons.

§ 6. The **Sadducees** (Zadokite priests) consisted mainly of certain aristocratic priestly families (Ac 4[6]) who held almost a monopoly of the high priesthood, and who played an influential and active part in the Sanhedrin, which under the Romans wielded considerable power. They were typical opportunists, and were bent above all things on keeping their own rights and privileges. Hence they were sensitive on the subject of popular disorder, which was likely to serve as an excuse to the Romans for displacing them (Jn 11[48]). It was a coalition of Pharisees and Sadducees which procured the death of our Lord, but in the period of the Acts the Sadducees were the more active persecutors. Religion with them was secondary, but they differed somewhat both in doctrine and in practice from the Pharisees (Ac 23[8]; cf. Edersheim, *Life and Times*, i. 314–321, etc.). They did not encumber themselves with the Pharisaic traditions, but took their stand upon the Pentateuch. They were notorious for strictness in judgment.

As contrasted with the Sadducees, the **Pharisees** (lit. Separatists or Purists) were essentially the religious party. They numbered more than 6000 (*Ant*. XVII. ii. 4), and were pledged to a high standard of life and scrupu-

* In *Ant*. XVIII. v. 2 Machærus is in the possession of Antipas, in the previous § it belongs to Aretas; but the reading of this latter passage is questionable (cf. Schürer, *NTZG* i. 362 n., 365 n. [*HJP* i. ii. 23, 25]).

lous performance of religious duties (Mt 23^{23}). Unfortunately, the high standard was outward rather than inward. The elaborate casuistry to which the Pharisees had recourse was used as a means of evading moral obligations (Mk 7$^{1-13}$|| 12$^{38-40}$||, Mt 23$^{13-33}$), and resulted in a spirit hard, narrow, and self-righteous.

Not exactly coextensive with the Pharisees, though largely to be identified with them (we read of 'scribes *of* the Pharisees,' Mk 2^{16} RV ; *i.e.* 'scribes who belonged to the party of the Pharisees'), were the Scribes (γραμματεῖς, νομικοί, νομοδιδάσκαλοι), or professed students of the law, who supplied the Pharisees with their principles. They had to a large extent taken the place of the priests as the preachers and teachers of Judaism. Their chief fields of action were the synagogues and the Rabbinical schools. The most highly respected of the scribes were the great religious authorities of the day. It was their successors who built up the Talmud. There were differences of opinion within the body (*e.g.* the rival schools of Hillel and Shammai, contemporaries of Herod the Great), but, without, their *dicta* were unquestioned. This veneration was, as a rule, only requited with contempt.

While the Pharisees at this date for the most part (though not entirely) held aloof from politics, on the ground that religion as they conceived it could be practised indifferently under any domination, and their own experiences under the national line, represented by Alexander Jannæus, had been the reverse of happy, the mass of the people were burning to throw off the yoke of the stranger. The party of action, which was prepared to go all lengths, was known as the Zealots.

One member of this party was numbered among the apostles (Mt 10⁴, Mk 3¹⁸, Lk 6¹⁵, Ac 1¹³). In the siege of Jerusalem they took the lead, and were distinguished at once by heroic courage and by horrible crimes.

The dynasty of the Herods had from the first claimed alliance with Hellenic culture. The founder of the dynasty had mixed with advantage to himself in the *haute politique* of his day; and he had signalized his reign by buildings in the Greek style, but on a scale of barbaric magnificence. The courts of the Herods must always have had a tincture of Hellenism about them. But the reaction against this was strong, and its influence probably did not extend very far, though it inspired the historians Nicolaus of Damascus, Justus of Tiberias, and Josephus. More likely to affect the lower and middle strata of the population would be the 'Greek cities' founded by the Syrian kings before the Maccabæan rising, such as the cluster known as Decapolis, for the most part east of the Jordan, with later foundations like the flourishing port of Cæsarea. But more important still would be the influence of the Jews of the Diaspora, constantly coming and going to the great feasts at Jerusalem, and with synagogues for their special use permanently established there (Ac 6⁹). The greatest of the centres with which the Jews were thus brought in contact were Alexandria and Antioch. And there is reason to think that the amount of intellectual intercourse and interchange was by no means inconsiderable.

There must have been other foreign influences at work, but rather by what might be called underground channels. The connexion of Palestine with Babylonia and the East, which goes back to immemorial antiquity, had been revived and deepened by the Captivity. It was kept up by intercourse with the Jews who remained in those regions. But whether or not they had come precisely in this way, there can be no doubt that Oriental, and indeed specifically Persian influences were present in the sect of the **Essenes**. The ceremonial washings, and the reverence paid to the sun, can hardly have had any other origin. The asceticism and community of goods have a Pythagorean cast, and may have come from Greece by way of Egypt, while the rejection of sacrifice and what we know of the speculative tendencies of the Essenes may well be native to the soil of Palestine. The Essene settlements were congregated near the Dead Sea.

B. Internal Conditions: the State of Religious Thought and Life.

§ 7. *General Conditions.*—To describe justly the state of Judaism in the time of Christ is a difficult and delicate thing. It is too apt to seem like an indictment of the Judaism of nineteen centuries, which not only on general grounds, but specially in view of the attitude of some Jewish apologists of the present day, a Christian theologian will be loth to bring. He will desire to make all the allowances that can rightly be made, and to state all the evidence (so far as he knows it) for as well as against. But at the same time he must not gloss over real faults and defects, without a statement of which Christianity itself can be but imperfectly understood.

Truth does not, as a rule, lie in compromises. And its interests will be perhaps best served if we set down without reserve both the darker and the brighter sides, only asking the reader to remember while he has the one before him, that the other is also there. That we attempt this difficult task at all is due to no wanton assumption of a right to judge, but to the unavoidable necessity that what is so intimately bound up with history should be seen in the full light which history throws upon it.

(a) *The Darker Side of the Contemporary Judaism.*— As we look broadly at the religious condition of Palestine in the time of our Lord, there can be little doubt that it was in need of a drastic reformation. This is the impression inevitably conveyed by the Gospels, and by the searching criticisms of St. Paul. Nor is it belied by the witness of Josephus, and in particular by the outbreak of untamed passion, with the horrors to which it gave rise, in the Jewish War. And although it may be easy to make a selection from the Talmud of sayings of a different character, it can hardly be questioned that the same source supplies proof enough that the denunciations of the Gospels were not without foundation. There is too evident a connexion between the inherent principles of Judaism and the defects charged against it to permit us to regard these as devoid of truth.

(i.) The idea of God was perhaps the strongest side of Judaism, but it was too exclusively transcendent. It had no adequate means of spanning the gulf between God and man. The faults of Judaism were those of Deism. It had one tender place, the love of Jehovah for

[handwritten margin note: ...ish idea of ...ce of God ...from Christian]

Israel. But this fell some way short of the Christian idea of the Father in heaven, the God who not only loves a single people, but whose essence is love. Judaism also largely wanted the mystical element which has played such an important part in Christianity. The Johannean allegory of the Vine and the Branches, which agrees so closely with the teaching of St. Paul, the whole conception of immanent divine forces circulating through the organism, has no true analogy in it.* (ii.) But the most disastrous feature of Rabbinical Judaism was its identification of morality with obedience to written law. 'Duty, goodness, piety,—all these are to the Jew equivalent terms. They are mere synonyms for the same conception—the fulfilment of the law. A man therefore is good who knows the law and obeys it; a man is wicked who is ignorant of it and transgresses it' (Montefiore, *Hibbert Lectures*, p. 479). This identification of morality with law led to a number of serious evils. (iii.) Law can deal only with overt action. Hence there was an inevitable tendency to restrict the field of morals to overt action. Motive was comparatively disregarded. It is doubtless true that the Rabbis frequently insist on rightness of motive. A religion which in its Sacred Books included the Prophets as well as the Law could not do otherwise. But the legal conception was too deeply ingrained not to tell its tale. If it had not been so, there would have been no need for the Sermon on the Mount; and the address, 'Scribes and Pharisees,

---

* The comparison of Israel to a vine is not unknown to Judaism, but in a wholly different application (see Wünsche, *Erläut. d. Evang.* on Jn 15[1]).

hypocrites,' would have had no point. (iv.) Another consequence of the stress laid on overt acts was the development of an elaborate doctrine of salvation by works. We need not suppose that this doctrine was universally held and always consciously acted upon; but it cannot be denied that there was in Judaism a widespread opinion that might be expressed in the terms, 'so much keeping of the law, so much merit'; and the idea of a 'treasure of merit,' which each man stores up for himself, is constantly met with. (v.) In one sense the keeping of the law was very hard. The labours of the scribes had added to the original and primary laws an immense mass of inferential law, which was placed on the same footing of authority. This portentous accumulation of precepts was a burden 'grievous to be borne.' (vi.) Not only so, but a great part of this additional law was bad law. It was law inferred by a faulty system of exegesis. Even where the exegesis was *bonâ fide*, it was in a large proportion of cases unreal and artificial. But there was a great temptation to dishonesty, for which the way was left open by the exaggerated stress laid on acts, and the comparative ignoring of motive. In the dead level of written law the relative degrees of obligation were disregarded. Hence there were a number of precepts which were positively immoral (*e.g.* Corban, Mk 7[11. 12]‖). (vii.) A further defect in the legal conception of religion was its intellectualism. The Talmud bears witness to what is little less than an idolatry of learning, and that, we must remember, Rabbinical learning. With religion converted into science, and the science in great part no science, we may well say,

'If the light that is in thee be darkness, how great is
the darkness!' The Scholasticism of the Middle Ages
had no such unchallenged supremacy; it was not the
one all-pervading ideal. (viii.) For the mass of the
population the double law, traditional as well as
original, could not but be a burden. The accumulation of precepts not possessed of moral value is always
a thing to be deprecated. And however much we may
allow for the fact that the observance of all these
precepts was not expected of every one, there still
remained enough to be a real incubus. And yet, on
the other hand, the performance of the full Pharisaic
standard was not so very difficult for persons of leisure,
who deliberately made up their minds to it. It did
not mean, or at least it might be understood as not
meaning, more than a life mechanically regulated.
But then it is easy to see that the existence of this
class, consciously setting itself above its neighbours,
and able, without any excessive strain, to make good
its pretensions, must have inevitably engendered a
feeling of self-righteousness or spiritual pride. The
parable of the Pharisee and the Publican (Lk 18$^{11-13}$)
must needs have been typical. (ix.) What the Pharisee
was to the ordinary Jew, that the Jew was to the rest
of mankind. However politically inferior, the Jew
never lost his pride of race, and with him this pride of
race was a pride of religious privilege. The Zealot
sought to translate this into political domination, but
the Pharisee was content to retire into the fortress of
his inner consciousness, from which he could look with
equanimity at the rise and fall of secular powers.
(x.) This particular form of pride had a tendency to

aggravate itself as time went on. 'To make a fence round the law' was a fundamental principle of Judaism. And in a like spirit the privileged people was tempted to make a fence round itself, and to dwell apart among the nations. Institutions which had had for their object to keep the nation clear of idolatry, were extended when the dangers of idolatry were past, until it required a revolution to say with St. Paul, 'There is neither Jew nor Greek.' (xi.) Worst and most disastrous of all was the tendency to fall back upon national privilege as a substitute for real reformation of life. We can see alike from the Gospels and from St. Paul how constantly the Jews had upon their lips, 'We have Abraham to our father' (Lk 3^8, Jn $8^{33. 39}$, Ro 2^{17-20}). It is admitted that 'the Jews were somewhat too confident of their assured participation in the blessedness of eternal life; all Israelites, except very exceptional and determined sinners, were believed to have their share in it' (Montefiore, *Hibb. Lect.* p. 482).

(β) *The Brighter Side of the Contemporary Judaism.*—The above is a long and a serious catalogue of charges, partly resting upon the logic of the creed, but also too much borne out by positive testimony. It seems conclusively to prove that not only reformation, but a thoroughgoing reformation, was needed.

And yet there is another side which the Christian teacher ought to emphasize more fully than it has been the custom to do.

(i.) In the first place, we have to remember that Judaism is professedly the religion of the OT. It is based upon a Book which includes the Prophets and the Psalms (to use the familiar description *a potiori*

2

parte) as well as the Law. And however much Judaism proper gave precedence to the Law, it could not forget the other parts of the volume, or run wholly counter to their spirit. It is not too much to say that even in the Talmud we can see at every turn how the spirit of legalism was corrected by an influence which is ultimately derived from what are rightly called the evangelical portions of OT. We shall see to what an extent Christianity itself is a direct development of these.

(ii.) The evidence of NT, severe as it is upon the whole, yet is not all of one tenor. Its pages are sprinkled over with Jewish characters who are mentioned in terms of praise: Zacharias and Elisabeth, Simeon and Anna, Nathanael, Nicodemus, and Joseph of Arimathæa, the young ruler, and the scribe who was pronounced to be 'not far from the kingdom of God' (Mk 12^{34}). We must not forget that there are parts of NT itself which in recent years have been claimed by Christian scholars as thinly veneered products of Judaism (Ep. of James, Apoc.). Whatever we may think of these particular instances, there are others (such as *Didaché* and the *Testaments of the Twelve Patriarchs*) in which it is highly probable that a Jewish original has been adapted to Christian purposes. And our present investigation will bring before us many examples in which, while Christianity corrects Jewish teaching, it nevertheless takes its start from it, and that not only from the purer original, but in its contemporary form.

(iii.) The panegyrists of the Talmud have at least right on their side to this extent, that single sayings can frequently be quoted from it in disproof of the sweeping allegations brought against it by its assailants. There are grains of fine wheat among its chaff. Some of these are referred, on what seems to be good authority, to a time anterior to the coming of Christ. The 'golden rule' is attributed to Hillel. The story is that when Shammai drove away an inquirer who desired to be taught the whole Torah while he stood on one foot, the man went to Hillel, who said : 'What is hateful to thyself do not to thy fellow; this is the whole Torah, and the rest is commentary' (Taylor, *Pirqe Aboth*, p. 37). Another great saying is ascribed to Antigonus of Soko : 'Be not as slaves that minister to the lord with a view to receive recompense; but be as slaves that minister to the lord without a view to receive recompense; and let the fear of Heaven be upon you' (*ib.* p. 27). There is a fair number of such sayings. If we take the treatise from which the last is directly quoted, we shall see in it what is probably not an unfair representation of the better Judaism in the time of Christ, with its weaknesses sufficiently indicated, but with something also of its strength.

(iv.) It is right also to bear in mind that the Judaism of this date had no lack of enthusiasts and martyrs. Akiba in particular, though a Jew of the Jews, cannot but command our admiration (see Taylor, *ut sup.* p. 67 ff.). And in a different category his fortitude is matched by the *mitis sapientia* of Hillel, of whom it was said that his gentleness brought men 'nigh under the wings of the Shekinah' (*ib.* p. 37).

(v.) A favourable impression on the whole is given by the numerous pseudepigraphic works which belong

in the main to the two centuries on each side of the
Christian era. The oldest parts of the Book of Enoch
may possibly be earlier, just as some outlying members
of the Baruch literature are probably later. The most
typical writings are the Book of Enoch and the Psalms
of Solomon (which can be dated with tolerable certainty B.C. 70–40), the Book of Jubilees and the
Assumption of Moses (which may be taken as roughly
contemporary with the founding of Christianity), and
the Fourth Book of Ezra (2 Es) and the Apoc. of
Baruch, both after the fall of Jerusalem in A.D. 70.
These writings show in varying degrees most of the
characteristic infirmities of Judaism, but they also
show its nobler features in a way which sometimes,
and especially in the two latest works, throws the
infirmities into the shade.*

It is a moot point how far the pseudepigrapha can be taken as
representative of the main currents of Judaism. Montefiore,
writing in 1892, says, 'It must be remembered that the apocalyptic
writings lie for the most part outside the line of the purest Jewish
development, and often present but the fringe or excrescence,
and not the real substance of the dominating religious thought'
(*Hibb. Lect.* p. 467). On the other hand, Charles has no difficulty
in assigning the different portions to recognised party divisions in
Judaism. Schürer in like manner describes their standpoint as
that of 'correct Judaism,' adding, however, that they are 'not
products of the school, but of free religious individuality' (*HJP*
III. ii. 49). Similarly, Baldensperger speaks of 4 Ezra and Baruch
as free from the spirit of casuistry, and not 'absorbed in the
Halachic rules' (p. 35, ed. 1). This verdict would apply in some

---

* For a closer and more exact but still tentative analysis and
dating, the reader may be referred to the editions by R. H.
Charles of *Enoch* (1893), *Secrets of Enoch* and *Apoc. of Baruch*
(1896), *Assumption of Moses* (1897); or for a judicious representation of average opinion, to Schürer, *HJP* II. iii. 54 ff.

degree to this class of literature generally.   It is perhaps in the main of provincial origin, or at least somewhat outside the beaten tracks of Jewish teaching.   The Pss. of Solomon and Bk. of Jubilees would be nearest to these.   It is very probable that 4 Ezr and Apoc. Bar were directly affected by the ferment of thought caused by the birth of Christianity.

When we endeavour to put together the impressions which we derive from these various sources, we may perhaps say that the outcome of them is that Judaism at the Christian era had all the outer framework of a sound religion if only the filling in had been different. The Jew knew better than any of his contemporaries in Greece or Rome or in the East what religion was.   He had a truer conception of God, and of the duty of man towards God; but on the first head he had much still to learn, and on the second he had many faults to be corrected in the working out of detail.

The Jew had at least a profound seriousness on the subject of religion.   Where this was wanting, the man was no true Jew.   And even allowing for all the external influences which told against this, there was among the Jews probably less of professed atheism, indifference, levity, than there has ever been in any other society, ancient or modern.   The Jew had also an intense feeling of loyalty to this society.   His love of what we should call his Church rose to a passion.   It is this which makes the apocalypses which followed the fall of Jerusalem so pathetic.   The faith of men has probably seldom received a shock so severe.   The authors of these apocalypses feel the shock to the uttermost.   They grope about anxiously to find the meaning of God's mysterious dealings; but their faith in Him is unshaken.   They are divided between

passionate grief and resignation: 'Two things vehe-
mently constrain me: for I cannot resist thee, and my
soul, moreover, cannot behold the evils of my mother'
(Apoc. Bar 3³).

§ 8. *The Special Seed-plot of Christianity.*—In general
terms it may be said that when we seek for affinities to
Christianity, we find more of them the farther we recede
from the centre of official Judaism.   The one thing to
which Christianity is most opposed is the hard, dry,
casuistic legalism of the Pharisee.   If we are right in
thinking of the apocalyptic literature as in the main
provincial, we shall not be surprised to find the points
of contact with it become more numerous.   Wherever
there are traces of a fresher and deeper study of the
Psalms and Prophets, there we have a natural kinship
for the Christian spirit.

Now there is one class among whom this continuity
with Psalms and Prophets is specially marked.   It has
been observed * that there is a group of Psalms (of
which perhaps 9. 10. 22. 25. 35. 40. 69. 109 are the
most prominent) in which the words translated in EV
'poor,' 'needy,' 'humble,' 'meek' are of specially
frequent occurrence.   It appears that these words have
acquired a moral meaning.   From meaning originally
those who are 'afflicted' or 'oppressed' (by men), they
have come to mean those who in their oppression have
drawn nearer to God and leave their cause in His hands.
They are the pious Israelites who suffer from the
tyranny of the heathen or of their worldly countrymen,

---

* See esp. Rahlfs, עָנִי *und* עָנָו *in den Psalmen*, Göttingen, 1892 ;
and Driver, *Parallel Psalter*, Oxf. 1898, Glossary, *s.v.* 'poor.'

and who refuse to assert themselves, but accept in a
humble spirit the chastening sent by God. As there
were many such in every period of the history of Israel,
they might be said to form a class. Now there is other
evidence that this class still existed at the Christian era.
They are the *mansueti et quiescentes* of 4 Ezr (2 Es) 11^{42}.
They are just the class indicated in Ps-Sol $5^{18f.}$ 'Who
is the hope of the needy and the poor beside thee, O
Lord? And thou wilt hearken: for who is gracious
and gentle but thou? Thou makest glad the heart of
the humble by opening thine hand in mercy.' (Compare also the reff. in Ryle and James, p. 48, and Index,
s.v. $\pi\tau\omega\chi\acute{o}s$). The special NT designation is $\pi\tau\omega\chi o\grave{\iota}$
$\tau\hat{\omega}$ $\pi\nu\epsilon\acute{\upsilon}\mu\alpha\tau\iota$ (Mt 5^3). And a better expression of the
spirit in question could not easily be found than the
Magnificat (Lk 1^{46-55}). It is clear that the group which
appears in Lk 1. 2, not only Joseph and Mary, but
Zacharias and Elisabeth, Simeon and Anna, all answer
to this description. They are those who look for 'the
consolation of Israel,' 'the redemption of Israel' (Lk
$2^{25. 38}$), and who looked for it rather by fasting and
prayer than by any haste to grasp the sword. There
was no organized party, no concerted policy; but we
cannot doubt that there were many devout souls
scattered throughout the country, and in just the kind
of distribution which the chapters Lk 1. 2 would
suggest, some for shorter or longer periods making
their way to Jerusalem, but the greater number dis-
persed over such secluded districts as the 'highlands'
($\acute{\eta}$ $\grave{o}\rho\epsilon\iota\nu\acute{\eta}$, Lk 1^{39}) of Judæa and Galilee.

Here was the class which seemed, as it were, specially
prepared to receive a new spiritual impulse and to take

up a great movement of reformation. And other tendencies were in the air which were ready to contribute
to the spread of such a movement when it came. The
labours of the scribes had not been all wasted. There
is a good example in Mk 12^{32-34}—the happy combination
of Dt 4^{39} with Lv 19^{18}—which shows that even among
the Rabbis there were some who were feeling their way
towards the more penetrating teaching of Jesus.

One great transition had been made since Ezk 18.
The value of the individual soul was by this time fully
realized. The old merging of the individual in the
family and the clan had been fully left behind. Another
germ contained in the teaching of the prophets had
been developed. We can see from the case of the
Essenes that men's minds were being prepared for the
abolition of animal sacrifices, and along with the abolition of sacrifice for an end to the localized worship of
the temple. The great extension of the synagogue
services would contribute to the same result.

. The proselytizing zeal which the later Judaism had
displayed (Mt 23^{15}) operated in several ways. It was a
step in the direction of the ultimate evangelizing of the
Gentiles. It had created a class in which the liberal
influences of Græco-Roman education prevented the
purer principles of OT from lapsing into Judaic narrow-
ness and formalism, and in which it was therefore
natural that Christianity should strike root. We meet
with specimens of this class in the Gospels (Lk 7^{2-5}||,
Mk 15^{39}||) as well as in the Acts. And not only was
there created a class of recipients for the gospel, but in
the effort to meet the demands of these converts from
paganism there was a tendency to tone down and throw

into the background the more repellent features of Judaism. If it is true, as it probably is, that the so-called *Didaché* is a Christian enlargement of what was originally a Jewish manual for proselytes, it would be a good illustration of this process.

§ **9.** *The Messianic Expectation.*—But by far the most important of all the preparations for the gospel, negative as well as positive, both as demanding correction and as leading up to fulfilment, was the growth of the Messianic expectation, with the group of doctrines which went along with it.

The more the stress of the times was felt, and the more hopeless it seemed that any ordinary development of events could rescue the Jewish people from its oppressors, the more were its hopes thrown into the future and based upon the direct intervention of God. The starting-point of these hopes was the great prophecy in Dn 7. The world empires, one succeeding another, and all tyrannizing over the Chosen People, were to be judged, and Israel at last was to enter on the dominion reserved for it. The figure of the Son of Man who appears before the Ancient of days (Dn 7[13f.]) was not in the first instance a person : it was a collective expression, equivalent to the 'saints of the Most High' in v.[18]. The form of a 'man' is taken in contrast to the 'beasts,' which represent in the context the dynasties of the oppressors. In conflict with the last of these Israel is at first to be hard pressed, but God Himself will interpose by an act of divine judgment; the enemy will be crushed, and there will be given to Israel a kingdom which is universal and eternal.

This dominion is Israel's by right. It had not only been repeatedly promised from Abraham onwards, but it had been earned as a matter of desert. It was the complement of Israel's possession of the law. By its observance of the law Israel had acquired a right which no other nation could acquire. In the compact or covenant between Israel and Jehovah, Israel was doing its part, and it remained for God to do His.

The grand catastrophe by which this was to be brought about, the περιπέτεια in the tragedy of the nations, was to culminate in an act of judgment. The **day of the Lord,** conceived of by the prophets at first as a decisive battle in which God intervenes, gives place to a judicial act in which those who have oppressed His people are called to account, and the parts of oppressor and oppressed are reversed. To complete the justice of the case, those of the saints who have died in the times of distress must not be left out. There must be a resurrection. And the resurrection will usher in for them a state of lasting joy and felicity. Nature would share with man. There would be a 'new heaven and a new earth.' The tendency was to conceive of these somewhat literally and materially. Elaborate but at the same time prosaic pictures are given of the inexhaustible plenty which the saints (*i.e.* Israel as a people) are to enjoy. Their bliss is also sometimes compared to a great feast (cf. Lk 14[15]).

In the Book of Daniel, and, as it would seem for some time afterwards, the reign of the saints is conceived impersonally. It is the dominion of Israel, the Chosen People. But gradually there arises a tendency to go back to a more primitive stage of prophecy, and to see the kingdom as concentrated in the person of its King : there is a personal Messiah. This is conspicuously the case in the Psalms of Solomon (17. 18), the date of which is fixed between B.C. 70–40. The righteous King who is to rule over the nations is the Davidic King of the elder prophets. A personal King is also implied in *Orac. Sibyll.* iii. 49 f., 652–656. In the middle section of the Bk. of Enoch (chs. 37–71), which is also probably pre-Christian, the title 'Son of Man' is taken up from Daniel and distinctly identified with a person. Here, too, as in *Orac. Sibyll.* iii. 286, and *Apoc. Bar* 72^{2-6}, the Messiah is not only King but Judge (cf. Enoch 45^3 62^{8-13} 69^{27}). The execution of the judgment is handed over to Him by God. There is not absolute unity of view. Sometimes judgment is carried out by the Messiah, sometimes by God Himself (*e.g.* Enoch 90^{18-27}, *Ass. Mos.* 10^{3-10}). There is also some diversity as to the extent to which the resurrection is to be of the righteous, of Israel, or of all mankind. One view is that there are to be two resurrections, with a millennial reign between them.

The Sadducees held aloof from the Messianic expectation to which they were not clearly compelled by the few allusions in the Pentateuch, and which would have been only a disturbing element in their policy of making the best—for themselves—of things as they were. Some of the scribes must have also done what they could to discourage the belief. It is well known that Hillel is said to have asserted that the prophecies of the Messiah were fulfilled in Hezekiah. But there is abundant evidence that in spite of this the expectation was widely diffused. It must have been constantly preached in the synagogues of Palestine, and it certainly took a strong hold of the popular mind. It was differently received and understood by different hearers. With some quiet God-fearing souls, 'poor in spirit' like those who come before us at the beginning of the evangelical narrative in Lk I. 2, it was cherished secretly with awed and wistful longing (Lk 2$^{25. \, 38}$). With the mass of the population, as well teachers as taught, it took its place only too easily among the body of hard, narrow, materialized beliefs which were so characteristic of the time—a visible earthly kingdom reserved for Israel as its right, and carrying with it domination over other nations, with such unlimited command of enjoyment as a sovereign people might expect under conditions specially created for its benefit: all this introduced by supernatural means, wielded by One who is variously called 'Messiah' or 'Anointed,' 'the righteous King,' 'the Elect' or 'Son of Man,' not (if the question were pressed) in the strict sense God, though endowed by God with plenary powers, a fit Head for the Chosen People in its golden age, which was at last about to begin. And scattered among these masses there were many—some banded together under the name of Zealots, and thousands more who were ready to join them at the first signal—men not of dreams but of action, who were only waiting for the leader and the hour to put their hand to the sword and rise in revolt against the hated foreigners who oppressed them, prepared to take a fearful vengeance, and proud in the thought that in doing so they would be 'doing God service' and establishing His kingdom.

LITERATURE.—Vast stores of ordered material are contained in Schürer's great work originally called *Neutest. Zeitgeschichte* (*NTZG*), and now as in the Eng. tr., *Hist. of the Jewish People in the Time of Jesus Christ* (*HJP*). The Eng. tr. from the 2nd much enlarged ed. came out in 1885–90; a 3rd ed., still further enlarged, has begun to appear (vols. ii. and iii., 1898). The late Dr. Edersheim's *Life and Times of Jesus the Messiah* (revised eds. from 1886) is also full of illustrative matter. Other works by the same author may also be consulted; esp. *History of the Jewish Nation after the Destruction of Jerusalem under Titus* (2nd ed. carefully revised by H. A. White, 1896). Another very useful work is Weber's *System d. altsynagog. Paläst. Theol.*, now called *Jüdische Theologie* (2nd ed., somewhat improved, 1897). As there is always a danger of confusing Jewish teaching of very different dates, this book should be checked as far as possible by comparison with the *Pseudepigrapha*, Philo, NT, and the early Talmudic work *Pirqe Aboth* (*Sayings of the Jewish Fathers*, ed. Taylor, 1877, and enlarged in 1897). To these authorities should now be added G. Dalman, *Die Worte Jesu* (Bd. i. 1898 *fin.*; Eng. tr., *The Words of Jesus*, T. & T. Clark, 1902), the most critical and scientific examination of the leading conceptions of the Gospels that has yet appeared.

Mention may be made among older works of Drummond's *Jewish Messiah* (1877) and Stanton's *Jewish and Christian Messiah* (1887). Hausrath's *NT Times* (Eng. tr. 1878–80) is picturesquely written, but far less trustworthy than Schürer; and Wünsche's *Neue Beiträge z. Erläuterung d. Evv.* (1878) is much criticized. Montefiore's *Hibbert Lectures* (1892) and arts. in *JQR* form an attractive apology for Judaism.

CHAPTER III.

THE EARLY MINISTRY.

§ 10. WE shall now be in a position to approach the study of the Public Ministry of our Lord in the manner indicated at the outset. We shall be able to place ourselves at the standpoint of a sympathetic spectator. We shall have some rough conception of the kind of ideas which would be in his mind, and of the kind of conditions which he would see around him. We shall thus be able to follow the course of the Public Ministry with a certain amount of intelligence. We do not as yet attempt to penetrate the whole of its secret. Broadly speaking, we suppose ourselves to see what a privileged spectator might be expected to see, and no more. We reserve until a later stage the introduction of those special details of illuminative knowledge which, as a matter of history, were not accessible to the first spectators, but were only disclosed after a time. But we hold ourselves at liberty to collect and group the facts which were not removed from the cognizance of a spectator, in any way that may be most convenient to secure clearness of presentation.

31

It may be well to avail ourselves of this freedom, at once, before giving an outline of the ministry, to state summarily certain conclusions which seem to arise out of the study of it. We shall hold the threads in our minds more firmly if we see to what results they are tending.

The anticipated conclusions, then, are these : (i.) From the very first (*i.e.* from the Baptism) our Lord had the full consciousness of the Messiah, and the full determination to found the Kingdom of God upon earth. (ii.) From the very first He had also the deliberate intention of transforming the current idea of the Kingdom. (iii.) In order to make this transformation effective, it was necessary to begin with the idea of the Kingdom and not of the King. In other words, the personal Messianic claim had to be kept in the background. But (iv.) the transformation of the idea was only a preliminary to the permanent establishment of the Kingdom; and this establishment turned round the Person of the Messiah. So that in the end the history of the Kingdom centres in the personal history of the King.

With so much of preface we proceed to give an outline of the Public Ministry according to the periods into which it seems to fall.

A. Preliminary Period : from the Baptism to the Call of the Leading Apostles.*

Scene.—Mainly in Judæa, but in part also Galilee.
Time.—Winter A.D. 26 to a few weeks after Passover A.D. 27.
  Mt 3^1-4^{11}, Mk 1^{1-13}, Lk 3^1-4^{13}, Jn 1^6-4^{54}.

---

* The choice of *termini a quo* and *ad quem* is sometimes inclusive and sometimes not inclusive. The most salient points are chosen. Here the *term. ad quem* is not inclusive.

B. First Active or Constructive Period: the Founding of the Kingdom.

Scene.—Mainly in Galilee, but also partly in Jerusalem.

Time.—From about Pentecost A.D. 27 to shortly before Passover A.D. 28.

Mt 4^{13}–13^{53}, Mk 1^{14}–6^{13}, Lk 4^{14}–9^6, Jn 5.

C. Middle or Culminating Period of the Active Ministry.

Scene.—Galilee.

Time.—Passover to shortly before Tabernacles A.D. 28.

Mt 14^1–18^{35}, Mk 6^{14}–9^{50}, Lk 9^{7-50}, Jn 6.

D. Close of the Active Period: the Messianic Crisis in View.

Scene.—Judæa (Jn $7^{10ff.}$ 11^{54}) and Peræa (Mk $10^1\|$, Jn 10^{40}).

Time.—Tabernacles A.D. 28 to Passover A.D. 29.

Mt 19^1–20^{34}, Mk 10^{1-52}, Lk 9^{51}–19^{28} (for the most part not in chronological order), Jn 7^1–11^{57}.

E. The Messianic Crisis: the Triumphal Entry, the Last Teaching, Passion, Death, Resurrection, Ascension.

Scene.—Mainly in Jerusalem.

Time.—Six days before Passover to ten days before Pentecost A.D. 29.

Mt 21^1–28^{20}, Mk 11^1–16^8 [16^{9-20}], Lk 19^{29}–24^{52}, Jn 12^1–21^{23}.

The chronology adopted in this article, not as certain, but as on the whole the best of current systems, is in substantial agreement with that of the art. Chronology of the New Testament. It differs from that in the writer's first work, *The Authorship and Historical Character of the Fourth Gospel* (London, 1872), by placing the Crucifixion in the year A.D. 29 rather than A.D. 30.

A. Preliminary Period: from the Baptism to the Call of the Leading Apostles.

§ 11. *Scene.*—Mainly Judæa, but in part also Galilee.

3

A

eminary Period

Time.—Winter A.D. 26 to a few weeks after Passover A.D. 27.

Mt 3^1–4^{11}, Mk 1^{1-13}, Lk 3^1–4^{13}, Jn 1^6–4^{54}.

The Public Ministry of our Lord begins with
His Baptism. (i.) This will therefore be the
first point to attract our attention, and some
explanation will be needed as to the Baptist and
his mission. (ii.) Along with the Baptism we
must needs take the Temptation, as a glimpse
vouchsafed by Jesus Himself, and early and
widely published, of the principles which were to
determine the nature of His Ministry. (iii.) After
this will come the first preliminary gathering of
a few loosely attached followers, and the first
miracle at Cana in Galilee. (iv.) Then the visit
to Jerusalem for the Passover of the year 27, with
a short stay in the South. (v.) Then we have a
return to Galilee, followed by a brief period of
partial retirement, leading up to the Call of the
four chief apostles.

Allusions, more or less explicit, to the Baptism
and to the ministry of John, are found in all four
Gospels; the other events of this period are recorded only in the fourth — unless we are to
identify the Healing of the Nobleman's Son
(Jn 4^{46-54}) with that of the Centurion's Servant
(Mt 8^{5-13}, Lk 7^{1-10}).

e Baptism

§ **12.** i. *The Baptist and the Baptism.*—Our survey of
contemporary Judaism has shown us that 'the kingdom
of God' was a phrase in almost every man's mouth.
It meant, in point of fact, to the majority 'a kingdom

for Israel' far more than a 'kingdom of God.' But though in a more or less indefinite sense it was understood to be near, no time had as yet been actually announced for it. Men were on the watch, but rather for the signs of the coming than for the actual coming itself.

We are not surprised, therefore, to find that the news that a prophet had appeared who preached the approaching coming of the Messiah, caused a widespread excitement.* The aspect of this coming, which he put in the forefront, was the aspect of judgment. The axe was laid to the root of the trees, and the fruitless tree would be burned (Mt 3^{10}, Lk 3^9).

The prophet who made this announcement bore the name of John. The scene of his preaching was the wilderness of Judæa, near the lower course of the Jordan where it fell into the Dead Sea. In this wilderness he had lived in solitude for some time before he began his prophetic mission. His whole appearance was sternly ascetic. He seems to have adopted deliberately a garb and a manner of life resembling those of Elijah, probably not so much in anticipation of the verdict which was to be afterwards passed upon him (Mt 11^{14}) as because he took Elijah for his model.

His character and his mission alike were severely simple. His soul was possessed with a strong conviction, wrought in him in precisely the same manner in which such convictions were wrought in the prophets

* Stress can hardly be laid on the form of announcement in Mt 3^2, which would make the Baptist anticipate exactly the announcement of Jesus. This would seem to be due to the editor. The older version describes the Baptist as 'preaching a baptism of repentance for remission of sins' (Mk 1^4).

of the OT, that a great crisis was near at hand. What lay beyond was dim, and, so far as the prophet had a definite picture before him, it was probably not very different from that which presented itself to his countrymen.   But he saw clearly that the crisis would take the form of a judgment, and that there would be a judge, a personal judge, with a mission vastly greater than his own.   At the same time, it is also borne in upon him that the preparation required by this coming judgment is a moral reformation.   This he sees intensely; and again he goes back behind the teaching of his day to that of the ancient prophets.   That which is required is not merely a stricter performance of the law, but a deep inward change—a change spontaneously expressing itself in right action.

Once more, and indeed very conspicuously, he made good his resemblance to the older prophets by clothing this leading idea of his in an expressive symbolical act.   The rumour of him brought the people to him in crowds; and one by one, as they confessed to him their sins and convinced him of the reality of their repentance, he took them down into the running waters of the Jordan; he made them plunge in or let the waters close over their heads, and then he led them out again with the consciousness that they had left their sinful past behind them, and that they were pledged to a new life.

The process was called 'Baptism'; and John, from the fact that it constituted the main outward expression of his mission, was called 'the Baptist.' The act bore a certain resemblance to those ceremonial washings with which the Jews were familiar enough, and which held a specially prominent place in the ritual of the Essenes. But it differed from all these in that it was an act performed once for all, and not repeated from day to day. The lesson of it was that of Jn 13^{10}: he who was once bathed in this thorough and searching fashion did not need to have the act repeated; the effect was to last for life.

The movement took hold especially of the lower and what were thought to be the more abandoned classes. John was kept fully employed in the work of confessing and baptizing, but he did not allow it to be forgotten that all this pointed forward to another mission greater than his own. The presentiment grew upon him that part of his task as prophet was to name this mightier successor. And again, after the manner of the older prophets, he knew that it would be made manifest to him whom he was to name.

Presently the sign was given. Among those who came to be baptized was one who passed for a relative of his own, with whom possibly, though perhaps not probably, he may have had some intercourse in boyhood (cf. Jn 1^{31}). As with others who before their baptism were called upon to confess, so also with this kinsman John had some converse, and if we may accept what is found only in a single narrative,* at first refused to baptize Him. His scruples are set aside, but it is not

---

* Resch (*TU.* x. ii. 57), in his later opinion, regards this narrative as belonging to the oldest evangelical document; but the passages which he has collected in support of this view might quite well be explained as paraphrastic allusions to the canonical Matthew. The Gospel according to the Hebrews as used by the Ebionites (Epiph. *Hær.* xxx. 13) had a similar scene after the Baptism of Jesus (Resch, *Agrapha*, p. 345 f.).

until the actual baptism that the full truth bursts upon him. Still, the analogy of the older prophecy is maintained. A sign is given such as that which Isaiah offered to Ahaz (Is 7^{11}). From the Fourth Gospel we should gather that it was seen in prophetic vision by the Baptist (Jn 1^{32-34}); from the Synoptics we should gather that it was seen in like vision by the baptized (Mk 1^{10}, Mt 3^{16} 'he saw'). And to prophetic sight was joined also the prophetic hearing of a voice from heaven, proclaiming in words that recalled at once Ps 2^7 and Is 42^1 'Thou art my beloved Son, in thee I am well pleased.'

(a) *The Baptist's Hesitation.*—The incident of Mt $3^{14f.}$ is open to some suspicion of being a product (such as might well grow up by insensible degrees in the passing of the narrative from hand to hand) of the conviction which later became general among Christians, that their Master was without sin, and of the difficulty which thence arose of associating Him with a baptism 'of repentance.' We cannot exclude this possibility. But, on the other hand, the difficulty is for us, too, a real one, and the solution given, while it has nothing under the circumstances inconsistent or improbable, is attractive by its very reserve. 'To fulfil all righteousness'=to leave undone nothing which God had shown to be His will. In a general movement which embraced all the more earnest-minded in the nation, it was right that He too should share. It would not follow that the symbolical act of Baptism should have precisely the same significance for every one who submitted to it. For the main body it denoted a break with a sinful past and a new start upon a reformed life. For the Messiah it denoted a break simply, the entrance upon a new phase in the accomplishment of His mission. It took the place with Him of the 'anointing,' which marked the assumption of the active work to which they were called by the kings and prophets of old. This 'anointing' was the 'descent of the Spirit.' The Baptism of the Messiah was Baptism 'with the Spirit,' wherewith He was to baptize. The significance of Baptism in His case was positive rather than negative.

(β) *The Voice from Heaven.*—It has been too readily assumed by some distinguished writers (*e.g.* Usener) that the oldest version of the voice from heaven was in exact agreement with Ps 2⁷ 'Thou art my [beloved] Son : this day have I begotten thee.' In two of the three Synoptics the reading is undoubtedly ἐν σοὶ [ᾧ] εὐδόκησα [ηὐδ-]. It is true, however, that in Lk 3²² an important group of authorities has ἐγὼ σήμερον γεγέννηκά σε. This is the reading of the larger branch of the Western text (D a b c *al. codd. nonnull. ap.* Aug. Juvenc. *al.*). A similar reading is found in Justin, *c. Tryph. bis* and in other writers, and both readings are combined in the Ebionite Gospel as quoted by Epiphanius. [The evidence is collected in full by Resch, *Agrapha*, p. 347 ff.] On the other hand, it is by no means certain that in some of these cases the Ps is not directly quoted, and in all assimilation to the text of the Ps lay very near at hand. Even the Western text of Luke is divided, a smaller but very ancient branch (including e) agreeing with the mass of the Gr. MSS. There can be little doubt that not only the Canonical Gospels, but the ground document on which they are based, had the common reading. The competing reading was a natural application of Ps 2⁷, and it fell in so readily with views which in different forms circulated rather widely in the 2nd cent., that we cannot be surprised if it met with a certain amount of adoption. See, further, below.

(γ) *Apocryphal Details.*—The story of the Baptism underwent various apocryphal amplifications and adornments. One of the earliest of these is the appearance of a bright light (Codd. Vercell. *et* Sangerm. *ad* Mt 3¹⁵ ; Ev. Ebion. *ap.* Epiph., Ephraem Syr.) or of a fire upon the Jordan (Just. *c. Tryph.* 88, *Prædicatio Pauli ap.* Ps.-Cypr. *de Rebapt.* 17 *al.*). The most elaborate working up of this kind of material is found in the Syriac *Baptismal Liturgy of Severus* (Resch, *Agrapha*, p. 361 ff.).

(δ) *The Synoptic and Johannean Versions.*—When a prophet began his prophetic career, he received clear proof of the reality of his call most often through some powerful inner experience or vision (*e.g.* Is 6), but also at times through Divine revelation to another (*e.g.* 1 K 19¹⁶). We may regard the events of the Baptism as a Divine authentication of this kind of the Mission of Jesus. But if so, there would be nothing incongruous in supposing that this authentication was vouchsafed, both to the Messiah Himself and to the Forerunner, just as a similar authentication was vouchsafed to St. Paul and to Ananias (Ac 9²ff· ¹¹ff·). We are therefore not in any way compelled to choose between the

Synoptic and Johannean versions as to the incidence of the supernatural signs.   The two versions may quite well be thought of as
supplementing rather than contradicting each other.

The Baptism of Jesus undoubtedly marks the beginning of His public ministry.   How much more was
it than this?   The Judaizing Ebionites of the 2nd century, who never rose above the conception of Christ as
an inspired prophet, and some Gnostic sects which
separated the Man Jesus from the Æon Christus, start-
ing from the Synoptic narrative, and combining it with
Ps 2^7, dated from the Baptism the union of the human
and the Divine in Christ in such a way that they are
sometimes described as making the Baptism a substitute for the supernatural Birth.   We can imagine how,
to those who had the story of the Baptism before them,
but who had not yet been reached by the tidings of
those earlier events round which the veil of a sacred
privacy had been drawn, and which (as we shall see)
only made their way to general knowledge by slow
degrees and after some length of time had elapsed,
should regard the descent of the Holy Ghost as a first
endowment with Divinity.   The fact that it was not till
then that Jesus began to perform His 'mighty works,'
would seem to give some colour to the belief.   And it
would be likely enough that a passing phase of Christian
thought, based upon imperfect knowledge, would sur-
vive in certain limited circles.   But the main body of
the Church did not rest in this contracted view, which
was really inconsistent with the Christology revealed
to us in the earliest group of St. Paul's Epistles.   It
accepted, and, through such leaders as Ignatius of
Antioch, emphasized strongly the earlier chapters of the

canonical narrative; and the contents of those chapters gave shape to the oldest form (which can hardly be later than Ignatius) of the Apostles' Creed. Already, before the 1st century was out, St. John had presented what was to be the Catholic interpretation of the relation of the Baptism to the Godhead of Christ. Far back at the very beginning of all beginnings, the Divine Word had already been face to face with God, and was Himself God; so that, when the same Word entered into the conditions of humanity, this did not denote any loss of Godhead which was inherent and essential. Much less could the Godhead of the incarnate Christ be supposed to date from the signs which accompanied the Baptism. The object of these signs was rather to inaugurate the public ministry of the Messiah, that He might be 'manifested to Israel' (ἵνα φανερωθῇ τῷ Ἰσρ., Jn 1³¹). Though the Greek is different, the idea is the same as that in Lk 1⁸⁰, where it is said of the Baptist himself that he was in the desert 'till the day of his showing unto Israel' (ἕως ἡμέρας ἀναδείξεως αὐτοῦ πρὸς τὸν Ἰσρ.). Whether or not the signs were in the first instance seen by more than the Messiah Himself and the Baptist (and it is probable that they were not), they were made public by the Baptist's declaration (Jn 1²⁹⁻³⁴), so that in any case there was a real 'manifestation to Israel.'

No doubt there was more than this. Besides the outward manifestation, a new epoch opened for the Son of Man Himself. But the nature of this we can describe only by its effects. The evangelists evidently have before their minds the analogy of the prophetic call and prophetic endowment. After the events of the

Baptism Jesus is 'full of the Holy Spirit' (Lk 4¹, cf. Mt 4¹, Mk 1¹²). And He applies to Himself the prophetic language of Is 61¹ 'The Spirit of the Lord is upon me; because the Lord hath anointed me to preach good tidings unto the meek,' etc. (cf. Lk 4¹⁸; it is probably this allusion to 'anointing with the Spirit' which has led to the incident in Lk being placed thus early). In the Gospel according to the Hebrews this is expressed even more emphatically than in the canonical Gospels: 'Factum est autem cum ascendisset Dominus de aqua, descendit fons omnis Spiritus sancti et requievit super eum et dixit illi: Fili mi in omnibus prophetis exspectabam te, ut venires et requiescerem in te. Tu es enim requies mea, tu es filius meus primogenitus qui regnas in sempiternum' (Hieron. *ad Jes.* xi. 1).

We have only to add that from this time onwards the rôle of the Messiah is distinctly assumed. The 'mighty works' very soon begin; disciples begin to attach themselves, at first loosely, but with increasing closeness; and there is a tone of decisive authority both in teaching and in act.

LITERATURE.—There is a strange mixture of fine scholarship and learning, with bold, not to say wild, speculation on the subject of this section in Usener's *Religionsgeschichtliche Untersuchungen*, 1 Teil, Bonn, 1889. With this may be compared Bornemann, *Die Taufe Christi durch Johannes in d. dogmatischen Beurteilung d. Christl. Theologen d. vier ersten Jahrhunderte*, Leipzig, 1896. *John the Baptist*, by the late Dr. H. R. Reynolds (3rd ed. 1888), represents the *Congregational Lecture* of 1874, and deals more with the career of John than with the questions which arise out of the Baptism of Jesus; but it does not leave these untouched so far as they had at that date come into view.

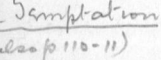

§ 13. ii. *The Temptation.*—We decline to speculate

where the data fail us. But one remarkable glimpse is afforded us into the state of the inner consciousness of the Son of Man after His Baptism. Strictly speaking, this would not as yet have been available to the spectator. It was probably not at this early date that it was disclosed, even to those nearest and dearest to Him. Still, the disclosure must have been made by the Lord Himself during His lifetime; and the extent to which it has found its way into all the Synoptics shows that it must have had a somewhat wide diffusion among the main body of the disciples. For this reason, as well as for the advantage of introducing it at the place which it occupies in the narratives, we shall not hesitate to touch upon the Temptation here, though it might perhaps more strictly come under the head of ' Supplemental Matter.'

The narratives of the Temptation are upon the face of them symbolical. Only in the form of symbols was it possible to present to the men of that day a struggle so fought out in the deepest recesses of the soul. There are two instances of such struggle in the life of the Redeemer—one at the beginning and the other at the end of His ministry (Lk 4^{13} comp. with 22^{53}). In both, the assault comes from without, from the personal Power of Evil. It is impossible for us to understand it, in the sense of understanding how what we call temptation could affect the Son of God. It could not have touched Him at all unless He had been also, and no less really, Son of Man. He vouchsafed to be tempted in order that He might be in all points like unto His brethren (He 4^{15}).

The Temptation clearly belongs to the beginning of

the Ministry.   It would have had no point before; and
the issue on which it turned had evidently been decided
before the public life of Jesus began, as that life
throughout its whole course followed the law which
was then laid down.   The Temptation implies two
things.   It implies that He to whom it was addressed
both knew Himself to be the Messiah whom the Jews
expected, and also knew Himself to be in possession of
extraordinary powers.   To say that He was now for
the first time conscious of these powers, is more than
we have warrant for.   But, in any case, it was the first
time that the problem arose how they were to be exercised.   Were they to be exercised at the prompting of
the simplest of all instincts—the instinct of self-preservation?   Were they to be exercised in furtherance of
what must have seemed to be the first condition on
which His mission as the Messiah could be accomplished—to convince the world that He had the mission,
that it was for Him to lead and for them to follow?
And, lastly, when He came forward as the Messiah,
was it to be as the Messiah of Jewish expectation?
Was His kingdom to be a kingdom of this world?
Was it to embrace all the secular kingdoms and the
glory of them, to enfold them in a system more powerful and more magnificent than theirs, brought about by
supernatural means, with no local limitations like even
the greatest of past empires, but wide as the universe
itself and indestructible?   Was it to be a real restoring
of the kingdom to Israel?   Was Jerusalem to be its
centre, in a new sense the 'city of the Great King'?

All these questions Jesus answered for Himself
absolutely in the negative.   There did not enter into

His mind even a passing shadow of the ambition which marked the best of earthly conquerors.   He was determined not to minister in the least to the national pride of the Jews.   Still less would He work out a new pride of His own.   He did not desire in any sense *volitare per ora*.   Even the most natural cravings of the nature which He had assumed He refused to satisfy so long as their satisfaction ended with Himself.

These principles are involved in the narrative of the Temptation.   They are laid down once for all; and the rest of the history shows no swerving from them.   At the same time it must be remembered that, although the decision had been reached by Jesus Himself, it was not yet known except so far as He was pleased to reveal it.   Partly, the revelation was made by acts and the self-imposed limits of action.   The clearest revelation was the story of the Temptation itself.   But neither the one nor the other was wholly understood.

§ **14.** iii. *The First Disciples and the Miracle at Cana.*—At this point we leave for some time the Synoptic narrative and follow rather that in the Fourth Gospel, which, it must be confessed, comes to us with very considerable verisimilitude.   If we had only the Synoptic Gospels we should have to suppose that our Lord gathered about Him a band of disciples abruptly and suddenly, capturing them as it were by the tone of authority in His command.   In St. John we have the steps given which led up to this, and which make it far more intelligible.

From this Gospel it would appear that Jesus remained for some time in the neighbourhood of the Baptist;

that the Baptist more than once indicated Him in a marked and indeed mysterious way (Jn 1²⁹ 'The Lamb of God, which taketh away the sin of the world'; cf. v.³⁶);* and that one by one several of John's disciples began to attach themselves, as yet more or less loosely, to His person. The Baptist's testimony, strengthened by first impressions, awoke in them the belief that at last the 'mightier than he' predicted by the Baptist had come (Jn 1⁴¹). Such a belief at this time and under these circumstances would need no elaborate demonstration. It would be accepted in a tentative way, awaiting verification from events, and, of course, only with those contents which accorded with current Jewish opinion.

The home of Jesus was still, as it had been for some thirty years of His life, at Nazareth; and at the time when He began to collect followers round Him, He was already on the point of returning thither (Jn 1⁴³). He had not as yet separated Himself from the domestic life of His family. It was as an incident in this life that He went to a marriage feast at the village of Cana (prob. = *Kâna el-Jelîl* rather than *Kefr Kenna*) in the company of His mother and some at least of His newly-found disciples. Here occurred the first of those 'signs' which were to be one conspicuous outcome of His mission. No wonder that it impressed itself vividly on the memory of one who was present, and that it con-

---

* The words are remarkable, especially as coming thus at the very threshold. It is possible that the evangelist may have been led to define somewhat in view of later events and later doctrines (for the allusion seems to be to Is 53). But the context, including the deputation from Jerusalem, is so lifelike and so thoroughly in accordance with probabilities, that the saying has a presumption in its favour.

firmed his incipient faith (Jn 2¹¹).   We shall speak of
these signs in their general bearing presently.

§ 15. iv. *The first Passover.*—There would seem to
have been some connexion between the family at
Nazareth and Capernaum,* as the whole party now
spend some days there (Jn 2¹²).   But the Passover was
near, and Jesus, with at least some of His disciples,
went up to it.   In connexion with this Passover, St.
John places, what has the appearance of a somewhat
high-handed act, the expulsion of buyers and sellers
from the outer court of the temple (Jn 2¹³⁻²²).   The
Synoptics place a similar act in the last week of the
Ministry (Mk 11¹⁵⁻¹⁸ ‖).   It is possible that such an act
may have happened twice; but if we are to choose, and
if we believe the Gospel to be really by the son of
Zebedee, we shall give his dating the preference—the
more so as in these early chapters the dates are given
with great precision, and apparently with the intention
of correcting a current impression.

This act was the first definite assumption of a public
mission to Israel, and its scene was fitly chosen at the
centre of Israel's worship.   It was the act, not as yet
necessarily of one who claimed to be the Messiah, but
of a religious reformer like one of the ancient prophets.
It was naturally followed by a challenge as to the right

* The site of Capernaum has been much debated.   At one time
it seemed as if the suffrage would go for *Tell Ḥûm*, but of late
there has been a reaction in favour of *Khân Minyeh* (see the art.
in Hastings' *DB*, *HGHL* p. 456 f., and von Soden, *Reisebriefe*
(1898), p. 160 f., who quotes a resident, Père Biever).   Buhl,
however, *GAP* p. 224, supports *Tell Ḥûm*, which the writer now
accepts (see *Journ. of Theol. Studies*, Oct. 1903).

of such an assumption. To this the enigmatic reply was given, ' Destroy this temple, and in three days (*i.e.* in a short time, cf. Hos 6²) I will raise it up '; which seems to be rightly glossed in Mk 14⁵⁸—the Jewish Church with its visible local centre should give place to the Christian Church with its invisible and spiritual centre (cf. Jn 4²¹ᶠ·). The saying made an impression at the time, and was brought up at the trial of Jesus to support a charge of blasphemy ; the disciples at a later date referred it to the Resurrection (Jn 2²¹ᶠ·).

A striking feature in the Johannean version of His visit to Judæa is the way in which the work of Jesus in connexion with it takes up the work of the Baptist, and fills in conspicuous gaps in the narrative of the Synoptics. The cleansing of the temple is an act of reformation which follows up the call to repentance. In John alone of the authorities have we a distinct statement that Jesus adopted the practice of baptism (3²² 4¹), though no other account of the origin of the Christian Sacrament is so natural. We find also that the necessity for baptism and the ' new birth ' which went with it is made the subject of a discourse with the Sanhedrist Nicodemus. The writer of the Gospel had been himself a disciple of John the Baptist, and still kept up his connexion with him, and knew what went on in his circle (Jn 3²³ᶠᶠ·). At the same time he seems to expand the discourses which he records with matter of his own (3¹⁶ᶠᶠ· ³¹ᶠᶠ·).

§ 16. v. *Retirement to Galilee.*—Soon after this John the Baptist was arrested by Herod Antipas, and Jesus retired into Galilee. On the way He passed through Samaria, and paused at Jacob's well near the village of

Sychar (now generally identified with *'Askar*), where His teaching made a marked impression (Jn 4^{39-42}). The Samaritans had a Messianic expectation of their own (Jn 4^{25}) ; and if the narrator has not defined what took place in the light of subsequent events, Jesus claimed to fulfil this expectation.   This was contrary to His policy for some time to come in dealing with Israel (Mk 1^{44}), but He may possibly have used greater freedom among non-Israelites.

The events of Jn 2^{13}–4^{45} may have occupied three or four weeks, but hardly more.   At the time when our Lord arrives in Galilee the impression of His public acts at the Passover was still fresh (Jn 4^{45}).   This would lead us to explain the latter half of Jn 4^{35} as a description of the state of things actually existing; the cornfields were at the time 'white for the harvest,' and 'Say not ye,' etc., will be a proverb.   But, that being so, a difficulty would be caused if the incident of the plucking of the ears of corn (Mk $2^{23\text{ff.}}$) were in its place chronologically, as the crops would still be in much the same condition as during the journey through Samaria, though the wheat harvest was going on be- tween Passover and Pentecost, and all the events im- plied in Mk 1^{14}–2^{22} would have intervened.   The time is really too short for these.   It is more probable that they were spread over some months.   We must conceive of our Lord as returning to Galilee with the few disciples with Him still in the state of loose attachment character- istic of this period, and Himself remaining for a while in comparative privacy.   The disciples had returned to their occupations when He takes the new and decisive step involved in the call described for us in the Synoptics.

4

The Synoptic Chronology.—If Mk 2²³ ‖ is to be taken as strictly consecutive with the events that precede, it would follow that the call of the leading apostles took place at least a week or two before the cutting of the ripened wheat, *i.e.*, as we might infer, before rather than some time after the Passover season. In that case the Johannean and Synoptic narratives would not be easy to combine. But the sequence of incidents in Mark (Eating with sinners, 2¹³⁻¹⁷; Fasting, 2¹⁸⁻²³; Two incidents relating to the Sabbath, 2²³–3⁶) suggests that we have here rather a typical group of points in the controversy with the Pharisees than a chronicle of events as they happened in order of time. In that case the call of the apostles might fall in the autumn, and the plucking of the ears of corn might belong to the end rather than the beginning of the period upon which we are about to enter.

The Healing of the Nobleman's Son.—As the narratives have come down to us, there are no doubt real differences between the story of the healing of the Nobleman's Son (Jn 4⁴⁶⁻⁵⁴) and that of the Centurion's Servant (Mt 8⁵⁻¹³ ‖). We must, however, reckon with the possibility—it cannot in any case be more—that they are two versions of the same event, arising out of the ambiguity of παῖς and δοῦλος. Years ago (*Fourth Gospel*, p. 100 f.) the writer had taken this view, which has since been adopted by Weiss (*Leben Jesu*, i. 423 ff. ; Eng. tr., T. & T. Clark). A similar question may be raised in connexion with the common features of the narratives Lk 5¹⁻¹¹, Jn 21¹⁻¹¹. There, too, there may have been some confusion (*Fourth Gospel*, p. 267 ; cf. Loofs, *Die Auferstehungsberichte*, p. 32). Such instances mark the limits of a laxer or stricter interpretation of the historicity of the documents, between which we are not in a position to decide with absolute certainty.

B. FIRST ACTIVE OR CONSTRUCTIVE PERIOD : THE FOUNDING OF THE KINGDOM.

§ 17. *Scene.*— Mainly in Galilee, but also partly in Jerusalem.

Time.—From about Pentecost A.D. 27 to shortly before Passover A.D. 28.

Mt 4¹²–13⁵³, Mk 1¹⁴–6¹³, Lk 4¹⁴–9⁶, Jn 5¹⁻⁴⁷.

In this period the points to notice are: (i.) The Call, Training, and Mission of the Twelve, followed perhaps by a larger number (the Seventy of St. Luke); (ii.) the gradual differentiation of the ministry of Jesus from that of John Baptist, and its assumption of a much larger scope; (iii.) a full course of teaching on the true nature of the Kingdom of God (or of Heaven); (iv.) the performance of a number of Messianic works, chiefly of healing; (v.) the effect of these works on the common people as seen in a great amount of superficial enthusiasm, but without as yet much intelligent apprehension of the object really in view; (vi.) the growing hostility of the scribes and Pharisees caused by a more and more declared divergence of principle; (vii.) the very gentle indirect and gradual putting forward by Jesus of His claim as the Messiah.

Up to the point which we have now reached there had been no definite 'founding' of a society; no steps had been taken towards the institution even of a new sect, much less of a new religion. The Baptism of Jesus had been attended by circumstances which marked Him out in a highly significant manner; but the general knowledge of these circumstances was vague, and even in those who were not unacquainted with them they awoke expectations rather than convictions, and these, too, were vague and left for the future to define. For the rest little as yet had occurred to define them. A certain number of disciples had gathered round Jesus in the most easy and natural manner, just as disciples had gathered round many a Rabbi before

Him.   These simply came and went as inclination took them; they were not as yet bound by any closer ties to His person.   He had gone about quietly with some of them in His company, but nothing very startling had happened.   The expulsion of the buyers and sellers from the temple was a prophetic act, and two 'signs' had occurred at a considerable interval; but this was little to what the Jews expected in their Messiah.   So far Jesus had worked side by side with the Baptist, and on very similar lines.   If His disciples took a share in baptizing (Jn 4[2]), it was in the same kind of baptizing as that of John.   It was a baptism 'of repentance,' and in no sense baptism 'into the name of Christ.'

The period on which we are now entering marks a great advance.   The work which Jesus came to perform now took its distinctive shape.   What had gone before was of the nature of foretaste, hints, foreshadowings; now the strokes follow each other in quick succession by which the purpose of Jesus is set clearly before those who have eyes to see.   We may take these one by one.

§ 18. i. *The Call, Training, and Mission of the Twelve* (*and of the Seventy*).—The first step is one which evidently struck the imagination of the followers of Jesus, because it is placed in the forefront of the Synoptic narrative.   It is, in fact, the real beginning of the Public Ministry.   Among those who had been the first to seek a nearer acquaintance with the new Prophet were two pairs of brothers, both from Capernaum, and both fishermen by trade.   When Jesus returned to Galilee they all went back to their ordinary occupations, and they were engaged in these when suddenly they saw Him standing by the shore of the lake, and received a peremptory command to follow Him (Mk 1^{16-20}||). This 'following' meant something more than anything they had done as yet; they were to 'be with him' (Mk 3^{14}), so that they might receive His teaching continuously and in a manner systematically. They were encouraged to ask questions, and their questions were answered. Special and full explanations were given to them which were not given to others (Mt 13^{34}). The teaching of Jesus was not esoteric, but there was this inner circle to whom peculiar advantages were given for entering into it.

The call which was issued in the first instance to the four, Peter and Andrew, James and John, was gradually extended. The one other instance particularized in the Gospels is that of Levi, the son of Alphæus, to whom was given—possibly by Jesus Himself (Weiss, *Leben Jesu*, i. 503)—the name of 'Matthew' (= 'given by God'). A like call proceeded to others, till the number was made up to twelve (lists in Mk 3^{16-19}, Mt 10^{2-4}, Lk 6^{14-16}, Ac 1^{13}). The persons chosen belonged to the middle and lower classes. Some must have been fairly well-to-do. Not only did the fishermen own the boats they used, but the father of James and John had 'hired servants' (Mk 1^{20}), and John was acquainted with the high priest * (*i.e.*, perhaps, with members of his household, Jn 18^{15}). Matthew was of the despised class of 'publicans.' The second Simon

---

* Hugo Delff (*Gesch. d. Rabbi Jesus v. Nazareth*, p. 70 ff.), distinguishing between the Apostle John and the author of the Fourth Gospel, makes the latter a Jew of priestly family.

belonged to the party of Zealots. One, the second Judas (like his father, Simon, Jn 6^{71} 13^{26} RV), was a native of Kerioth in Judæa. They were chosen evidently for a certain moral aptitude which they showed for the mission to be entrusted to them. Judas Iscariot possessed this like the rest, but wrecked his fair chances. The choice and call of Jesus did not preclude the use of common free-will.

The course of teaching in which the Twelve were initiated covered a considerable part of that of which an outline will presently be sketched, especially its first two heads. It is summarized in the phrase 'the mystery of the Kingdom' (Mk 4^{11}||). Of course it is not to be thought that the disciples at once understood all that was told them. Very far from it. They had much to unlearn as well as to learn, and they showed themselves slow of apprehension. But the form of teaching adopted by Jesus was exactly fitted for its object, which was to lodge in the mind principles that would gradually become luminous as they were interpreted by events and by prolonged if slow reflection.

Jesus Himself knew full well how unripe even the most intimate of His disciples were to carry out His designs. After a time—we may suppose early in the year 28—He sent out the Twelve on a mission to villages and country districts which He was not able to visit at once Himself (Mt 10$^{1ff.}$ ||). But they were not to attempt to teach. Some of the wonderful works which Jesus did Himself they also were empowered to do ; but the announcement which they were to make by word of mouth was limited to the one formula with

which both John and Jesus had begun : 'The kingdom
of heaven is at hand' (Mt 10[7]).

In one Gospel mention is made of a mission which seems to be
supplemental to this. Luke speaks not only of the Twelve being
sent out, but also of Seventy sent out like the Twelve by twos (Lk
10[1ff.]).] When we observe that the instructions given to them
are substantially a repetition of those already given to the
Twelve, the question lies near at hand whether we have not in
this incident a mere doublet of the preceding, the number seventy
(*var. lect.* seventy-two) representing in current symbolism the
nations of the known world (cf. Gn 10)—being gradually substituted in the oral tradition of Gentile Churches for the number
twelve, which seemed to point specially to Israel. We note also
that Luke omits the restrictions of Mt 10[5]. But, on the other
hand, Luke connects with the return of the Seventy a little group
of sayings (Lk 10[18, 20]) which have every appearance of being
genuine, and so increase the credibility of the narrative which
leads up to them. And there is reason to think that one at least
of the special sources to which Luke had access came from just
such a quarter as that indicated by the Seventy—not the innermost, but the second circle of disciples. He may therefore have
had historical foundation for his statement. Nor need it perhaps
mean more than that Jesus did not draw any hard-and-fast line at
the Twelve, but made use of other disciples near His person for
the same purpose.

§ **19.** ii. *Differentiation of the Ministry of Jesus from
that of John the Baptist.*—We have just seen that John,
Jesus Himself, and the apostles all opened their ministry
with the same announcement. They also made use of
the same rite—baptism. But there the resemblance
ceased. These were only the links which bound the
stage of preparation to the stage of fulfilment. Looking back upon the work of John, Jesus pronounced
that the least of His own disciples was greater than
he (Mt 11[11]||). It was the difference between one who
was within the range of the Kingdom and one who was

without it. The work of John was perfectly good and appropriate as far as it went. Its character was indicated by the 'preaching of repentance,' with which it stopped short. In full keeping with this was John's ascetic habit and mode of life. The abandonment of this by Jesus was the first outward sign of divergence which struck the eye of the world (Mk 2^{18-22} ||, Mt $11^{18f.}$ ||). But the inward divergence was far greater. John inherited the old idea as to the nature of the Kingdom and of the Messiah. While impressed with the necessity of a moral reformation as leading up to it, there is nothing to show that in other respects John's conception of King and Kingdom differed from that of his countrymen. But Jesus came to revolutionize not only the conception but the mode of carrying it out. Hence it was that towards the end of his day, with the despondency of one whose own work seemed wrecked, and who was himself confined in a dungeon, and with the disappointment natural to one who saw or heard of but few of the signs which he had expected as in process of fulfilment, John sent to inquire if Jesus were the Messiah indeed, or, in other words, if the great hope and the great faith to which he had himself given expression had proved delusive. As yet Jesus had but in part, and that very covertly, declared Himself; it was impossible all at once to open the eyes of John to the full mysteries of the Kingdom; and therefore Jesus contented Himself with appealing from the current idea to one of the fundamental passages of ancient prophecy, the higher authority of which John would recognize (Mt 11^5 ||). At the same time He hinted that patience and insight were necessary for a true faith; anything less than this might easily stumble (Mt 11^6‖).

§ 20. iii. *Preaching of the Kingdom.*—In the meantime the crowds of Galilee, and especially the Twelve, enjoyed the privilege which John did not. They were having expounded to them in full the new doctrine of the Kingdom of God (or of heaven). This doctrine is of such far-reaching importance, and is so intimately bound up with the rest of our Lord's teaching, that it has seemed best to reserve the fuller account of it for separate and connected treatment at the end of this section. In so doing we are following the example of the First Evangelist, who has massed together a body of teaching at an early place in his Gospel (Mt 5-7), not that it was all spoken on the same occasion, but as a specimen of the general tenor of the teaching of which it formed part. We have a similar example of grouped specimens of teaching in Mt 13. It must suffice to add here (*a*) that the main subject of the teaching at this period would seem to have been the nature of the Kingdom and the character required in its members: such sayings as Mt $7^{22f.}$ are more in keeping with the later cycle of teaching, and were probably spoken later. (*b*) It must be remembered that the vast majority of those who listened to this teaching heard it only by fragments. It was like the seed-corn scattered in various kinds of ground (Mk 4^{1-20}‖): it was not to be expected that even under the most favourable circumstances it should germinate and bear fruit all at once. Clearly, the Twelve themselves did not take in its full significance. But it is much that they should have remembered so much of it as they did, and that when their eyes were more fully opened they should have been able to set it down so coherently.

§ **21.** iv. *The Messianic Works.* — Another marked characteristic of this period is the number of miraculous works of healing, etc., which are attributed to it and evidently belong to it.   Once more we may follow the example of the First Evangelist by treating these works, which are so much the subject of discussion in modern times, by themselves.   We assume here the result which we seem to reach in the section devoted to them. We assume that the miracles are historical; and we observe only that they bear the general character indicated in the reply of Jesus to John the Baptist. They are predominantly works of mercy; and they are a direct, and as we believe conscious, fulfilment of the most authentic of ancient prophecies, as contrasted with the mere signs and wonders for which the contemporary Jews were looking.   Here, as in other things, we note at once (*a*) that Jesus condescends to put Himself at the level of those to whom He was sent. Miracles were to them the natural credentials of any great prophet, and especially of the Messiah.   Jesus therefore did not refuse to work miracles.   That He should work them was part of the conditions of the humanity which He assumed.   But (*b*) though He condescended to work miracles, it was only miracles of a certain kind. He steadily refused to perform the mere wonders which the critics of His claims repeatedly challenged Him to perform.   In other words, He made His miracles almost as much a vehicle of instruction as His teaching.   Those which He did perform fell into their place as the natural accompaniment of one who as in character so novel and unexpected a King was founding so novel a Kingdom.

§ **22.** v. *Effect on the Populace.*—It is a confirmation of the view taken above and based on the Fourth Gospel,—that the call of the Twelve was preceded by a preliminary and more sporadic ministry—that from the first day on which the regular ministry began it attracted great attention and was attended by great, if superficial, success among the populace of Galilee (Mk 1^{32-34}||). Nor did the success of this first day stand alone; it was frequently repeated, and indeed gives the character to the whole of this period (Mk $2^{2.12}$|| 3^{7-10}|| ^{32}|| 4^{1}|| 5^{21}||, Lk $7^{16f.}$). Both the miracles and the teaching of Jesus made a strong impression. The people were struck by the difference between the acts and words of Jesus and those of the teachers to whom they were accustomed. Acts and words alike implied a claim to an authority different in kind from that of the most respected of the Rabbis (Mk 1^{27}||, Mt $7^{28f.}$). The Rabbis interpreted the law as they found it; Jesus laid down a new law (Mt $5^{21.22}$ etc.), and when He spoke, it was with an air of command. It must not, however, be supposed that Jesus was at once recognized as the Messiah. The testimony of the Baptist had reached but few, and was by this time generally forgotten. The construction put upon the commanding attitude of Jesus was that described in Lk 7^{16} 'A great prophet is arisen among us; and God hath visited His people.' Still less can it be supposed that there was any adequate recognition of the change which Jesus came to work in the current conceptions of religion.

§ **23.** vi. *Effect upon the Pharisees.*—The populace came to Jesus with simple and credulous minds, and they did not resist the impression made upon them, though it lacked depth and permanence (Mk $4^{5f.}$ ‖). Our documents are doubtless right in representing the first signs of opposition and hostility as coming from the religious leaders, the scribes and Pharisees. They are also clearly right in representing the growth of this opposition as gradual. At first Pharisees joined freely in social intercourse with Jesus and His disciples, and even invited them to their own tables (Lk $7^{36ff.}$ probably belongs to this early period). They could not deny the possibility of a prophet arising, and they repeatedly sought to test after their manner whether Jesus were really a prophet sent from God or no (Mt $12^{38ff.}$‖ $16^{1ff.}$ $19^{3ff.}$‖, Jn $7^{47ff.}$, cf. $1^{19ff.}$). But their suspicions were soon aroused. It was evident that the teaching and manner of the life of Jesus conflicted greatly with their own. There was a freedom and largeness of view about it which was foreign to their whole habits of thought. (*a*) In such matters as fasting, the practice of Jesus and His disciples was different (Mk $2^{18ff.}$, Mt $6^{16ff.}$ etc.). Worse than this, Jesus appealed expressly to those classes which they scrupulously avoided (Mk 2^{15-17}‖ etc.). (*b*) Not only did Jesus direct His ministry especially to those whom they regarded as outcast and irreclaimable, but He made some direct attacks upon themselves. At first these attacks may have been slightly disguised (as in Mt $6^{1ff.}$, where the Pharisees are not mentioned by name), but they constantly increased in directness and severity. (*c*) One of the first topics on which they came into collision was in regard to the keeping of the Sabbath. Mark has collected a little group of incidents bearing upon this (Mk 2²³–3⁶), the first of which, from the mention of the ripe corn, appears, as we have seen, to belong to the second year of the ministry, but belongs to an early phase in the conflict. To the same effect is the incident related in Jn 5¹ᶠᶠ·, and Luke contributes another (Lk 13¹¹⁻¹⁷). (*d*) The Pharisees were also honestly shocked at seeing Jesus adopt a tone and assume prerogatives which seemed to them to encroach upon the honour of God (Mk 2⁵⁻¹¹‖).

(C) Sabbath

(d) Jesus' a... high prerogative

It is interesting, and throws a favourable light on the documents, to note how carefully the distinction is marked between (*a*) the local scribes and Pharisees such as were to be found scattered throughout Galilee (Mk 2⁶·‖ ¹⁶·‖ ¹⁸· ²⁴ 3⁶‖, Lk 7³⁶); (*b*) the scribes who came down from Jerusalem (Mk 3²²), apparently emissaries from the hierarchy, like the deputation of Jn 1¹⁹; and (*c*) the Herodians (Mk 3⁶), the dynastic party of the Herods, who with quite different motives acted in alliance with the Pharisees. The Herodians are mentioned again in Mk 12¹³‖. The name is otherwise almost unknown to history, though the party is known to have existed. Josephus has οἱ τὰ Ἡρώδου φρονοῦντες, but not Ἡρωδιανοί. This is a pure reflexion of the facts of the time—facts which soon passed away, and which fiction would never have recovered. See, further, *DB*, art. HERODIANS.

§ 24. *The Self-Revelation of Jesus.*—Although Jesus assumed these high prerogatives, and although, as we have seen, He both spoke and acted with an authority which permitted no question, He showed a singular reticence in putting forward Messianic or Divine claims. It is remarkable that from the first those possessed

Self Revelation Jesus

checked
[?] of demons

o (p 112)

with demons publicly confessed Him for what He was;
but it is no less remarkable that He checked these
confessions: 'He suffered not the demons to speak,
because they knew him' (Mk 1³⁴‖ 3¹² [Mt 12¹⁶]).   He
imposed a like injunction of silence on one healed of
leprosy (Mk 1⁴⁴‖).   The farthest point to which Jesus
went in the way of self-revelation at this early period
was by taking to Himself the special title 'Son of
Man.'   There was probably some precedent for the
identification of this title with 'Messiah,' but it was at
least not in common use, and therefore served well to
cover a claim which was made but in no way obtruded.
A fuller discussion of the title will be found below
(p. 91 ff.).

This marked reticence of Jesus in regard to His own
Person is clearly part of a deliberate plan.   One of its
motives was to prevent the rash and reckless violence
which one who appealed to the Messianic expectation
was sure to excite (Jn 6¹⁵).   But it was in full keeping
with the whole of His demeanour and with the special
character which He gave to His mission.   The first
evangelist rightly sees in this a fulfilment (which we
believe here as elsewhere to have been conscious and
deliberate) of the prophecy Is 42¹⁻³ 'My servant . . .
shall not strive, nor cry aloud; neither shall any one
hear his voice in the streets,' etc.

It is impossible for us to think of the Jesus portrayed
in the Gospels as forcing His claims upon the attention
of the world.   He rather let them sink gently into the
minds of His disciples until they won an assent which
was not only free and spontaneous, but also more
intelligent than it could have been if enforced simply by

authority. But, apart from this, it was essential to the development of His mission that the teaching of the Kingdom should precede, and precede by a sufficient interval, the public self-manifestation and offer of the King. The first thing to be done was to change the character and revolutionize the moral conceptions of men. This was to be the work of quiet teaching. The hour for the Leader to come forward was the hour when teaching was to give place to action. Hence it was well that at first and for some time to come the King should remain, as it were, in the background, until the preparation for His assuming His kingship was complete.

CHAPTER IV.

TEACHING AND MIRACLES.

The Teaching of Jesus.

a. General Characteristics of the Teaching.

§ 25. (1) *Its Relation to the Teaching of the Baptist and to that of the Scribes.*—We have seen that Jesus began by taking up not only the announcement of the Baptist that the Kingdom of God was at hand, but also his call to reformation of life and the rite of baptism by which that call was impressed upon the conscience. We are also expressly told that the call to repentance was part of the apostolic commission (Mk 6^{12}). And we find it no less insisted upon after the resurrection (Lk 24^{47}, Ac 2^{38} 3^{19} 5^{31} 11^{18} 17^{30} 20^{21} 26^{20}).

This is clear proof of the continuity which bound together the teaching of Jesus with that of the Baptist. The starting-point of both was the same. And yet this starting-point was very soon left behind. The heads of the Baptist's teaching are soon told; the teaching of Jesus expands and ramifies in a thousand directions. It is like passing from the narrow cleft of the Jordan to a Pisgah-view over the whole Land of Promise.

5

Although it was permitted to the Baptist to prepare the way for the teaching of Jesus, so far as even to enunciate its opening lesson, the place of the Baptist is quietly assigned to him; and it is a place outside the threshold of the Kingdom : 'He that is but little in the kingdom of heaven is greater than he' (Mt 11[11]∥).

If Christ thus drew a line between His own teaching and that of John, still more marked was the difference between it and other contemporary teaching. John was at least a prophet, and spoke with the full authority of a prophet (Mt 11[9, 13]). The scribes had no original authority at all; they did but interpret a law which they had not made. Jesus spoke with an authority not only above that of the scribes (Mk 1[22]∥), but higher still than that of John. He is the legislator of a new law (Mt 5[22] etc.), the founder of that Kingdom which John did not enter.

§ 26. (2) *Its Universal Range.*—With this commanding character of the teaching of Jesus there goes a corresponding width of outlook. We began with a rapid survey of the state of parties and opinions in Palestine at the time of Christ. But the object of this survey was not to explain the teaching of Jesus by affiliating it to any existing school. It was remarked of Him that He had had no regular training (Jn 7[15]). He was not a Pharisee, not a Sadducee, not an Essene, not an Apocalyptist. The direct affinities of the teaching of Jesus were with nothing so transitory and local, but rather with that which was most central in OT. We might call it the distilled essence of OT: that essence first clarified and then greatly enlarged, the drop became a crystal sphere.

We are speaking, of course, of the substance, and of the main part of the substance, of the teaching of Jesus. The mere fact that it was conditioned by time and space involved that it should be addressed to a given generation in a language which it understood. Nor was it wholly without definite and particular applications—sidelights, so to speak, upon that space in history within which it falls. But history itself has shown that in the main it transcends all these conditions, and is as fresh at the end of eighteen centuries as when first it was delivered.

§ 27. (3) *Its Method.*—This wonderful adaptability in the teaching of Jesus is accounted for in part by its extreme simplicity. If it had been a doctrine of the schools, something of the fashion of the schools would have adhered to it. But, as it was, it was addressed chiefly to the common people—sometimes to congregations in synagogues, sometimes to the chance company collected in private houses, more often still to casual gatherings in the open air.

And the language in which the teaching was couched was such as to appeal most directly to audiences like these. As a rule it takes hold of the simplest elements in our common humanity, 'das allgemein Menschliche.' The trivial incidents of everyday life are made to yield their lessons: the sower scattering his seed, the housewife baking her cakes or sweeping the house to find a lost piece of money, the shepherd collecting his sheep, the fishermen drawing in their net. Sometimes the story which forms the vehicle for the teaching takes a higher flight: it deals with landed proprietors, and banquets, and kings with their subjects. But even then there seems to be a certain deliberate simplification. The kings, for instance, are those of the popular tale rather than as the courtier would paint them.

Parables

§ **28.** (4) *The Parables.*—We have been naturally drawn into describing that which is most characteristic in the outward form of the teaching of Jesus—His parables. The Greek word παραβολή is used in the NT in a wider sense than that in which we are in the habit of using it. In Lk 4²³ it = 'proverb.' In Mt 15¹⁵ (comp. with vv.¹¹· ¹⁶⁻²⁰) it = 'maxim,' a condensed moral truth, whether couched in figurative language or not. It covers as well brief aphoristic sayings (*e.g.* Mk 3²³ 13²⁸‖, Lk 5³⁶ 6³⁹) as longer discourses in which there is a real 'comparison.' But these latter are the 'parables' in our modern acceptation of the term: they are scenes or short stories taken from nature or from common life, which present in a picturesque and vivid way some leading thought or principle which is capable of being transferred to the higher spiritual life of man. The 'parable' in a somewhat similar sense to this had been employed in OT and by the Rabbis, but it had never before been employed with so high a purpose, on so large a scale, or with such varied application and unfailing perfection of form.

Parables 1)
and
) Parallelism

We may say that the parables of Jesus are of two kinds. In some the element of 'comparison' is more prominent. In these the parable moves as it were in two planes—one that of the scene or story which is made the vehicle for the lesson, and the other that of the higher truth which it is sought to convey; the essence of the parable lies in the parallelism. In the other kind there is no parallelism, but the scene or the story is just a typical example of the broader principle which it is intended to illustrate. The parables in Mt 13, Mk 4 all belong to the one class, several of those in the later chapters of St. Luke (the Good Samaritan, the Rich Fool, the Rich Man and Lazarus, the Pharisee and the Publican) belong rather to the other.

There is a group of sayings in the Fourth Gospel to which is given the name παροιμία rather than παραβολή (Jn 10⁶, cf. 16²⁵· ²⁹), though the latter term would not have been inappropriate, in which Jesus uses the method of comparison to bring out leading features in His own character and person. In this way He speaks of Himself as the Good Shepherd, the Door of the sheep, the Vine, the Light of the World. These sayings form a class by themselves, and from the peculiar way in which they are worked out—the metaphor and the object explained by the metaphor being not kept apart but blended and fused together—are commonly classed under the head of 'allegory' rather than 'parable.' This is another instance in which we draw distinctions where the Greek of the NT would not have drawn them.

§ 29. (5) *Interpretation of the Parables.*—To this day there is some difference of opinion as to the interpretation of the parables. The Patristic writers as a rule (though with some exceptions) allow themselves great latitude of interpretation. Any point of resemblance to any detail of the parable, however subordinate, justifies in their eyes a direct application of that detail. A familiar instance is the identification of the 'two pence,' which the Good Samaritan gives to the host, with the two Sacraments. An opposite modern school would restrict the application to the leading idea which the parable expresses. It is, however, fair to remember that the parables are meant to illustrate the laws of God's dealings with men; and as the same law is capable of many particular applications, all such applications may be said with equal right to be included in the parable. For instance, the parable of the Two Sons may be as true for individuals or for classes as it is for nations or groups of nations. The parable of the Great Banquet to which the invited guests do not come, and which is then thrown open to others who were not invited, no doubt points directly to the first reception of the gospel, but it is equally appropriate to every case where religious privilege is found to give no advantage, and the absence of religious privilege proves no insuperable hindrance. Any such range of application is legitimate and interesting; nor does the aptness of the lesson to one set of incidents make it any less apt to others where a like principle is at work. Every parable has its central idea, and whatever can be related to that idea may be fairly brought within its scope. To press mere coincidences with the picturesque accessories of a parable may be permissible as rhetoric, but can have no higher value.

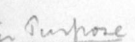

§ **30.** (6) *The Purpose of Teaching by Parables.*—If

we had before us only the fact of parabolic teaching,
with the parables as they have come down to us and
the actual psychological effect which they are seen to
exercise, we should probably not hesitate as to the
reason which we assigned for them.   The parabolic
form is, as it were, a barb to the arrow which carries
home truth to the mind.   The extreme beauty of this
mode of teaching, handled as it is, has been universally
acknowledged.   If simplicity is an element in beauty,
we have it here to perfection.   But when simplicity
is united to profundity, and to a profundity which
comes from the touching of elemental chords of human
feeling,—a touching so delicate, so sure, and so self-
restrained, which reminds us of the finest Greek art
with an added spiritual intensity which in that art was
the one thing wanting,—we have indeed a product
such as the world had never seen before and will not
see again.   We seem to be placed for the moment at
the very centre of things : on the one hand there is laid
bare before us the human heart as it really is or ought
to be, with all its perversities and affectations stripped
away ; and on the other hand we seem to be admitted
to the secret council-chamber of the Most High, and to
have revealed to us the plan by which He governs the
world, the threads in all the tangled skein of being.
No wonder that the parables have exercised such an
attractive power, not over any one class or race of men,
but over humanity wherever it is found.

Then the nature of the parable, at once presenting
a picture to the mind and provoking to the search for
a hidden meaning or application beneath it, would seem
to be exactly suited to the pædagogic method of Jesus,

which always calls for some responsive effort on the part of man, and which prefers to produce its effects not all at once, but rather with a certain suspense and delay, so that the good seed may have time to germinate and strike its roots more deeply into the soil.

This natural action of the method of teaching by parables seems so obvious, that we might well be content not to seek any further.   But when we turn to the Gospels, we find there stated a motive for the adoption of this method of teaching which is wholly different, and it must be confessed at first sight somewhat paradoxical.   All three Synoptists agree in applying to teaching by parables the half-denunciatory passage Is 6^{9-10}; they would make its immediate object not so much to reveal truth as to conceal it—at least to conceal it for the moment from one class while it is revealed to another, and its ulterior object to aggravate the guilt of those from whom it is concealed.   And, what is still more remarkable, all three Synoptists ascribe the use of this quotation to our Lord Himself, as though it really expressed, not merely the result of His chosen method of teaching, but its deliberate purpose.   What are we to make of this?   One group of critics would roundly deny that the words were ever used in this manner by our Lord.   Jülicher (*e.g.*) takes his stand on Mk 4^{33} 'with many such parables spake he the word unto them, *as they were able to hear it,*' which would seem to make the method a tender concession to slowness of apprehension rather than a means of aggravating it.   But, on the other hand, we observe that the quotation is attributed to our Lord in what must have been the common original of all three

Gospels, *i.e.* in one of our best and oldest sources. And while such passages as Jn 12$^{39-41}$ (where the same quotation is applied by the evangelist) and Ac 28$^{25-27}$ (where it is applied by St. Paul) would show that it was part of the common property of the apostolic age, the fact that it was so would be still more intelligible if the example had been set by our Lord Himself. Nor would it be less but rather more appropriate as coming from Him, if we regard it as summing up in a broad way what He felt was and must be for many of those among whom He moved the final outcome of His mission. The lesson is very similar to that of Jn 12$^{46-48}$. The Son of Man does not need to pass judgment on those who reject Him. His word judges them by an automatic process. That which is meant for their life becomes to them an occasion of falling, when from indolence or self-will it makes no impression upon them. This was the actual course of things; it was a course rendered inevitable by the laws which God had laid down, and which in that sense might be regarded as designed by Him. And inasmuch as the Son associates Himself with the providential action of the Father, it might be also spoken of as part of His own design. It is so, however, rather in the remoter degree in which, allowing for the contrariant action of human wills, whatever is is also ordained, than as directly purposed before the appeal has been made and rejected. It belongs to that department of providential action which is not primary and due to immediate Divine initiative, but secondary or contingent upon human failure.

There is then perhaps sufficient reason to think that

the words may after all have been spoken, much as we have them, by our Lord.   But granting this, we should still not be forbidden to surmise that they are some-what out of place.   Standing where they do they come to us with a shock of strange severity, which would be mitigated if they could be put later in the ministry, where they occur in St. John.   The transference may have been due to the position which the original pas-sage occupies in Isaiah, where it also serves as a sort of programme of the prophet's mission.   There, too, the arrangement may conceivably represent the actual historical order, but it may also represent the result of later experience, which for didactic effect is placed at the beginning of the career rather than at the end.

b. Contents of the Teaching.

§ 31. There are five distinctive and characteristic topics in the teaching of Jesus—

(1) The Fatherhood of God.
(2) The Kingdom of God.
(3) The Subjects or Members of the Kingdom.
(4) The Messiah.
(5) The Paraclete and the Tri-unity of God.

With that simplicity which we have seen to be so marked a feature in His teaching, Jesus selects two of the most familiar of all relations to be the types round which He groups His teaching in regard to God and man—the family and the organized state; God stands to man in the relation at once of Father and of King.   These two types by no means exclude each other, but each helps to complete the idea derived from the other without which it might be one-sided.   At the

same time, in different connexions, first one and then
the other becomes more prominent.   Thus, when stress
is laid upon the Divine attributes, God appears chiefly
in the character of Father; when attention is turned
to the complex relations of men to Him and to one
another, they are more commonly regarded under the
figure of a Kingdom.

§ 32. (1) *The Fatherhood of God.*—It has just been
said that the doctrine that God is Father by no means
excludes the doctrine that He is also King.   This idea,
too, is repeatedly put forward (Mt 5^{35} 18^{23} 22^2 etc.).
The title 'King' brings out what in modern language
we are accustomed to call the 'transcendence' of God.
But the recognition of this was, as we saw (p. 13, *sup.*),
a strong point in the contemporary Judaism, and therefore it needed no special emphasis.   It was otherwise
with the idea of Fatherhood.

Not that this idea was unknown to the pagan
religions, and still less to the religion of Israel.   From
Homer onwards Zeus had borne the name 'Father of
gods and men.'   But this was a superficial idea : it
meant little more than 'originator.'   This sense also
appears in the older Jewish literature, but with further
connotations added to it.   God is more particularly the
Father of His people Israel (cf. Dt 14^1 32^6, Jer 3^{19} $31^{9.\ 20}$),
in a yet deeper sense of the righteous in Israel (Is 63^{16}),
and, though not with the same wealth of meaning, of
the individual (Mal 2^{10}, Sir $23^{1.\ 4}$).

It is the tenderest side of the teaching of OT
(Ps 103^{13}) which is now taken up and developed.   It
becomes indeed the corner-stone of the NT teaching

about God.   The name 'Father' becomes in NT what
the name Jehovah (Jahveh) was in OT, the fullest
embodiment of revelation.   If it is prominent in the
apostolic writings, this is traceable ultimately to the
teaching of Jesus (cf. Ro 8[15] and comms.).   The title
belongs primarily to Jesus Himself as 'the Son' (ὁ
Πατήρ μου, esp. Mt 11[27]).   Through Him it descends
to His followers (ὁ Πατὴρ ὑμῶν, ὁ Πατήρ σου, Mt
5[16. 45. 48] 6[1. 4. 6. 8. 9. 14. 15] etc.).   But the love of God
as Father extends beyond these limits even to 'the
unthankful and evil' (Lk 6[35], Mt 5[45]).   The presentation of God as Father culminates in the parable of the
Prodigal Son.   Older conceptions of God find their
counterpart in the Elder Brother of this parable (Lk
15[25ff.] contrasted with v.[20]).   The application which
is thus made of the Fatherhood of God invests the
teaching of Jesus with wonderful tenderness and beauty
(Mt 6[32] 7[11] 10[29. 30], Lk 12[32] etc.).

§ 33. (2) *The Kingdom of God.*—If the conception of
God as Father does not exclude His majesty as King,
no more does the conception of His Kingdom exclude
that of children gathered together in His family.   Still,
the leading term to denote those active relations of
God with man, with which the mission of Jesus is
specially connected, is ἡ βασιλεία τοῦ θεοῦ or τῶν
οὐρανῶν.

The use of these terms suggests a number of questions which are still much debated.   (i.) Were both
names originally used?   Or if one is to be preferred,
which?   (ii.) What is the meaning of the phrase?
Does βασιλεία = 'kingdom' or 'reign'?   (iii.) When

we have determined this, with what order of ideas is the phrase to be associated? With the later Judaism? or with the teaching of the prophets? Or does it belong to the more novel element in the teaching of our Lord? (iv.) Is the Kingdom merely conceived of from the side of man or from the side of God? Is it something which man works out or which is bestowed upon him? (v.) Is it present or future? Was it in course of realization during the lifetime of Jesus Himself, or is it mainly eschatological? (vi.) Is it inward or outward? A moral reformation or the founding of a society? (vii.) Was the conception as at first framed national or universal?

These questions are put as alternatives. And they are usually so regarded. But it may be well to say at once that in almost every case there seems to be real evidence for both sides of the proposition; so that the inference is that the conception to which they relate was in fact many-sided, and included within itself a number of different *nuances*, all more or less valid. And the reason for this appears to be, that our Lord took up a conception which He found already existing, and although He definitely discarded certain aspects of it, left others as they were, some with and some without a more express sanction, while He added new ones. The centre or focus of the idea is thus gradually shifted; and while parts of it belong to so much of the older current conception as was not explicitly repealed, other parts of it are a direct expression of the new spirit introduced into it. The one element definitely expelled was that which associated the inauguration of the Kingdom with political violence and revolution.

(i.) *The Name.*—It is well known that the phrase ἡ βασιλεία τῶν οὐρανῶν for ἡ βασ. τ. θεοῦ is a peculiarity of the First Gospel (where it occurs thirty-two times), and that it receives no sanction from the other Synoptics. Neither can Jn 3[5], where the reading is distinctly Western, be quoted in support of it. Hence some have thought that it was a coinage of Matthew. It occurs, however, also in *Ev. sec. Heb.* (Handmann, p. 89); and the fact that βασ. τ. θ. is found in Mt 12[28] 21[31, 43] would go to show that the evangelist had no real objection to that form, while the corresponding phrase πάτηρ ὁ ἐν τοῖς οὐρανοῖς though it disappears from Lk 11[2] is verified by Mk 11[25]. Moreover, we know that 'heaven' was a common metonymy for 'God' in the language of the time (cf. also Mk 10[21], Lk 10[20] 12[33]), and that the particular phrase 'kingdom of heaven' (though not exactly in the sense usually assigned to it; see below under ii.) occurs repeatedly in the Talmud. It seems, therefore, on the whole probable that both forms were used by our Lord Himself. In any case they may be regarded as equivalents.

(ii.) *Meaning.* — The phrase in both its forms is ambiguous : it may mean either 'kingdom' or 'reign,' 'sovereignty,' 'rule' of heaven, or of God. It appears that in the Talmud the latter signification is the more common (Schürer, *NT Zeitgesch.*[3] ii. 539 n. [Eng. tr. II. ii. 171]; Edersheim, *Life and Times*, etc. i. 267 f.). And though the former is that more usually adopted by commentators, there seems to be no reason why recourse should not be had to the latter where it is more natural (as, *e.g.*, in Lk 17[20, 21]). The phrase covers both senses, and the one will frequently be found to shade off into the other. The best definition known to the writer is one given incidentally by Dr. Hort (*Life and Letters*, ii. 273), 'the world of invisible laws by which God is ruling and blessing His creatures.' This is the most fundamental meaning; all others are secondary. The 'laws' in question are 'a world,' inasmuch as they have a connexion and coherence of their own; they form a system, a cosmos within the cosmos; they come direct from 'heaven,' or from God; and they are 'invisible' in their origin, though they may work their way to visibility.

(iii.) *Associations.*—The sense just assigned was that which was most fundamental in the thought of Jesus. It was that which He saw ought to be the true sense, however much it might be missed by His contemporaries. It was deeper and subtler than the conception of Psalmist and Prophet, even than the bright and exhilarating picture of Ps 145$^{11-13}$, because it was compatible with any kind of social condition, and because it did not turn mainly on the majestic exercise of power. And if this was true of the later and more developed conception, much more was it true of the earlier notion of the theocracy, which was simply that of the Israelite State with a Prophet or Judge at the head instead of a King (1 S 12$^{7-12}$). The contemporaries of Jesus when they spoke of the 'Kingdom of God' thought chiefly of an empire contrasted with the great world-empires, more particularly the Roman, which galled them at the moment. And the two features which caught their imagination most were the throwing off of the hated yoke and the transference of supremacy from the heathen to Israel. This was to be brought about by a catastrophe which was to close the existing order of things, and which therefore took a shape that was eschatological.

This eschatological and catastrophic side Jesus did not repudiate, though He gave a different turn to it, but the essence of His conception was independent of all convulsions. The simplest paraphrase for 'the Kingdom of God' is the clause which follows the petition for the coming of the Kingdom in the Lord's Prayer : 'Thy will be done on earth, as it is in heaven.' The only difference is that the Prayer perhaps hints rather more at the co-operation of human wills. This is not excluded in the idea of the Kingdom, which is, however, primarily the working out of the Will of God by God Himself.

(iv.) *The Nature of the Kingdom: how far Supernatural ?*—The very name of the Kingdom 'of heaven *or* of God' implies that it has its origin in the world above. It 'comes' ($\check{\epsilon}\rho\chi\epsilon\sigma\theta\alpha\iota$, Mt 6^{10}, Mk 9^1, Lk 11^2 17^{20}; $\grave{\epsilon}\gamma\gamma\acute{\iota}\zeta\epsilon\iota\nu$, Mt 3^2 4^{17} 10^7 etc.; $\phi\theta\acute{\alpha}\nu\epsilon\iota\nu$, Mt 12^{28} = Lk 11^{20}); it is 'given' (Mt 21^{43}) and 'received' (Mk 10^{15} = Lk 18^{17}); it is 'prepared' by God (Mt 25^{34}); it is 'inherited' (*ib.*), and men 'enter into' it (Mt 5^{20} 19^{23}, Jn 3^5); it is an object of 'search' (Mt 6^{33} = Lk 12^{31}, Mt 13^{45}). All this means that it is not built up by the labour of man, it is not a product of development from below, but 'of the creative activity of God' (Lütgert, *Reich Gottes*, p. 26). It is a gift bestowed, not something to be done, but something to be enjoyed (' Nie eine Aufgabe, wohl aber eine Gabe,' Holtzmann, *NT Th.* p. 202, partly after Lütgert). It is a prize, the highest of all prizes (Mt 13[44-46]), corresponding to the *summum bonum* of pagan philosophy.

This part of the conception has a considerable range, according as the context points to the popular view of the Messianic Kingdom as implying outward conditions of splendour, abundance, and enjoyment, or as it points to what we have called the inner thought of Jesus, the invisible laws of God's working, taken into and welcomed by the individual soul, as in the parables of the Pearl and the Treasure in the Field.

These parables show that there is a place, though a subordinate place, left for human effort, the co-operation of the human will with the Divine. The process of 'seeking' implies both effort and renunciation. There must be a concentrating of the powers of the soul upon the Will of God, if that Will is to be really done; but where it is done it brings its own exceeding great reward (Lk 6[38]).

From this point of view it may be said, with Holtzman (*NT Th*. i. 202–207), that the negative side of the conception is the Forgiveness of Sins as the first condition of entrance into the Kingdom, and that the positive side of it is the active practice of Righteousness with the peace and contentment which that practice brings.

(v.) *Present or Future?*—There can be no real question that the Kingdom is presented in both lights as present and as future. Strictly speaking, the future is divided, and the notes of time are threefold—present, near future, and more distant future. Take, for instance, the following passages: Mt 12[28] (= Lk 11[20]) 'If I by the Spirit of God cast out demons, then is the

6

Kingdom of God come ($\check{\epsilon}\phi\theta\alpha\sigma\epsilon\nu$) upon you'; Mk 1[15] (= Mt 4[17]) 'The time is fulfilled, and the Kingdom of God is at hand' ($\check{\eta}\gamma\gamma\iota\kappa\epsilon\nu$); Mk 9[1] || 'There be some here . . . which shall in nowise taste of death till they see the Kingdom of God come ($\grave{\epsilon}\lambda\eta\lambda\upsilon\theta\upsilon\hat{\iota}\alpha\nu$) with power.' The only one of these passages about which there can be any doubt is the second (see above, p. 35), and even that belongs to the common groundwork of the Synoptic tradition, and it is supported by Mt 10[7]||. If the latest of these dates still falls within the lifetime of the then generation, there is a group of parables (the Mustard Seed, the Wheat and Tares, the Drag-net) which would seem at once to bring the Kingdom into the present, and to postpone its consummation.

These apparent inconsistencies are probably to be explained in the same way as others which we meet with. The future coming, the more or less distant coming, of which the Son Himself does not know the day or the hour, is the eschatological coming of the current expectation, which, if we follow our authorities, we must believe that Jesus also shared. There was, however, a certain ambiguity even in this expectation as popularly held: it was not clear exactly in what relation of time the coming of the Messiah and the establishment of His Kingdom stood to the end of all things. And this ambiguity was necessarily heightened by the peculiar nature of the coming of Christ, and the conviction which gradually forced itself upon the minds of the disciples that there must needs be a double Coming,—one in shame, the other in triumph; one therefore which for them was past, and another still in the future.

But, apart from all this, it will be apparent that the more distinctive conception of the Kingdom as the 'world of invisible laws' by which God works is not subject to the same limitations of time. In this sense it embraces the whole providential scheme of things from the beginning; though, as we have said, it is really a cosmos within the cosmos, and it has its culminating periods and moments, such as was above all that which dates from the Incarnation. The most characteristic expression of this aspect of the Kingdom would be the parables of the Leaven and of the Seed growing secretly.

(vi.) *Inward or Outward?*—A like conclusion holds good for the question which we have next to ask ourselves: Are we to think of the Kingdom of God as visible or as invisible? Is it an influence, a force or collection of forces, or is it an institution? We are familiar with the very common and often quite superficial identification of the Kingdom with the Church. Is this justified? Many recent writers answer this question emphatically, No (list with reff. in Holtzmann, *NT Th.* i. 208). And it is true that there are certain passages by which it seems to be excluded.

Conspicuous among these are the verses Lk 17[20, 21] Οὐκ ἔρχεται ἡ β. τ. θ. μετὰ παρατηρήσεως. οὐδὲ ἐροῦσιν, Ἰδοὺ ὧδε ἢ ἐκεῖ. ἰδοὺ γὰρ ἡ β. τ. θ. ἐντὸς ὑμῶν ἐστίν. A majority of leading German scholars, including Schürer (*Die Predigt. J. C.* p. 18) and Holtzmann (with a slight modification, 'in your reach'), take the last words as meaning 'in your midst,' the main ground being that they are addressed to the Pharisees. But Field seems to have shown (*Ot. Norv. ad loc.*) that this interpretation is lexically untenable ('no sound example'), and that the better rendering is *in animis vestris.*

But, on the other hand, parables like the Wheat and

the Tares and the Drag-net are most naturally explained of a visible community; and there can be no doubt that the popular expectation was of a visible kingdom, such as that in which the sons of Zebedee sought for a chief place.

If we keep to the clue which we have hitherto followed, the facts will be sufficiently clear. The Kingdom in its highest and most Christian sense is the working of 'invisible laws' which penetrate below the surface and are gradually progressive and expansive in their operation. But in this as in other cases spiritual forces take to themselves an outward form; they are enshrined in a vessel of clay, finer or coarser as the case may be, not only in men as individuals but in men as a community or communities. The society then becomes at once a vehicle and instrument of the forces by which it is animated, not a perfect vehicle or a perfect instrument,—a field of wheat mingled with tares, a net containing bad fish as well as good,—but analogous to those other visible institutions by which God accomplishes His gracious purposes amongst men.

(vii.) *National or Universal?*—The same principle holds good throughout the whole of this analysis of the idea of the Kingdom. The aptest figure to express it is that of *growth*. It is a germ, secretly and silently insinuated, and secretly and silently working until it puts forth first the blade, then the ear, then the full corn in the ear. It is a mistake to cut a section of that which is thus ceaselessly expanding, and to label it with a name which might be true at one particular moment but would not be true at the next. The Kingdom of God is not the theocracy of the OT, nor the eschato-

logical Kingdom of the Apocalypses, nor the Christian
Church of the present day, or of the Middle Ages, or of
the Fathers. These are phases through which it passes;
but it outgrows one after the other. For this reason,
because He foresaw this inevitable and continuous
growth, the chief Founder and permanent Vicegerent
of the Kingdom showed Himself, as we might think,
indifferent to the precise degree of extension which
it was to receive during His life on earth; He was
content to say that He 'was not sent but unto the lost
sheep of the house of Israel' (Mt 15^{24}), though within a
generation His gospel was about to be carried to the
ends of the then known earth. It was enough that the
seed was planted—planted in a soil suited to it, and
under conditions that ensured its full vitality, 'like a
tree by the streams of water, that bringeth forth its
fruit in its season, whose leaf also doth not wither.' It
is characteristic of God's processes that there is no
hurry or impatience about them; the Master was not so
anxious to reap immediate fruit as the disciple (Ro 1^{13}),
and therefore He calmly left it to His followers to see
'greater things' than He saw Himself (Jn 14^{12}); but
these 'greater things' are none the less virtually His
own.

§ **34.** (3) *The Members of the Kingdom.* — As the *The memb*
'Reign of God,' the βασιλεία τοῦ θεοῦ denotes certain
Divine forces or laws which are at work in the world;
as the Kingdom of God it was at most stages a society,
but at all stages a definite sphere or area, into which
men might enter, and, by entering, become partakers
of the same Divine forces or subject to the same Divine

laws. It was therefore a matter of much moment what
were the conditions of entrance into the Kingdom, and
what was the character impressed upon its members.
The two things run into each other, because it was
required of those who entered that they should possess
at least the germs of the character to be developed in
them.

(i.) *Conditions of Entrance.*—These are clearly laid
down : 'Except ye turn, and become as little children,
ye shall in no wise enter into the kingdom of heaven'
(Mt 18³). There was to be a definite change of mind, a
break with the sinful past. This was to be ratified by
submission to the rite of baptism, which, in the discourse with Nicodemus, is described as a new birth of
'water and Spirit' (Jn 3⁵). The entrance into the
Kingdom is something more than a deliberate act of
the man himself, it is a self-surrender to Divine influences. The response on the part of God is forgiveness, which is the permanent concomitant of baptism,
not only that of John, but also that in the name of
Christ (Mk 1⁴‖, comp. with Ac 2³⁸, Lk 24⁴⁷ etc.).

(ii.) *The Character of the Members.* — The typical
character of the members of the Kingdom is that of a
'little child,' in which the prominent features are
innocence, simplicity of aim, absence of self-assertion,
trustfulness, and openness to influences from above.
A sketch of such a character is given in the Beatitudes
(Mt 5³⁻⁹; the ‖ in Lk 6²⁰⁻²⁶ refers rather to conditions
or circumstances suited to the character). The Christian ideal here depicted stands out in marked contrast
to most other ideals of what is admirable in man. The
qualities commended ('poor in spirit' — where the

Matthæan gloss is in any case right in sense,—'meek,'
'merciful,' 'pure in heart,' 'peacemakers') are all of
the gentle, submissive, retiring order. And this is
fully borne out by other sayings, the cheek turned to
the smiter, the litigant forestalled, the requisition of
labour offered freely, and even doubled (Mt 5^{38-41}||),
enemies to be loved, persecutors to be prayed for (*ib.*
vv.$^{43. 44}$), the sword to be sheathed (Mt 26^{52}), the duties
of charity strongly inculcated (Lk 10^{25-37}), the duty of
forgiveness of injuries (Mt $18^{23ff.}$), service greater than
authority (Lk $22^{25ff.}$). And it is noticeable that the
same type of character is praised by St. Paul (Ro 12^{21}
'Be not overcome of evil, but overcome evil with
good'; cf. ch. 13). The whole duty of man is summed
up in love to God and love to one's neighbour (again cf.
Ro 13^{8-10}). We observe, too, that the ethical teaching
of Jesus is almost confined to that side of ethics which
touches upon religion. Allusions to civic and industrial
duties are very few, and those negative rather than
positive (Mt 18^{27} 22^{21} = Ro 13^{7}).

(iii.) *Paradoxes of Christianity.*—It is only natural
that these features in the teaching of Christ should be
taken hold of and made a charge against Christianity,
as they have been from Suetonius onwards (*Domit.* 15,
'contemptissimæ inertiæ,' of Flavius Clemens, probably
as a Christian; cf. Tertull. *Apol.* 42, 'infructuosi in
negotiis dicimur'). And it may be doubted whether
even yet the full intention of our Lord has been
fathomed, and the exact place of the specifically Christian ideal in relation to civic and social duties ascer-
tained. The following suggestions may be offered.

The precepts in question were probably addressed

in the first instance, not to promiscuous multitudes, but to the disciples. If certain passages (as Mt 5[1]) may be quoted to the contrary, it should be remembered that these introductory notes as to the circumstances under which discourses were spoken are among the least trustworthy parts of the Gospel tradition, and are often nothing more than vague conjectures of the evangelists. The type of character described bears on its face the marks of being intended for the little community of Christians (cf. Latham, *Pastor Pastorum*, p. 253).

As such we can see that it had a very special appropriateness. It was not an accident that Christianity is the religion of the Crucified. The Cross is but the culminating expression of a spirit which was characteristic of it throughout. Its peculiar note is *Victory through Suffering*. An idea like that of Islam, making its way by the sword, was abhorrent to it from the first. Jesus came to be the Messiah of the Jews, but the narratives of the Temptation teach us that, from the very beginning of His career, He stripped off from His conception of Messiahship all that was political, all thought of propagating His claims by force. A new mode of propagating religion was deliberately chosen, and carried through with uncompromising thoroughness. The disciple was not above His Master; and the example which Jesus set in founding His faith by dying for it, was an example which His disciples were called upon to follow into all its logical consequences. Christianity, the true Christianity, carries no arms; it wins its way by lowly service, by patience, by self-sacrifice.

History shows that there are no instruments of religious propaganda comparable to these. It also shows that the type of character connected with them is of the very highest attractiveness and beauty. Is it a complete type, a type to which we can apply the Kantian maxim, 'So act as if your action was to be a law for all human beings'? This would seem to be more than we ought to say. It is not clear that the Christian type would be what it is if it were not built upon, and if it did not presuppose, a certain structure of society, to which other motives had contributed. The ethical ideal of Christianity is the ideal of a Church. It does not follow that it is also the ideal of the State. If we are to say the truth, we must admit that parts of it would become impracticable if they were transferred from the individual standing alone to governments or individuals representing society. It could not be intended that the officers of the law should turn the cheek to the criminal. The apostles were to bear no sword, but the judge 'beareth not the sword in vain.'

May we not say that the functions of Christian morals —specifically Christian morals—are these? (1) At their first institution to form a vehicle, the only possible vehicle, for the Christian religion. So far as Christianity has taken a real and genuine hold upon society, it is through these means and no others. Other things may have commended it for a time, but no trust can be placed in them. (2) The Christian motive acting in the midst of other motives gradually leavens and modifies them, imparting to them something which they had not before. If we look round us at the

principles which at this moment regulate the action of
States, in their external or international relations as
well as those which are internal, we shall see that if
these principles are not wholly Christian, they are also
not pagan. They have a certain coherence, and they
mark a very conspicuous advance as compared with
the principles of the ancient world. Christianity has
shown a power of modifying what it does not altogether
supplant. The world even outside Christianity is still
God's world. It is a world of which the essential characteristic is that it is progressive; and it may conduce
most to this progress that it should be brought under
the influence of the Christian precept, not pure but in
dilution. And (3) may we not draw from this the
augury that in the end, at some time which we cannot
see, the social structure may be still more fully re-cast,
under the influence of Christianity: 'Nation shall not
lift up sword against nation, neither shall they learn
war any more'? We can conceive a condition of things
in which the Church became coextensive with the State,
and in which religion penetrated the body politic in a
sense in which it has never done so yet. When that
time came, conduct which now would be only quixotic
might be rational, and required by the public conscience.

When the verse Mt 5^{42} 'Give to him that asketh
thee,' etc., is criticized from the point of view of modern
political economy, the mistake is in applying a standard
which is out of place. In those days the natural and,
indeed, the only outlet of the kind for benefiting the
poor was almsgiving; and our Lord's main object
was to strengthen the motive, which was in itself a
thoroughly right one. It would have been in vain to

anticipate methods which God has evidently intended to be the result of long experience. The argument from analogy comes in here with great force. God *might* have removed many forms of human ill with a word; but as it is, He has been pleased to let improved methods, and the wisdom to use them, grow gradually and grow together. The advance which mankind slowly makes is a solid advance, and an advance not here and there, but all along the line.

We have seen that our Lord was not careful to guard against misunderstandings. It has been a salutary exercise for His followers to find out what was the true sense of His sayings for themselves.

§ 35. (4) *The Messiah.*—We are not concerned here with the very remarkable historical evolution of the claim of our Lord to be the Messiah, which will come before us in connexion with the narrative of His life. At present we have to do only with His teaching on the subject, and that mainly with reference to the deeply significant names by which His claim was conveyed.

(i.) **The Christ.**—We need not delay over the title 'Messiah,' 'Christ,' 'Anointed,' which is simply that of the current Jewish expectation. It is repeatedly applied to our Lord by others, and on three occasions, at least, expressly accepted by Himself (Jn 4²⁶, Mt 16¹⁷, Mk 14⁶¹· ⁶² ‖, cf. Jn 11²⁷); but only once does our Lord use the term of Himself (Jn 17³ Ἰησοῦν Χριστόν), and that in a passage where we cannot be sure that the wording is not that of the evangelist. In like manner the title 'Elect' (ἐκλελεγμένος, Lk 9³⁵; ἐκλεκτός, Lk

23^{35}), which is also current (cf. Enoch 40^5), is applied to our Lord, but not by Himself.

(ii.) **Son of David.**—Much the same may be said of another title which belongs to a prominent side of the expectation. 'Son of David' occurs several times (on the lips of the crowd at and before the triumphal entry, of the Syrophœnician woman, of Bartimæus, of the Pharisees), but Jesus Himself does not use it, and rather propounds a difficulty in regard to it (Mk 12^{35} ||).

(iii.) **Son of Man.**—The really characteristic title which occurs some eighty times in the Gospels, and is without doubt the one which Jesus chose to express His own view of His office, is 'the Son of Man.' Whereas the other titles are used by others of Him, this is used only by Him and of Himself. What He desired to convey by this is a question at once of no little difficulty and of great importance ('Die Frage gehört zu den verwickeltsten ja verfahrensten der ganzen neutest. Theologie,' Holtzmann).

The starting-point for this, as well as for the idea of the kingdom, is, we may be sure, Dn 7^{13}. The 'Son of Man' in that passage, as originally written, stood for Israel. The four world-empires are represented by beasts, the dominion that falls to Israel is that of a man. But in this as in other respects the passage was interpreted Messianically. In the Similitudes of the Book of Enoch (chs. 37–70) the Son of Man takes a prominent place. He is a person, and a superhuman person. It is He who holds the great judgment to which the Apocalyptic writings look forward. The attributes ascribed to Him are all more or less directly

connected with this judgment, which is at once to
vindicate the righteous, and finally to put down the
wicked.   The date of this portion of the Book of Enoch
has been much debated, but opinion at the present time
is still more preponderantly in favour of the view that
it is pre-Christian (between B.C. 94–64, Charles, *Enoch*,
p. 29 f.).   The language of the Gospels requires that the
title as applied to a person and to the Messiah should
be not entirely new.   It also requires that it should be
not perfectly understood and familiar (Mt 16^{13}, Jn 12^{34}).
It is probable that its use did not go beyond a small
circle, the particular circle to which the Similitudes of
Enoch belonged.   This, however, would be enough to
give the phrase a certain currency, and to make it at
least suggest association with the Messiah.

It is associated with Him, especially in His character as Judge, and as the chief actor in that series of
events which marks the end of the age, and the reversal
of the places of good and wicked.   This sense Jesus
did not discard.   It appears unmistakably in a number
of passages (Mt 13^{41} 16^{28} 19^{28} $24^{30\text{ff.}}$ $25^{31\text{ff.}}$ 26^{64} etc.).
But at the same time there can be no doubt that
He read into it a number of other ideas, new and
original, just as He read them into the conception of
the Kingdom.

What is most distinctive in this novel element in the
teaching of Jesus ?   There is an increasing tendency
among scholars to lay stress on the Aramaic original
of the phrase.   The Aramaic equivalent is said to mean
and to be the only way which they had of expressing 'Man' (generically, *i.e.* 'Mankind').   Hence the
attempt has been made to interpret the phrase im-

personally, and to get rid more or less of its Messianic
application (see Holtzmann, *NT Th.* i. 256 ff.). It is
true that an impersonal sense will suit such a passage
as Mk 2[28] 'The Sabbath was made for man . . .
therefore the Son of Man is Lord even of the Sabbath.'
At the same time this is by no means the necessary
sense. And Wellhausen, who is one of those who
most emphatically maintain the equation 'Son of Man'
= 'Man,' yet sees that the expression must have been
used by our Lord to designate His own person (*Israel.
u. Jüd. Gesch.*[2] p. 381). Nor can this conclusion really
be avoided by such an expedient as Holtzmann's, who
calls attention to the comparative rarity of the title in
the early chapters and early stages of the history (*e.g.*
in Mark only 2[10. 28]), and would explain it during this
period impersonally, and only after St. Peter's confession personally. Against this and against more
sweeping attempts (*e.g.* by Martineau, *Seat of Authority*,
p. 339) to get rid of the Messianic signification altogether, it may be enough to point out that if reasonable
critics like Holtzmann allow, and a narrative such as
that of the Temptation seems to prove, that Jesus from
the first really assumed the character of the Messiah,
and if our oldest authorities with one consent treat the
title Son of Man as in the later stages Messianic, it is
fair to presume that it is Messianic also in the earlier.
If the Similitudes of the Book of Enoch are pre-
Christian, this conclusion would amount almost to
certainty.

It is, however, fair to argue from the natural sense
of the phrase in Aramaic, that by His use of it, Jesus
did place Himself in some relation to humanity as a

whole.   And we are led to form the same inference by
the conspicuous use of the corresponding Hebrew in
Ps 8[4] 'What is man that thou art mindful of him?
and the son of man that thou visitest him?'   Here
the parallelism shows that 'son of man' = 'man.'   We
also know from He 2[6–10] that the psalm was at a very
early date applied to Jesus as the Messiah, and at a
still earlier date (the Baptism) we have the neigh-
bouring Ps 2[7] applied to Him.   It seems to follow, or
at least to be a very natural presumption, that these
two psalms early became an object of close study
to Jesus, and helped to give outward shape to His
conceptions.

Ps 8 seems specially adapted to fall in with these,
as it brings out with equal strength the two elements
which we know to have entered into the consciousness
of Jesus—the combination of lowliness with loftiness,
the physical weakness of man as contrasted with his
sublime calling and destiny.   We can see here the
appropriateness of the application of one and the same
title to Him who, on the one hand, had 'not where to
lay his head,' and who must needs 'go as it was written
of him,' and who yet, on the other hand, looked to come
again 'with power' in His Kingdom.

We do not like to use such very modern phraseology
as the 'ideal of humanity,' 'the representative of the
human race'; and yet it would seem that Jesus did
deliberately connect with His own person such ideas
as these : He fused them as it were into the central
idea of Messiahship, and we can see how the Jewish
conception of the Messiah was enlarged and enriched
by them.   If the Messiah comes out in the claim to

forgive sins, it is the Son of Man whose mission it was 'to seek and to save that which was lost' (Lk 19[10]), 'not to be ministered unto but to minister, and to give his life a ransom for many' (Mk 10[45]‖).

Here we have another connexion in which the name is frequently used. The prophecies of the Resurrection and of the Second Coming are closely associated with the fatal end of the First: 'The Son of Man must suffer many things, and be rejected by the elders, and the chief priests, and the scribes, and be killed, and after three days rise again' (Mk 8[31] etc.). If we ask for the OT original of this 'Saviour through suffering,' no doubt it is the Second Part of Isaiah, and especially Is 53. Still, it would be rather too much to describe this idea as embodied in the title 'Son of Man.' It is embodied in the *character* of the Son of Man as conceived by Jesus, but not exactly in the name. The name which expressed it was the 'Servant of Jehovah' (παῖς κυρίου); and this name was undoubtedly applied to Christ by the Church as soon as it began to reflect upon His life and mission (cf. Ac 3[13. 26] 4[27. 30], Mt 12[18]), but we have no evidence that Jesus used it of Himself. One reason for the choice of the name 'Son of Man' probably was that it admitted and favoured these associations, even if it did not directly suggest them.

This comprehensive and deeply significant title touched at the one end the Messianic and eschatological expectation through the turn which had been given to it in one section of Judaism (the Book of Enoch). At the other and opposite end it touched the idea of the Suffering Servant. But at the centre it is broadly based upon an infinite sense of brotherhood with toiling and struggling humanity, which He who most thoroughly accepted its conditions was fittest also to save. As Son of God, Jesus looked upwards to the Father; as Son of Man, He looked outwards upon His brethren, the sheep who had no shepherd.

(iv.) **Son of God.**—Only once in the Synoptics (Mt 27^{43}) and in a few places in the Fourth Gospel (Jn 10^{36}, cf. 5^{25} 9^{35} *var. lec.* 11^4) is it hinted that Jesus directly assumed this title. It is repeatedly given to Him by others—by the Baptist (Jn 1^{34}), by Nathanael (Jn 1^{49}), by Satan hypothetically (Mt 4^3), as also by the crowd (Mt 27^{40}), by the possessed (Mk $3^{11\|}$), by the disciples (Mt 14^{33}), by the centurion (Mk 15^{39} = Mt 27^{54}), and by evangelists (Mk 1^1 *v.l.* Jn 3^{18} 20^{31}).

At the same time it is abundantly clear that the title was really assumed from the indirect mode in which Jesus constantly speaks of God as 'My Father.' This is very frequent in the Synoptics as well as in St. John (Mt 7^{21} 10^{32} 11^{27} 15^{13} 16^{17} etc.). And although, as we have seen, the consciousness which finds expression in this phrase becomes the basis of an extended doctrine of the Divine Fatherhood ('the Father,' 'our Father,' 'thy Father,' 'your Father'), there is nevertheless a distinct interval between the sense in which God can be claimed as Father by men, even the innermost circle of the disciples, and that in which He is Father to the Son. In this respect the passage Mt 11^{27} = Lk 10^{22} is quite explicit (cf. also the graduated scale of being in Mk 13^{32} = Mt 24^{36}). Although this passage stands out somewhat conspicuously in the Synoptics, the context in which it occurs is so original and so beyond the reach of invention, while it supplies so marvellously the key

7

to that which distinguishes the history of Jesus from other histories, that doubt cannot reasonably be cast upon it. It is confirmed by the sense in which the title 'Son of God' is taken by the Jews—not merely by the populace but by the learned (Mt 27^{41-43}, cf. Mk $15^{31.\ 32}$, Jn 19^{7}). And, on the other hand, it confirms sufficiently the substantial accuracy of like passages in the Fourth Gospel (*e.g.* $10^{30.\ 38}$). We are thus prepared for the unanimity with which the Church at the earliest date fixed upon this title to convey its sense of the uniqueness of Christ's nature (Ac 9^{20}, Ro 1^{4}, Gal 2^{20}, Eph 4^{13}, He 4^{14} etc., 1 Jn 4^{15} etc., Rev 2^{18}).

This aspect of the question will come before us more fully later. We content ourselves for the present with observing that the teaching of Jesus, reserved and reticent as it is, presupposes as its background this wholly exceptional relation of 'the Son' to 'the Father.' From that as centre radiate a number of other relationships to His immediate disciples, to the Church of which they formed the nucleus, and to mankind. The Sonship of Jesus is intimately connected with His work as Messiah (Titius, p. 116). It is in this character that 'all things are delivered' to Him (Mt 11^{27}‖), in this character that He is enabled to give to the world a revelation of the Father (*ib.*), in this character that He carries out His work of redemption even to the death (Mk 14^{36}‖).

§ **36.** (5) *The Paraclete and the Tri-unity of God.*—In the earliest Epistles of St. Paul we find that the Son of God is placed side by side with the Father, and is associated with Him as the ground of the Church's being, the source of spiritual grace, and as co-operating with Him in the providential ordering of events (1 Th 1¹, 2 Th 1¹, 1 Th 3¹¹ᶠ·). It is difficult to describe the effect of the language used in any other terms than as attributing to the Son a coequal Godhead with the Father. And it is remarkable that St. Paul does this, within some twenty-two years of the Ascension, not as though he were laying down anything new, but as something which might be assumed as part of the common body of Christian doctrine.

We observe also that throughout the earliest group of Epistles there are frequent references to the work of the Holy Spirit as the one great force which lies behind at once the missionary activity and the common life of the Church of the apostolic age (esp. 1 Co 12–14, but cf. 1 Th 1⁵ᶠ· 4⁸ 5¹⁹ etc.). This, too, it is assumed that all Christians would understand.

How are we to account for the prevalence of such teaching at so early a date, and in a region so far removed from the centre of Christianity? It would be natural if the Lord Jesus Christ Himself in His intercourse with His disciples had prepared them to expect a great activity of the Holy Spirit, and if He had hinted at relations in the Godhead which made it threefold rather than a simple monad. Apart from such hints, the common belief of the Church respecting Christ Himself and the Holy Spirit seems very difficult to understand. Certain previous tendencies in Jewish thought might lead up some way towards it, but they would leave a wide gap unspanned.

When, therefore, we find that one Gospel ascribes to our Lord rather full and detailed teaching respecting

the Paraclete, which is explained to be another name
for the Holy Spirit (Jn 14[16. 26] 15[26]), when there is held
out a clear hope and promise of a new Divine influence
to take the place of that which is being withdrawn,
and when in another Gospel we are also told of the
institution* of a rite associated with a new revelation
of God under a threefold Name, that of Father, Son,
and Holy Spirit (Mt 28[19]), these phenomena are just
what we are prepared for, and just such as we should
have had to assume even if we had had no definite
record of them.   We may, then, regard them as
having received—whatever the antecedent claims of
the documents in which they are found—a very considerable degree of critical verification. , The single
verse 2 Cor 13[14] seems to require something very like
what we find in St. Matthew and St. John.

LITERATURE.—Much material of value will be found in the
works on the Biblical Theology of NT by Weiss, Beyschlag, and
esp. H. J. Holtzmann (1897).   Reference may also be made to
Bovon, *Théol. du NT*, Lausanne, 1897.   The most considerable
recent work on the Teaching of Jesus as a whole is Wendt's
Lehre Jesu, Göttingen, 1890 (Eng. tr., T. & T. Clark, Edin. 1892).
Bruce, *The Kingdom of God* (1890 and later) embraces the
Synoptic Gospels only.   In the last few years a number of monographs have appeared on the doctrine of the Kingdom and
points connected with it—all, it may be said, bringing out some
real aspect in the doctrine, though in the writer's opinion too
often at the expense of other aspects.   The series began with
two prize essays, *Die Lehre vom Reiche Gottes*, by Issel and
Schmoller (both Leiden, 1891), and includes treatises with similar
titles by Schnedermann (Leipzig, 1893, 1895, 1896), J. Weiss
(Göttingen, 1892), Lütgert (Gütersloh, 1895), Titius (Freiburg
i. B. u. Leipzig, 1895), Krop (Paris, 1897); also Bousset, *Jesu*

---

* Not, of course, the first institution, but its confirmation as a
rite and its first association with the triple formula.

Predigt in ihrem Gegensatz zum Judentum (Göttingen, 1892);
Paul, *Die Vorstellungen vom Messias u. vom Gottesreich* (Bonn,
1895); Lietzmann, *Der Menschensohn* (Leipzig, 1896); J. Weiss,
Die Nachfolge Christi (Göttingen, 1895); Grass, *Das Verhalten
zu Jesus* (Leipzig, 1895); Ehrhardt, *Der Grundcharakter d. Ethik
Jesu* (Freiburg i. B. u. Leipzig, 1895); Wiesen, *Die Stellung Jesu
zum irdischen Gut* (Gütersloh, 1895).

The Miracles of Jesus.

§ **37.** There has been a certain tendency of late to
recede from the extreme position in the denial of
Miracles. Harnack, for instance, writes in reference
to the Gospel history as follows: 'Much that was
formerly rejected has been re-established on a close
investigation, and in the light of comprehensive experience. Who in these days, for example, could
make such short work of the miraculous cures in
the Gospels as was the custom of scholars formerly?'
(*Christianity and History*, p. 63, Eng. tr.).

§ **38.** (i.) *Different Classes of Miracles.*—Partly this
change of attitude is due to the higher estimate which
would now be put on the value of the evangelical
sources generally, as to which something will be said
below. Partly it would be due to a change of view in
regard to the supernatural, which is no longer placed
in direct antagonism to the natural, but which is more
reasonably explained as resulting from the operation
of a higher cause in nature. And partly also it would
be due to the recognition of wider possibilities in
nature, 'more things in heaven and earth' than were
dreamt of in the narrow philosophy of the *Aufklärung*.

(*a*) In particular, it may be said that medical science would have no difficulty in admitting a large class of miracles of healing. All those which have to do with what would now be called 'nervous disorders,' all those in which there was a direct action of the mind upon the body, would fall into place readily enough. Given a personality like that of Jesus, the effect which it would have upon disorders of this character would be strictly analogous to that which modern medicine would seek to produce. The peculiar combination of commanding authority with extreme gentleness and sympathy would be a healing force of which the value could not easily be exaggerated.

A question would indeed still be left as to the treatment of the cases of what was called 'demoniacal possession.' There can be no doubt that Jesus Himself shared, broadly speaking, the views of His contemporaries in regard to these cases: His methods of healing went upon the assumption that they were fundamentally what every one, including the patients themselves, supposed them to be. We can well believe that this was a necessary assumption in order to allow the healing influences to operate. We must remember that all the ideas of the patient would be adjusted to the current belief, and it would be only through them that the words and acts of Christ could take effect. In the accounts of such miracles we see that there was a mutual intelligence between Healer and patient from the first (Mk 1$^{24f.}$|| ^{34}|| 5^6||). It was by means of this mutual intelligence that the word of command struck home.

We should be prepared, then, to say that this class

of miracles implied accommodation to the ideas of the
time. But when we speak of 'accommodation' on
the part of our Lord, we do not mean a merely
politic assumption of a particular belief for a particular
purpose. We mean that the assumption was part of
the outfit of His incarnate Manhood. There was a
certain circle of ideas which Jesus accepted in becoming
Man in the same way in which He accepted a particular
language with its grammar and vocabulary.

It would have been wholly out of keeping with the
general character of His Ministry if Jesus had attacked
this form of disease in any other way than through the
belief in regard to it which at that time was universal.
The scientific description of it has doubtless greatly
changed. But it is still a question which is probably by
no means so clear, whether, allowing for its temporary
and local character, the language then used did not
contain an important element of truth. The physical
and moral spheres are perhaps more intimately connected than we suppose. And the unbridled wickedness
rife in those days may have had physical effects, which
were not unfitly described as the work of 'demons.'
The subject is one which it is probable has not yet been
fully explored.

(β) There is, as we have seen, one large class of
diseases in regard to which the healing force exerted
by the presence and the word of Jesus has a certain
amount of analogy in the facts recognized by modern
medicine. We must not, however, treat that analogy
as going farther than it does. It does not hold good
equally for all the forms of disease which are described
as having been healed. Wherever the body is subject

to the action of the mind, there we can give an account
of the miracle which is to some extent—to a large extent—rational and intelligible. But in cases in which
the miracle involves a purely physical process, it will
not be possible to explain it in the same way.

This other class of miracles will fall rather under the
same head as those which were wrought, not upon man,
but upon nature. In regard to these miracles, the
world is probably not much nearer to a reasoned account than it was. It must always be remembered that
the narratives which have come down to us are the
work of those who expected that Divine action would
(as we should say) run counter to natural laws and not
be in harmony with them, and that the more Divine it
was the more directly it would run counter to them.
We may be sure that if the miracles of the first century
had been wrought before trained spectators of the
twentieth, the version of them would be quite different.
But to suppose this is to suppose what is impossible,
because all God's dealings with men are adapted to the
age to which they belong, and cannot be transferred to
another age. If God intended to manifest Himself
specially to the twentieth century, we should expect
Him to do so by other means. We are then compelled
to take the accounts as they have come down to us.
And we are aware beforehand that any attempt to
translate them into our own habits of thought must be
one of extreme difficulty, if not doomed to failure.

§ 39. (ii.) *Critical Expedients for eliminating Miracle.*
—In view of the difficulty of giving a rational (*i.e.* a
twentieth century) version of miracle, it is not surpris-

ing that recourse should be had to critical expedients for explaining away Miracle altogether; in other words, to account for the narratives of miracles without assuming that objective facts corresponding to them really occurred. The expedients most in favour are: (*a*) imitation of similar stories in OT; (β) exaggeration of natural occurrences; (γ) translation of what was originally parable into external fact. These are causes which have about them nothing violent or incredible, and we may believe that they were to some extent really at work. The question to *what* extent, will depend mainly upon the nature of the evidence for miracles and the length of time interposed between the evidence and the events. This will be the next subject to come before us. We may, however, anticipate so far as to say that whatever degree of verisimilitude belongs to the causes suggested in themselves, they do not appear to be adequate, either separately or in combination, to account for the whole or any large part of the narratives as we have them. And there is the further consideration, on which more will also be said presently, that something of the nature of miracle, something which was understood as miracle, and that on no insignificant scale, must be assumed to account for the estimate certainly formed by the whole first generation of Christians of the Person of Christ.

§ **40.** (iii.) *The Evidence for the Gospel Miracles in general.*—Coming to the question as to the evidence for the Miracles recorded in the Gospels, there are three main observations to be made: (*a*) that the evidence for all these miracles, generally speaking, is strong;

(β) that the evidence for all the different classes of miracles is equally strong; (γ) that although for the best attested miracles in each class the evidence is equal, there is a difference between particular miracles in each class; some are better attested than others.

(*a*) It is unnecessary to repeat what has been already said (p. 4, *sup.*) about the general character of the Gospel History.   The critical student must constantly have in mind the question to what state of things the different phases of that history as it has come down to us correspond.   Does it reflect conditions as they existed after A.D. 70 or before?   And if before, how far does it reflect the later half of that period, and how far the earlier?   How far does it coincide with a section of Christian thought and Christian life (*e.g.*) taken at the height of the activity of St. Paul; and how far does it certainly point to an earlier stage than this? In other words, how much of the description contained in the Gospels belongs to the period of consequences, and how much to the period of causes?

Every attempt to treat of the life of our Lord should contribute its quota to the answer to these questions. And it is becoming more and more possible to do this, not merely in a spirit of superficial apologetics, but with a deep sense of responsibility to the truth of history.   And the writer of this article strongly believes that the tendency of the researches of recent years has been to enhance and not to diminish the estimate of the historical value of the Gospels.

all diff. classes
made in
ory

(β) This applies to the Gospel records as a whole, in which miracles are included.   It is natural next to ask, What is the nature of the particular evidence for

Miracles? How is it distributed? Does the distribution correspond to the distinction which we have drawn between the easier and the more difficult Miracles? If it did, we might suppose that the former class had better claims to credence than the latter.

But an examination of the documents shows that this is not the case. Without committing ourselves to all the niceties of the Synoptic problem, there are at any rate broad grounds for distinguishing between the matter that is found in all the three Synoptics, in the First and Third, and in one only of the Three. Whether the ultimate groundwork is written or oral, the three-fold matter represents that groundwork, and is therefore, if not necessarily the oldest, at least the most broadly based and authoritative. There is reason to think that the double matter is also very ancient. It consists largely of discourse, but some few narratives seem to belong to it. The peculiar sections of the different Gospels vary considerably in their character, and it is natural to suppose that they would have the least antecedent presumption in their favour. Some confirmatory evidence would be needed for facts which rested upon their testimony alone.

Now, if it had happened that the Nature-Miracles had been confined to sections of this last kind, while the Miracles of Healing—and especially the Healing of nervous diseases—had entered largely into the Double and Triple Synopsis; or—inasmuch as discourse more often bears the stamp of unmistakable originality than narrative—if the miracles of one class had appeared only in the form of narrative, while the allusions in discourse were wholly to miracles of the other, then the inference would have lain near at hand that there was a graduated scale in the evidence corresponding to a like graduated scale in the antecedent probability of the miracle.

But this is not the case. Miracles of all the different kinds occur in all the documents or sources. The Triple Synopsis contains not only the healing of demoniacs and paralytics, but the healing of the issue of blood (Mk 5^{25} ||), the raising of Jairus' daughter (*ib.* ^{38} ||), the stilling of the storm (*ib.* 4^{37} ||), the feeding of the five thousand (*ib.* 6^{35} ||). This last miracle is found not only in all three Synoptists, but also in Jn $6^{5 \text{ff.}}$. And there is this further point about it, that if we regard the miracles generally as a gradual accretion of myth and not based upon fact, we should undoubtedly assume that the feeding of the four thousand (Mk 8^1, Mt 15^{32}) was a mere duplicate of it. But it is probable that this story also belonged to the fundamental source, in spite of its omission by Luke. In that case both the feedings of a multitude would have had a place in the oldest of all our authorities, and the first growth in the tradition would have to be pushed back a step farther still. We should thus have a nature-miracle not only embodied in our oldest source, but at its first appearance in that source already pointing back some way behind it.

(γ) It thus appears that the evidence, externally considered, is equally good for all classes of miracles. It is not, as we might expect, that the evidence for the easier miracles is better than that for the more difficult, leaving us free to accept the one and reject the others. We cannot do this, because the best testimony we have embraces alike those miracles which imply a greater deviation from the ordinary course of nature and those in which the deviation is less.

It does not, however, follow that within the different classes of miracles the evidence for particular miracles is equal. When Prof. Goldwin Smith insists that all the miracles recorded in the Gospels stand or fall together, he is going in the teeth, not so much of anything peculiar to the study of the Gospels, but of the historical method generally. And the examples which he gives are unfortunate. ' We cannot pick and choose. The evidence upon which the miraculous darkness and the apparition of the dead rest is the same as that upon which all the other miracles rest, and must be accepted or rejected in all the cases alike' (*Guesses at the Riddle of Existence*, p. 160). No critical student needs to be told that the evidence for the apparitions of the dead (Mt $27^{52f.}$) belongs just to that stratum which carries with it the least weight. The authority for the darkness is much higher, but its miraculous character need not be magnified. Any unusual darkening of the sky would naturally strike the imagination of the disciples ; and it might be not contrary to nature and yet also not accidental.

§ **41.** (iv.) *The Quality of the Evidence.*—So far we have spoken of the external character of the evidence. It is speaking within the mark to say that a large part of the evidence for the Gospel miracles, including some of those that are most miraculous, is separated from the facts by an interval of not more than thirty years. We may be pretty sure that before that date, and even much before it, stories of miracles like those recorded in the Gospels circulated freely among Christians, and were a common subject of teaching by catechists and others.   We now proceed to ask, What is the quality of the narratives in which these stories occur?   What features are there in the stories themselves which throw light upon their historical value?

e Temptation
see p 42 - 5)

(*a*) We are met at the outset by the Temptation.   If there is anything certain in history, it is that the story of the Temptation has a real foundation in fact, for the simple reason that without such a foundation it would have occurred to no one to invent it.   It suits exactly and wonderfully the character of Jesus as we can now see it, but not as it was seen at the time.   Men were trying to apprehend that character; they had a glimpse here and a glimpse there; but they cannot have had more than dim and vague surmises as to what it was as a whole.   But whoever first told the story of the Temptation saw it as a whole.   We have therefore already drawn the inference that it was first told by none other than Jesus Himself.   And by that inference we stand.   There is nothing in the Gospels that is more authentic.

But the story of the Temptation presupposes the possession of supernatural powers.   It all turns on the question how those powers are to be exercised.   It not only implies the possession of power to work such miracles as were actually worked, but others even more remarkable from the point of view of crude interference with the order of nature.   The story of the Temptation implies that Jesus *could* have worked such miracles if He had willed to do so; and the reason why

He did not work them was only because He did not will.

The keynote which is struck by the Temptation is sustained all through the sequel of the history. We can see that the Life of Jesus was what it was by an act of deliberate renunciation. When He says, as the end draws near, 'Thinkest thou that I cannot beseech my Father, and he shall even now send me more than twelve legions of angels?' (Mt 26^{53}), the lesson holds good, not for that moment alone, but for all that has preceded it. The Public Ministry of Jesus wears the aspect it does, not because of limitations imposed from without, but of limitations imposed from within.

Here lies the paradox of the Miracles of Christ. He seems at once to do them, and so to guard against a possible misuse, that it is as if He had not done them. The common idea of miracles was as a manifestation of Divine power. Jesus gave the manifestation, and yet He seemed so to check it from producing its natural effect that it is as though it did not serve its purpose. It really serves His purpose, but not the purpose which the world both then and since has ascribed to Him.

(β) We have seen that the principles laid down at the Temptation governed the whole public life of Jesus. He steadily refused to work miracles for any purely self-regarding end. If the fact that He works miracles at all is a sympathetic adaptation to the beliefs and expectations of the time, those beliefs are schooled and criticized while they are adopted (Mt 12^{39} ‖ 16$^{1f.}$, Jn 4^{48}), the element of mere display, the element of self-asser tion, even of self-preservation, is eliminated from them.

They are studiously restricted to the purposes of the mission.

Now this carefully restricted character in the miracles of Jesus is unique in history. Among all the multitude of wonders with which the faith, sometimes superstitious, but more often simply naïve, of the later Church adorned the lives of the saints, there is nothing quite like it. We may say with confidence that if the miracles of Jesus had been no more than an invention, they would not have been what they are. We can see in the evangelists a certain dim half-conscious feeling of the self-imposed limitations in the use of the supernatural by Christ. But we may be very sure that they have this feeling, because the limitations were inherent in the facts, not because they formed part from the first of a picture which they were constructing *a priori*.

(γ) There are three kinds of restriction in the miracles of our Lord. The limitation in the subject-matter of the miracles is one; the limitation in the conditions under which they are wrought is another (Mt 13^{58} || 15$^{24. 26}$); and the limitation in the manner in which they are set before the world is a third. In a number of cases, after a miracle has been performed, the recipient is strictly cautioned to maintain silence about it (Mk 1^{34} || demoniacs, 1^{44} || leper, 3^{12} demoniacs, cf. Mt 12^{16}, Mk 7^{36} deaf and dumb, 8^{26} blind). This hangs together with the manifest intention of Jesus to correct not only the current idea of miracles, but the current idea of the Messiah as one endowed with supernatural power. If He was so endowed, it was not that He might gather about Him crowds and establish a carnal kingdom such as the Jews expected.

This, too, is a very original feature. It is certainly not one that the popular imagination would create, because the motive to create it was wanting. It is not to be supposed that the popular imagination would first correct itself and then embody the correction in a fictitious narrative. Here again we are driven to the conclusion that the narrative truly reflects the facts.

(δ) In yet another way do the accounts of the miracles work in with the total picture of the Life of Christ. They have a didactic value, which makes them round off the cycle of the teaching. This fact perhaps leaves some opening for the possibility that here and there what was originally parable may in course of transmission have hardened into miracle. An example of such a possibility would be the withering of the Fig-tree (Mk 11$^{12-14.\ 20.\ 25}$ || compared with Lk 13$^{6-9}$). But, on the other hand, it is just as possible that parable and miracle may stand side by side as a double enforcement of the same lesson. The story of the Temptation is proof that Jesus would not hesitate to clothe His teaching in a form at once natural and impressive to that generation, though it is less so to ours. In this He only takes up a marked characteristic of the OT Prophets.

§ 42. (v.) *Historical Necessity of Miracles.*—The truth is that the historian who tries to construct a reasoned picture of the Life of Christ finds that he cannot dispense with miracles. He is confronted with the fact that no sooner had the Life of Jesus ended in apparent failure and shame, than the great body of Christians—not an individual here and there, but the mass of the Church— passed over at once to the fixed belief that He was God.

8

By what conceivable process could the men of that day have arrived at such a conclusion, if there had been really nothing in His life to distinguish it from that of ordinary men? We have seen that He did not work the kind of miracles which they expected. The miracles in themselves in any case came short of their expectations. But this makes it all the more necessary that there must have been something about the Life, a broad and substantial element in it, which *they could recognize* as supernatural and divine—not that we can recognize, but which they could recognize with the ideas of the time. Eliminate miracles from the career of Jesus, and the belief of Christians, from the first moment that we have undoubted contemporary evidence of it (say A.D. 50), becomes an insoluble enigma.

§ **43.** (vi.) *Natural Congruity of Miracles.*—And now, if from the belief of the Early Church we turn to the belief of the Church in our day, there a different kind of congruity appears, but a congruity that is no less stringent. If we still believe that Christ was God, not merely on the testimony of the Early Church, but on the proof afforded by nineteen centuries of Christianity, there will be nothing to surprise us in the phenomena of miracles. 'If the Incarnation was a fact, and Jesus Christ was what He claimed to be, His miracles, so far from being improbable, will appear the most natural thing in the world. . . . They are so essentially a part of the character depicted in the Gospels, that without them that character would entirely disappear. They flow naturally from a Person who, despite His obvious humanity, impresses us throughout as being at home in two worlds. . . . We cannot separate the wonderful life, or the wonderful teaching, from the wonderful works. They involve and interpenetrate and presuppose each other, and form in their insoluble combination one harmonious picture ' (Illingworth, *Divine Immanence*, pp. 88–90).

If we seek to express the *rationale* or inner congruity of miracles in Biblical language, we shall find this abundantly done for us in the Gospel of St. John. Miracles arise from the intimate association of the Son with the Father in the ordering of the universe, especially in all that relates to the redemption of man. When challenged by the Jews for healing a sick man upon the Sabbath, Jesus replied, ' My Father worketh even until now (*i.e.* since, and in spite of the institution of the Sabbatical Rest), I am working also' (Jn 5^{17}); the same law holds for the actions of the Son as for the conservation of the universe. And He goes on, ' Verily, verily, I say unto you, The Son can do nothing of himself, but what he seeth the Father doing: for what things soever he doeth, these the Son also doeth in like manner. For the Father loveth the Son, and showeth him all things that himself doeth: and greater works than these will he show him, that ye may marvel' (*ib.* vv.$^{19, 20}$). Many other passages at once suggest themselves to the same effect (Jn 3^{35} $8^{28f.}$ 14^{10}). The Son is ' sent' by the Father, and He is invested with full powers for the accomplishment of that mission ; or rather with reference to it and for the purpose of it, He and the Father are one (Jn 10^{30}).

The sayings of this character are all from the Fourth Gospel. But there is a near approach to them in the well-known passage Mt 11^{27} || (' All things have been delivered unto me of my Father'); and this does but form a natural climax to others, which, without it, would seem to leave something wanting and incomplete.

§ **44.** (vii.) *The Unexplained Element in Miracles.*— When all the above considerations are borne in mind, some may think that there is a residuum which is not wholly explained—not so much as to the fact of miracles, or as to their congruity with the Person of Jesus, but rather as to the method of particular miracles in the form in which they have come down to us. It is quite inevitable that there should be such a residuum, which is only another name for the irreducible interval which must, when all is done, separate the reflective science-trained intellect of the twentieth century from the naïve chroniclers of the first. Jesus Himself would seem to have been not without a prescience that this would be the case. At any rate there is a permanent significance, unexhausted by the occasion which gave rise to it, in His reply to the disciples of the Baptist, while appealing to works which, however beneficent, would, He knew, fail to realize all the Baptist's expectations : 'Blessed is he that shall find no scandal—or stumbling-block—in me' (Mt 11⁶ ‖). There was doubtless something left in the mind of John which he could not perfectly piece together with the rest of such mental outfit as he had. And so we may be sure that it will be in every age, though age after age has only helped to strengthen the conviction that the modes of thought of the *Zeitgeist* may and do continually change, but that the worth for man of the Person of Jesus does not change, but is eternal.

LITERATURE.—Probably the best work in English at the present moment on the presuppositions of the Gospel Miracles would be Illingworth's *Divine Immanence* (1898), a sequel to his *Bampton Lectures* (1894). It may be worth while to compare Gore, *Bamp. Lect.* (1891). On the other hand, Mozley's lectures on the same foundation for 1865 have reference rather to a phase of the controversy which is now past. There is, of course, much on the subject in the various treatises on Apologetics ; and articles are constantly appearing in magazines, as well as shorter monographs, both British and Foreign. The present writer cannot say—or at least cannot remember—that he has gained as much from these several sources as in the case of the teaching of Jesus. He would like, however, to mention with gratitude, *Grounds of Theistic and Christian Belief*, by Dr. G. P. Fisher of Yale (New York, 1883 ; revised edit. 1903), a very clear and temperate statement of the evidence for the Gospel Miracles on older lines ; the chap. on Miracles in Dr. A. B. Bruce, *Chief end of Revelation* (3rd ed. 1890) ; and three short lectures, entitled *The Supernatural in Christianity* (by Drs. Rainy, Orr, and Marcus Dods, in reply to Pfleiderer, Edinb. 1894).

The most considerable attempt in English to construct Christianity without Miracles is Dr. Edwin A. Abbott's *The Kernel and the Husk* (1886), and *The Spirit on the Waters* (1897). With this may be compared Dr. Salmon's *Non-miraculous Christianity* (*and other Sermons*).

There are well-known systematic works on the Gospel Miracles by the late Archbishop Trench and Dr. A. B. Bruce.

CHAPTER V.

THE LATER MINISTRY.

C. MIDDLE OR CULMINATING PERIOD OF THE ACTIVE MINISTRY.

§ **45.** *Scene.*—Galilee, with an excursion across the northern border.

Time.—Passover to shortly before Tabernacles A.D. 28.

Mt 14^1–18^{35}, Mk 6^{14}–9^{50}, Lk 9^{7-50}, Jn 6.

This is a period of culminations, in which the prophecy of Simeon begins to be conspicuously fulfilled : ' Behold, this child is set for the falling and rising up of many in Israel, and for a sign which is spoken against ' (Lk 2^{34}). The main culminations are (i.) of the zeal of the populace, followed by their disappointment and falling away ; (ii.) the still greater embitterment of the scribes and Pharisees ; (iii.) the awakening at last of a more intelligent faith in the disciples, reaching its highest point in St. Peter's confession ; (iv.) the Divine testimony to Jesus in the Transfiguration ; (v.) the consciousness of victory virtually won in

Jesus Himself (Mt 11$^{25-30}$, Lk 20$^{17-24}$); (vi.) at the same time He sees clearly, and begins to announce the seeming but transient catastrophe, the final humiliation and exaltation, in which His work is to end.

The time of this period is clearly marked by the occurrence of the Passover of the year A.D. 28 at its beginning, and the Feast of Tabernacles (in October of the same year) at the end. It is probable that within these six months all the salient events referred to below may be included. The place is, broadly speaking, Galilee, beginning with the shores of the lake (Jn 6); but in the course of the period there falls a wider circuit than any that had been hitherto taken. In this circuit Jesus touched on, and probably crossed, the borders of the heathen districts of Tyre and Sidon (Mk 7^{24}‖); He then returned eastwards through the neighbourhood of Cæsarea Philippi (Mk 8^{27}‖); and He finally returned to Capernaum, not directly, but after taking a round to the east of the lake and through Decapolis (Mk 7^{31}). The motive was probably not so much on this occasion extended preaching as to avoid the ferment excited among the population of Central Galilee. Observe Mk 7^{24} and the strict injunctions of secrecy in Mk 7^{36} 8^{30}‖ 9^{9}‖. If we may follow our authorities (Mk 7$^{32ff.}$ 8$^{1ff.}$ $^{11ff.}$) there was a certain amount of active work at the end of the circuit; but Mt 11$^{20ff.}$ appears to mark the practical close of the Galilæan ministry.

The greater part of this circuit lay within the dominions, not of Herod Antipas, where Jesus had hitherto mainly worked, but of his brother Philip. Now we know that the hostility to Him was shared by

the Pharisees with the partisans of Herod (Mk 3^6 and
p. 61 above; cf. also Mk 8^{15}).   We have also, but
probably at a still later date, threats, which, if not
actually made by Herod Antipas, were at least plausibly
attributed to him (Lk 13^{31}).   In any case, it is likely
enough that intrigues were on foot between the two
allied parties of the Pharisees and Herodians; and
some writers, of whom Keim may be taken as an
example, have attributed to these what they describe as
a 'flight' on the part of Jesus.   They may have had
something to do with His retirement.

This division of our Lord's Life includes several
narratives (the Feedings of the Five and Four Thousand,
the Walking on the Water, the Transfiguration) which
sound especially strange to modern ears.   We must
repeat the warning, that if a twentieth century observer
had been present he would have given a different account of the occurrences from that which has come
down to us.   But the mission of Jesus was to the first
century and not to the twentieth.   His miracles as
well as His teaching were adapted to the mental habits
of those to whom they were addressed.   It is wasted
ingenuity to try, by rationalizing the narratives, to
translate them into a language more like our own.
Essential features in them are sure to escape in the process.   It should be enough to notice that the narratives
in question all rest on the very best historical authority.
They belong to the oldest stratum of the evangelical
tradition.   And more than this: if we suppose, as it is
not unreasonable to suppose, that the Feedings of the
Five and of the Four Thousand are different versions of
the same event, this would throw us back some way

behind even that oldest stratum; because we should
have to allow an additional period of time for the two
versions to arise out of their common original (see
p. 108 *sup.*). This would carry us back to a time when
numbers must have been living by whom the truth of
that which is reported might be controlled. In the case
of the Feeding of the Five Thousand, we have the confirmatory evidence of the Fourth Gospel, which for
those who believe the author to have been an eye-
witness must be little less than decisive.

§ **46.** i. *The Enthusiasm and Falling-away of the
Populace.*—It was just before the Passover of the year
28 that the impression which Jesus had made on the
people of Galilee seemed to reach its climax. This was
the result of what is commonly known to us as the
Feeding of the Five Thousand. The fact that the
Passover was so near at hand accounts for a special
gathering of pilgrims, or those preparing for the
journey, from the Galilæan towns. In such a mixed
multitude there would doubtless be many Zealots and
enthusiastic expectants of the 'deliverance of Israel.'
The miracle convinces these that they have at last
found the leader of whom they are in search. They are
aware that hitherto He had shown no signs of en-
couraging the active measures which they desired;
and therefore they hasten to seize the person of Jesus in
order to compel Him to put Himself at their head, with
or against His will. He, however, retires from them;
and their disappointment is complete when on the next
day the more determined among them, after following
Him at no little trouble into the synagogue at Caper-

naum, find themselves put off with what they would regard as a mystical and unintelligible discourse. This is a turning-point in what had been for some time a gathering movement on the part of many who were willing to see in Jesus a Messiah such as they expected, but who were baffled and drew back when they found the ideal presented to them so different from their own. And the crisis once past, every possible precaution was taken to ensure that it should not recur (Mk $7^{24.\ 36}\ 8^{30}\|$ $9^9\|$, as above).

Are the two Feedings of Mk $6^{30-46}\|$ and Mk $8^{1-9}\|$ to be regarded as two events or one? Besides the general resemblance between the two narratives, a weighty argument in favour of the latter hypothesis is, that in the second narrative the disciples' question appears to imply that the emergency was something new. They could hardly have put this question as they did if a similar event had happened only a few weeks before. The different numbers are just what would be found in two independent traditions. The decision will, however, depend here (as in the instances noted above) on the degree of strictness with which we interpret the narrative generally.

The discourse in the synagogue at Capernaum, Jn 6^{26-51}, works up to one of those profound truths which fixed themselves especially in the memory of the author of the Fourth Gospel. It is not a direct reference to the Sacrament of the Lord's Supper, but it is a preparatory statement of the deep principle of which that Sacrament is the expression. We shall have more to say on this head below (see p. 165).

§ 47. ii. *Widening Breach with the Pharisees.*—More than one incident occurs in this period which points to the increasing tension of the relations between Jesus and the Pharisees (Mk $8^{11.\ 15}$). But the decisive passage is Mk $7^{1-13}\|$, the severity of which anticipates the denunciations of the last Passover. In this Jesus cuts away root and branch of the Pharisaic traditions and exposes their essential immorality. From this time onwards the antagonism is open and declared.

§ **48**. iii. *The Climax of Faith among the Twelve; St. Peter's Confession.*—We have seen how the enthusiasm of the multitudes reached its climax after the Feeding of the Five Thousand, but did not recover from the rebuff which it then received, and from that time more or less collapsed, until it flamed up for a moment at the triumphal entry. The Twelve were in a better position to enter into the mind of their Master, and it was but natural that they should be more steadfastly attached to His person. Hence their faith survived the shocks which it was continually receiving, and St. Peter gave the highest expression which it had yet received, when, in reply to a direct question, he exclaimed, 'Thou art the Christ [the Son of the Living God]' (Mt 16^{13-20} ‖). Jesus marked His sense of the significance of the confession by words of warm commendation. He attributes it, indeed, to a direct inspiration from Heaven. The value of the confession stands out all the more clearly when it is compared with the doubts of the Baptist (see above, p. 56). We are not to suppose that St. Peter had by any means as yet a full conception of all that was implied in his own words. He still did not understand what manner of Messiah he was confessing; but his merit was, that in spite of the rude shocks which his faith had been receiving, and in spite of all that was paradoxical and enigmatical in the teaching and actions of his Master, he saw through his perplexities the gleams of a nature

which transcended his experience, and he was willing
to take upon trust what he could not comprehend.

It would be out of place to attempt here to discuss the conflict-
ing interpretations of the blessing pronounced upon St. Peter.
We can only say that, although it is not adequate to explain the
blessing as pronounced upon the confession and not upon St.
Peter himself, it is nevertheless distinctly pronounced upon St.
Peter *as confessing*. It is in the fact that there is at last one who,
in the face of all difficulties, recognizes from his heart that Jesus
is what He is, that the first stone, as it were, of the Church is
laid ; other stones will be built upon and around it, and the edifice
will rise day by day ; but the beginning occurs but once, and the
beginning of the Christian Church occurred then. It is not to
detract from the merit of St. Peter—which so far as the building up of the Church is concerned was as high as human merit
could be—if we interpret the blessing upon him in the light of
1 Co 3^{11}. The Church has but one foundation, in the strict sense,
Jesus Christ. It was precisely to this that St. Peter's confession
pointed. But that confession was the first of all like confessions ;
and in that respect might well be described as the first block of
stone built into the edifice.

§ **49.** iv. *The Culminating Point in the Missionary
Labours of Jesus.*—God seeth not as man seeth. To
the average observer, even to one who was acquainted
with St. Peter's confession, it would seem to be the
solitary point of light in the midst of disappointment
and failure. A retrospect of the Galilæan ministry
seemed to show little but hard-heartedness, ingratitude,
and unbelief (Jn 12$^{37-40}$). Our Lord Himself can only
denounce woe upon the cities which enjoyed most of
His presence (Mt 11$^{20-24}$ ||). And yet about the same
time two sayings are recorded which mark a deep
inward consciousness of success. The ministry which
might seem to be in vain was not really in vain, but
potential and in promise ; to the eye which saw into the

future as well as into the present, and which looked
into the inmost counsels of the Father, the crisis might
even be regarded as past.   One of these sayings is Lk
10[18].   The success of the disciples in casting out
demons draws from Jesus the remark that the power of
the prince of darkness is broken.   And about the same
time, as if ingratitude and opposition counted for
nothing, He pours out His thanks to the Father: 'I
thank thee, O Father, Lord of heaven and earth, that
thou didst hide these things from the wise and understanding, and didst reveal them unto babes; yea,
Father, for so it was well-pleasing in thy sight' (Mt
11[25f.]‖).   The next verse in both Gospels contains the
clearest expression in the Synoptics of that sense of
oneness with the Father which is brought out so
pointedly in John.   And the verses which follow in
Matthew are that wonderful invitation: 'Come unto
me,' etc.   He who understands this group of sayings
has found his way to the heart of Christianity.

§ **50.** v. *The Transfiguration.*—To the confession of
the apostle and to the words of thanksgiving, which
are also words of serene contentment and inward
assurance, there was not wanting an outward Divine
sanction.   This was given in the scene which is known
to us as the Transfiguration (Mk 9[2-8]‖).   The narrative
of the Transfiguration reminds us, in more ways than
one, of those of the Baptism and Temptation.   Once
again the apostles hear words which seem to come
from Heaven confirming the mission of their Master.
At the same time they see a vision which brings out
the significance of that mission in a way for which as

yet they can hardly have been prepared. The appearance of Moses and Elijah by the side of, and as it were ministering to, Jesus, symbolized the Law and the Prophets as leading up to and receiving their fulfilment in the Gospel.

It is impossible not to see the appropriateness of this Divine testimony to the mission of Jesus occurring just where it does. That unique relationship of the Son to the Father, which forms the constant background of the narrative of the Fourth Gospel, and is not less the background—real, if not so apparent—of the Synoptics, could not but assert itself from time to time. And what time could be fitter for a clear pronouncement of it than this, when outward circumstances were for the most part so discouraging, and when the prospect was becoming every day nearer and more certain of the fatal and terrible end! If the Son must needs go down into the valley of the shadow of death, the Father's face will shine upon Him for a moment before He enters it with a brightness which will not be obscured.

As bearing upon the essentially historical character of the narrative, however difficult and even impossible it may be for us to reconstruct its details in such a way that we could be said to understand them, note (1) the significance of the appearance of Moses and Elijah at a time when that significance can have been but very imperfectly apprehended by the disciples, and when there was absolutely nothing to suggest such an idea to them ; and (2) the Transfiguration comes within the cycle of events in regard to which a strict silence was to be observed. This striking and peculiar stamp of genuineness was not wanting to it. We may note also (3) the random speech of St. Peter (Mk 9^5 ‖) as a little graphic and authentic touch which had not been forgotten.

It might be supposed that the enlargements in Lk $9^{31f.}$ were merely editorial, but, like not a few added details in this Gospel, they become more impressive upon reflexion. The other evangelists throw no light upon the subject of the converse between the glorified figures ; Luke alone says that they 'spake of his decease which he was about to accomplish at Jerusalem.' This was, we may be sure, the subject which deeply occupied the mind of Jesus at this time : and it is hardly less certain that the particular aspect of it which would be most present to Him would be its relation to the prophetic Scriptures of OT (and the Law also had its prophetic side). We might expect an appearance of Isaiah rather than Elijah ; but Elijah was the typical prophet, and the Jews expected his appearing (cf. Wetstein on Mt 17³). The other peculiar detail in Luke, that 'Peter and they that were with him were heavy with sleep,' may well seem confirmatory of the view (*e.g.*) of Weiss and Beyschlag, that the scene was presented to the three apostles in divinely caused vision.

§ 51. vi. *The Prophecies of Death and Resurrection.* —The period we are describing is a kind of water-shed, which marks not only the summit of the ascent but the beginning of the descent. We have seen how this was the case with the enthusiasm of the multitude : it was also the case with Christ Himself. The confession of St. Peter was immediately followed, and the Transfiguration both preceded and followed, by distinct prophecies of the fatal end which was to close His ministry—an end fatal in the eyes of men, but soon to be cancelled by His resurrection. As these prophecies will meet us again in the next period, to which they give its dominant character, we will reserve the discussion of them till then.

D. CLOSE OF THE ACTIVE PERIOD: THE MESSIANIC CRISIS IN VIEW.

§ 52. *Scene.*—Judæa (Jn 7¹⁰ff. 11⁵⁴) and Peræa (Mk 10¹‖, Jn 10⁴⁰).

Time.—Tabernacles A.D. 28 to Passover A.D. 29.

Mt 19¹–20³⁴, Mk 10, Lk 9⁵¹–19²⁸ (for the most part not in chronological order), Jn 7¹–11⁵⁷.

In this period we may note more particularly (i.) the peculiar section of St. Luke's Gospel which might on a superficial view seem to be placed in this period; (ii.) that portion of the Johannean narrative which really belongs to it; (iii.) the general character of our Lord's Teaching at this time; (iv.) in particular, the prophecies of Death and Resurrection; and (v.) the hints which are given of a special significance attaching to these events.

The time of this period extends from the Feast of Tabernacles in A.D. 28 to the Passover of A.D. 29. There is more difficulty in mapping out the distribution of its parts topographically.   We have some clear landmarks if we follow the guidance of the Fourth Gospel. The events of the section Jn 7^1–10^{21} partly belong to the Feast of Tabernacles and in part follow at no great interval after it. We have again in Jn 10^{22} a clear indication of time and place, the Feast of Dedication at Jerusalem. This would be towards the end of December. After that, Jesus withdrew beyond Jordan to the place where 'John was at the first baptizing' (Jn 10^{40}). Here He made a lengthened stay, and it was from hence that He paid His visit to Bethany for the raising of Lazarus. Then He again retired to a city called Ephraim on the edge of the wilderness north-east of Jerusalem, where He remained until the Jews began to gather together to attend the Passover (Jn 11^{55}). We have thus a fairly connected narrative extending from the beginning of the year to the Passover of A.D. 29, the scene of which is in part Judæa and in part Peræa. We have also a fixed point covering, perhaps, about a fortnight in the latter half of October, and localized at Jerusalem. But what of the seven or eight weeks which separate this from the Feast of

9

Dedication? Is it probable that Jesus returned to Galilee and continued His ministry there? It does not seem so. The solemn and deliberate leave-taking from Galilee is not likely to have been so broken. The principal objection to this view would be that the secret and unexpected visit to Jerusalem at the Feast of Tabernacles does not seem consistent with the solemnity of this leave-taking. We may, however, suppose that the Galilæan ministry was practically complete before this date, and that strong expressions like those of Lk 9^{51}, if they are to be taken as they stand, refer to one of the later journeys.

§ 53. i. *The so-called Peræan Ministry.*—There is a long section of St. Luke's Gospel, Lk 9^{51}–18^{34}, which has been often treated as a single whole and as containing the record of a special ministry, identified with the last journey towards Jerusalem, and having for its scene the lands beyond the Jordan. This is based upon the fact that the beginning of the section coincides with Mk 10^1, Mt 19^1, and that the end of it brings us to the approach to Jericho (Lk 18^{35}). It is true that some part of the time preceding the last Passover was spent in Peræa. We know this on the joint testimony of the other Synoptists and St. John (Mk 10^1, Mt 19^1, Jn 10^{40}). But to suppose that the whole section must be localized there is to misunderstand the structure and character of St. Luke's Gospel. It is far more probable that he has massed together a quantity of material derived from some special source to which he had access, and which could not be easily fitted into the framework supplied to him by St. Mark.

When we come to examine these materials in detail, it would seem probable that they belong to very different periods in our Lord's ministry. Some incidents, for instance, appear to assume those easier relations to the Pharisees which we have seen to be characteristic of the earlier period (Lk 11[37] [but not vv.[42-54]] 14[1ff.]). It would be natural also to refer to this or the middle period the three parables of ch. 15 (Weiss, *Leben Jesu,* i. 507). On the other hand, some of the incidents are practically dated by their co-incidence with the other Gospels; while others, like the severer denunciations of the Pharisees and eschatological sections such as Lk 13[22-30] 17[20]–18[8], are referred to the later period by their subject-matter. It would be wrong to lay too much stress on mere symmetry; but when a natural sequence suggests itself, it may be accepted as having such probability as can be attained. The document which St. Luke is using in this part has preserved for us discourses of the utmost value, and it is largely to them that the Gospel owes its marked individuality.

§ **54**. ii. *The Johannean Narrative of this Period.*— The historical value of the Fourth Gospel comes out strongly in this period. Rarely has any situation been described with the extraordinary vividness and truth to nature of ch. 7 (see esp. vv.[11-15. 25-27. 31. 32. 40-52]). Not less graphic are the details of ch. 9; and there is marked precision in the statements of Jn 10[22f. 40f.] 11[54-57]. We note a special intimacy with what passes in the inner counsels of the Sanhedrin (Jn 7[47-52] 11[47-53]). This intimate knowledge might have been derived through Nicodemus or through the connexion hinted at in Jn 18[15].* But, apart from the peculiar verisimilitude of these details, some such activity as that described in these chapters is required to explain the great cata-strophe which followed. It is impossible that Jesus

* The theory of Delff has been mentioned above (p. 53 *sup.*); but it turns too much upon a single set of data, and leads to an arbitrary dissection of the Gospel.

should have been so much a stranger to Judæa and
Jerusalem as the Synoptic narrative would at first sight
seem to make Him.   For the steps which lead up to
the end we must go to St. John.

of teaching of
period

§ **55**. iii. *The general Character of the Teaching of
this Period.*—There are no doubt portions of the teaching of this period preserved in the Synoptics.   But
except those contained in Mk 10$^{1-45}$‖ they are difficult
to identify with certainty.   For the greater part of our
knowledge of it we are indebted to St. John, and we
may observe that the teaching now begins to take a
new character.   Hitherto it has been mainly concerned
with the nature of the Kingdom; henceforward greater
stress is laid on the person of the King.   We have
already noted the remarkable verse Mt 11^{27}‖ 'All
things have been delivered unto me of my Father: and
no one knoweth the Son save the Father; neither doth
any know the Father save the Son, and he to whom-
soever the Son willeth to reveal him.' This verse may
be said to represent the text which the discourses in St.
John set in various lights.   We have now the self-
revelation of the Son as the central life-giving and
light-giving force of humanity.   As He is the living
Bread (Jn 6), so is He the living Water (Jn 7$^{37f.}$); He
is the Light of the world (Jn 8^{12} 9^5); He is the Good
Shepherd (Jn 10^{11}), the Resurrection and the Life (Jn
11^{25}).   If we suppose that these discourses were really
held, we shall understand better than we could do
otherwise the state of Christian thought which meets
us when we open the first surviving Epistles of
St. Paul.

§ 56. iv. *The Prophecies of Death and Resurrection.*— *Prophecies of Resurrection*
From the time of St. Peter's confession Jesus began in
set terms to foretell that His mission would end in His
death, soon, however, to be followed by His resurrec-
tion (Mk 8[31] ||).   At the moment of His highest triumph,
marked by the Transfiguration, the same solemn prediction is repeated (Mk 9[31]), and again yet a third time
towards the end of the period with which we are now
dealing (Mk 10[32-34] ||).

(*a*) Even an ordinary observer might have seen that
the signs of the times were ominous.   St. Peter's confession showed no more than one adherent whose fervid
faith might be supposed capable of resisting a pressure
of life or death.   Herod Antipas and his faction were
hostile.   The Pharisees were yet more hostile, and their
bitterness was growing every day.   Within the period
before us two deliberate attempts were made on the life
of Jesus (Jn 8[59] 10[39]).   And with the certainty that
the course on which He was bent would include nothing
to conciliate these antagonisms, it was clear where they
would end.

(*b*) But the foresight of Jesus took a wider range
than this.   He had laid it down as a principle that it
was the fate of prophets to be persecuted (Mt 5[12] 23[34. 37]).
In particular, He had before Him the example of the
Baptist, whose fate He associated with His own
(Mk 9[12f.] ||).

(*c*) But there was a deeper necessity even than this.
At the Betrayal, to him who drew sword in His defence
Jesus replied calmly, 'How then should the Scriptures
be fulfilled, that thus it must be?'   And this is His
consistent language (comp. Lk 24[25f. 44. 46] etc.).   The

mind of Jesus was steeped in the ancient prophecies. He had Himself, as we have seen, deliberately fused the conception of the conquering Messiah with that of the Suffering Servant of Jehovah, and He as deliberately went the way to fulfil these prophecies in His own person. There was nothing accidental about His Death. He 'set His face steadfastly' on the road which led to it.

(*d*) When we look into its lessons we are carried even behind the fulfilment of prophecy. We shall have to speak presently of the extraordinary novelty of the turn which Christ gave to His mission. Others had conquered by the exercise of force; He was the first to set Himself to conquer by weakness, patience, non-resistance. And the natural and inevitable consummation of this new method of conquest was Death.

(*e*) In all this He was carrying out, and knew that He was carrying out, the Will of the Father. It was conceivable that that Will might have yet ulterior objects even beyond those, deep enough as we might think, which we have been considering. That Jesus ascribed to His Death such an ulterior object, we are led to believe by the way in which He speaks of it. The two places in which He does so must next engage our attention.

§ 57. v. *Significance of the Death of Jesus.*—The first of the passages to which allusion has just been made is Mk 10^{45} ‖ ‘For verily the Son of Man came not to be ministered unto, but to minister, and to give his life a ransom for many.’ We observe here that Jesus brings His Death under the category of service, and regards it

as the climax of a life of service.   This is one way of
stating the great paradox to which we have just alluded.
The kings of the Gentiles exercise lordship over their
subjects; but such was not to be the ambition of the
disciples of Christ; rather the very opposite; and it was
Christ Himself who set them the example.   At the end
of the avenue stood a cross, and the Saviour of men
walked up to it as if it had been a crown.   It is a question of pressing interest how much farther we may go
than this : is the λύτρον ἀντὶ πολλῶν to be interpreted
by the ἀπολύτρωσις and ἱλαστήριον of Ro $3^{24f.}$, and by
the language of other similar passages?   By itself we
could not say that it compelled such an interpretation;
but there is nothing forced in supposing that the early
Church knew and followed the mind of its Founder.
In that case we should have reason to think that Jesus
Himself had hinted at the sacrificial character of His
Death, and that He too regarded it as propitiatory.

If this passage suggests a sacrificial aspect of one
kind, the other is more explicit in bringing out sacrificial associations of another.   All the extant accounts
of the institution of the Eucharist connect the Blood
shed upon the Cross with the founding of a '[new]
Covenant.'   This is certainly an allusion to the inauguration of the first Covenant with sacrifice (cf. Ex
24^{4-8}, He 9^{18-23}), and the death of Christ is clearly
regarded as the Sacrifice inaugurating the second (see
below, p. 166).

In other words, the momentous question came before
the mind of Jesus, whether the New Dispensation which
He was founding was or was not like the Old in including the idea of Sacrifice?   He deliberately answered that

it was. And He deliberately foresaw, and as deliberately accepted, the consequence, that the Sacrifice of this New Dispensation could be none other than the Sacrifice of Himself.

That which gives this particular Death a value which no other death could have had, is (*a*) the fact that it is the Death of the Messiah, of One whose function it is to be the Saviour of His people, and whose Death, like His Life, must in some way enter into the purpose of the whole scheme of salvation; and (β) the further fact that although the Death is a necessity in the sense that it was required for the full development of God's gracious purpose, it was nevertheless a purely voluntary act on the part of the Son, an expression of that truly filial spirit in which He made the whole of the Father's purpose His own. 'The good Shepherd layeth down his life for the sheep. . . . Therefore doth the Father love me, because I lay down my life, that I may take it again. No one taketh it away from me, but I lay it down of myself. I have power to lay it down, and I have power to take it again. This commandment received I from my Father' (Jn 10[11. 17f.]). It follows (γ) that however much it may be right to conceive of the Death of Christ as a Sacrifice, and a sacrifice which has for its object the 'remission of sins' (Mt 26[28]), we must not in connexion with it set the justice of God against His mercy, or think of Him as really turning away His face from the Son of His love.

LITERATURE.—The subject of these last two sections not only comes into the field of New Testament Theology in general and treatises (like Wendt's and others named above) on the Teaching of Christ, but it necessarily occupies a prominent place in discussions of the Doctrine of the Atonement. Among these may be mentioned especially Ritschl's *Rechtfertigung u. Versöhnung*, vol. ii. of which goes elaborately into the exegesis of the leading passages (ed. 2, 1882), and a recent treatise by Kähler, *Zur Lehre von der Versöhnung* (Leipzig, 1898), which gives prominence to the relation of the doctrine to the Life of Christ. A lengthy monograph by Schwartzkopff deals directly with our Lord's predictions of His Passion (*Die Weissagungen Jesu Christi von seinem Tode*, u.s.w., Göttingen, 1895; Eng. tr., T. & T. Clark); and 'Christ's Attitude to His Death' is the title of some striking articles by Dr. A. M. Fairbairn in *Expos.* 1896, ii., and 1897, i.

CHAPTER VI.

THE MESSIANIC CRISIS.

E. The Messianic Crisis: the Triumphal Entry, the Last Teaching, Passion, Death, Resurrection, Ascension.

§ **58.** *Scene.*—Mainly in Jerusalem.

Time.—Six days before Passover to ten days before Pentecost A.D. 29.

Mt 21^1–28^{20}, Mk 11^1–16^8 [vv.$^{9-20}$ an early addition], Lk 19^{29}–24^{52}, Jn 12^1–21^{23}.

This series of momentous events has naturally furnished much matter for discussion and controversy, some of it very recent. (i.) Our first duty will be to sketch rapidly the course of the events with special reference to the motives of the human actors in them. (ii.) We must consider the debated points in the chronology of the last week. (iii.) We shall have to discuss the eschatological teaching which the Synoptists place in this period. (iv.) A number of points, critical and doctrinal, will meet us in connexion with the Last Supper. (v.) We shall have in like manner to consider both the attestation and the significance of the crown-

ing event of all, the Resurrection. This will
include some discussion of the Appearances which
followed.   Lastly (vi.), as our subject is the Life
of Christ and not the Gospels, we must, even
though in so doing we cross the threshold of St.
Luke's 'second treatise,' follow the steps of the
Master to His Ascension.

§ 59. i. *The Action and the Actors.*—Our four Gospels,
taken together, in part convey and in part suggest a
view at once clear and probable of the course of events
which led to the Crucifixion, and of the motives which
impelled the several actors in them.   We have seen
that the Fourth Gospel is needed to explain the
heightened enmity which had so tragic an issue.   A
residence in Jerusalem and Bethany of four days would
not be enough to account for the overtures to Judas.
The events of the Feast of Tabernacles, the Feast of
Dedication, and the Raising of Lazarus, with the
knowledge that Jesus had been teaching and making
disciples at no great distance from Jerusalem, supply
what is wanted.   And in the case of the Last Week the
touches which the Fourth Gospel adds to its predecessors supplement them effectively.

(*a*) *The Populace.*—In the Triumphal Entry we seem
to see a gleam once more of the enthusiasm which had
followed the Feeding of the Five Thousand.   It was
probably quite as superficial.   We may imagine the
crowd made up in part of those who had been impressed
by recent teaching beyond the Jordan or in Jerusalem
itself, or by the news of the still more striking miracle
wrought upon Lazarus: besides these, there would

doubtless be a contingent of pilgrims from more distant Galilee, the remnant of the crowds who had at one time or another followed Jesus there. But it would be too much to expect that all, or even many of these, had acquired an intelligent insight into the character of Him whom they were cheering. They were still in the twilight of their old Jewish expectations. They supposed that the moment had at last come when the hopes which they cherished would be realized, and when before the crowds assembled for the Passover Jesus would at last put Himself forward as the Leader for whom they were waiting. Nothing, however, came of this seeming appeal to their enthusiasm. A few discourses in the temple, partly levelled against the religious authorities they were most accustomed to reverence, but containing not a word of incitement against the Romans, and that was all. What wonder if their enthusiasm died away, and if in some of the fiercer among them it changed to bitter and angry disappointment! Doubtless some of these Zealots mingled with those who cried 'Crucify him, crucify him'; it was natural that they should prefer one of their own trade, like Barabbas; but the crowds in Jerusalem at Passover time were so great that many of these fanatics may have had no personal acquaintance with Jesus at all. The choice between Jesus and Barabbas would seem to them a choice between a mock leader, a dreamer of dreams, who offered them nothing but words, and a true son of the people, who had shown himself ready to grip the sword in the good cause.

(b) *The Traitor.*—It is possible that Judas Iscariot may have shared something of these feelings. In the

lists of the apostles he is usually named next to a
Zealot. The long course of training which he had
undergone may have failed to purge his mind of the
carnal expectations of his countrymen. It may have
been a sudden access of disappointment, greater than
ever before, because the hopes by which it had been
preceded had been greater, which impelled him to seek
his interview with the members of the Sanhedrin. It
has even been suggested that he did what he did in
order to compel his Master to declare Himself, and
with the belief that He would at last exert for the
deliverance of the nation the supernatural powers with
which He was endowed. For this we have no sufficient
warrant; and we are told expressly (Jn 12⁶ RV text and
most Comms.) that Judas was guilty of petty pilfering
from the common fund, and therefore may infer that he
was accessible to the temptations of avarice. Still, few
men act from motives that they cannot at least make
plausible to themselves; so that a mixture of obstinate
and misguided patriotism is more probable than pure
malignity. If Judas had not been at least capable of
better things, it is not likely that he would have been
chosen to be one of the Twelve.

(c) *The Pharisees.*—By this time between Jesus and
the Pharisees there is open war. Insidious questions
are still put to Him, but only in order to 'ensnare him
in his talk' (Mt 22¹⁵ ‖).   And on His side Jesus replied
to their treachery by the sternest denunciations. It
need not be supposed that all 'scribes and Pharisees'
were equally the object of these. We know that Nicodemus and Joseph of Arimathæa were members of the
Sanhedrin; we do not know that they belonged to the

Pharisees

party of the Pharisees, but we cannot doubt that there
were some Pharisees like-minded with them; just as we
learn from the Acts that after the Resurrection a number
of the 'priests' (Ac 6[7]) and at least some Pharisees (*ib.*
15[5]) became Christians.

(*d*) *The Sadducees.*—With the last week of our Lord's
life, or rather, if we may trust St. John, as far back as
the Feast of Tabernacles (Jn 7[45]), a new party comes
into prominence. The Sanhedrin begins to take official
action against Jesus; and although the Pharisees had
some footing in that body, its policy was more determined by the Sadducees, to whom belonged most of the
'chief priests,' and in particular Caiaphas, the acting
high priest, and his yet more influential father-in-law
and predecessor Annas. As against Jesus the two
parties of Pharisees and Sadducees acted together, but
their motives were different. The Pharisees were
jealous for their authority and traditions, which were
openly assailed. The Sadducees themselves rejected
these traditions,—they were selfish politicians, who
played their own game. Their motto was *quieta non
movere*. They dreaded any kind of disturbance which
might give the Romans an excuse to take the power
out of their hands (cf. Jn 11[48]). It is curious to note
how from this time onwards the bitterest opposition
comes from the Sadducees, while leading Pharisees are
neutral or even favourable (Ac 4[34-39] 23[9]).

(*e*) *Pilate.*—The position of things is this. The Jews
(*i.e.* primarily the Sanhedrin) were bent upon bringing
about the death of Jesus. Now they themselves had not
the power of life and death (Jn 18[31]). According to the
Talmud, they lost it forty years before the destruction

of Jerusalem, which would be about this very time. It is probable, however, that they did not long continue to possess it after the annexation of Judæa by the Romans. This being the case, they could only act through the instrumentality of the Roman governor. This necessitated the putting forward of different reasons from those that really weighed with themselves. Rather we should say that there were really three sets of reasons : (i.) The real motive of the Sanhedrin was jealousy of its own authority,—on the part of the Sadducees fear of disturbance, on the part of the Pharisees resentment of the attacks upon themselves and their traditions, and with some of the most patriotic among them perhaps disgust at a Messiah who was not a Messiah in any sense which they could comprehend. (ii.) The ostensible reason, which with some may have been sincere enough, was the charge of blasphemy against God. This charge they tried to bring home, but for a time could not (Mk 14^{59}||), until at last they caught at the confession of Jesus Himself. On the strength of this He was condemned (Mk 14$^{62-64}$). (iii.) This charge, however, was not one which they could bring before the governor, and therefore they changed their ground. St. Luke, who in all these scenes draws upon special and good information, states the accusation with more precision than the other Synoptists. 'We found this man perverting our nation, and forbidding to give tribute to Cæsar, and saying that he himself is Christ a king' (or 'an anointed king,' RVm; Lk 23^{2}).

· With this charge it is that the leaders of the Sanhedrin come before Pilate. Pilate has the rough

Roman sense of justice, and he feels that the charge is not proved. He sees no evidence that Jesus is really a formidable conspirator, or even a conspirator at all against the State. He therefore desires to release Him; but the Jews insist, the leaders being backed by the clamour of the crowd. The Sanhedrists know *the people loud* the weak point in Pilate's armour, and they fasten upon *Pilate, weak* it: 'If thou release this man, thou art not Cæsar's *point* friend: every one that maketh himself a king speaketh against Cæsar' (Jn 19¹², a most lifelike touch). For themselves they protest their loyalty. 'We have no king but Cæsar' (Jn 19¹⁵). For many of the Sanhedrin, Pharisees as well as Sadducees, this would be true, and those for whom it was not would discreetly hold their peace. To this pressure Pilate in the end gives way, washing his hands of the responsibility. He might have taken a nobler course, but he felt insecure of his position; he knew that the Jews had matter of just complaint against him; and sooner than face their malice, with the inconveniences which it might cause, he let them have their will.

LITERATURE.—With this section may be compared two works of imagination: Dr. Edwin A. Abbott, *Philochristus*, London, 1878; and *As Others Saw Him*, London, 1895 (written from a Jewish point of view, but sympathetic and instructive). Also Chwolson, *Das letzte Passamahl Christi*, etc., St. Petersburg, 1892, Anhang: 'Das Verhältniss d. Pharisäer, Sadducäer u. der Juden überhaupt zu Jesus Christus' (minimizing the opposition of the Pharisees, and laying the blame upon the Sadducees. The writer was a distinguished Orientalist, Christian, but of Jewish birth).

§ 60. ii. *The Chronology of the Last Week.*—A number *the Chronology of last week* of chronological difficulties meet us in the narrative of

10

this Last Week.   (1) The *primâ facie* view would
certainly be that the Anointing at Bethany was placed
by Mark *two* days (Mk 14^1) and by John *six* days (Jn
12^1) before the Passover.   (2) The common opinion is
that the Crucifixion took place on a Friday, and the
Last Supper on the evening of Thursday; but it has
also been argued that the two events took place on
Thursday and Wednesday.   (3) There is a much larger
division of opinion as to the date of the Crucifixion in
the Jewish calendar, and the relation of the Last Supper
to the Paschal Meal.   The Synoptists seem to identify
the two, whereas St. John expressly places the Last
Supper before the Passover, and would make the
Crucifixion fall on Nisan 14.   (4) The authorities also
appear to differ as to the time of day occupied by
the Crucifixion.   According to Mk 15^{25} the time of the
Crucifixion itself was the 'third hour' (= 9 a.m.);
according to Jn 19^{14} the trial was not quite over by
the 'sixth hour' (= noon), and therefore the Crucifixion
was still later.

Of these discrepancies No. 2 need not detain us.
The view that the Crucifixion took place upon a
Thursday is almost peculiar to Dr. Westcott (*Introd.
to the Study of the Gospels*, p. 322, ed. 3).   It turns
upon a pressing of the phrase 'three days and three
nights' in Mt 12^{40}, along with the probability of confusion between 'preparation *for the Passover*' and the
more ordinary use of the word in the sense of 'preparation *for the Sabbath*' (*i.e.* Friday).   The phrasing of
Mt 27^{62} is somewhat peculiar, but not really less so on
this way of reckoning than the other, because the day
described as the 'morrow after the Preparation' would

be itself the weekly παρασκευή. And Mt 12⁴⁰ is due only to the evangelist, and is not supported by the other authorities. [On the length of the interval between the Crucifixion and the Resurrection see esp. art. CHRONOLOGY OF NT in Hastings' *DB* i. 410ᵇ (with Field, *Ot. Norv.* iii. p. 7, there referred to), and Wright, *NT Problems*, p. 159 ff.]

No. 1 is commonly removed by treating the note of time in Mk 14¹‖ as referring to the events of vv. 1. 2. 10. 11 and not to the intervening narrative of vv.³⁻⁹. In support of this, Meyer-Weiss (ed. 8, *ad loc.*) points to analogous cases of intrusive matter in Mk 3²²⁻³⁰ 4¹⁰⁻²⁵ 6¹⁴⁻²⁹ 7²⁵⁻³⁰. On the other hand, M'Clellan (*Gospels*, p. 472 f.) restricts the application of Jn 12¹ to the arrival at Bethany, which, according to him, was on the afternoon of Friday, Nisan 8. The Anointing he would place on the evening of Tuesday, Nisan 12. Either view is possible, and neither can be verified. If we think that the fourth evangelist deliberately corrects his predecessors, we shall probably give the preference to him. On such a point Mark is not a first-hand authority, and the connexion between his placing of the Betrayal and of the Anointing may well be loose.

As to (4) the difference in regard to the hour of the Crucifixion, attempts have been made with some persistence to prove that St. John used a different mode of reckoning time from that in common use. The writer of this was at one time inclined to look with favour on these attempts. If the premiss could be proved, the data would work out satisfactorily. But, in view of the articles by Mr. J. A. Cross in *Class.*

Rev. 1891, p. 245 ff., and by Prof. Ramsay in *Expositor*, 1893, i. 216 ff., it must definitely be said that the major premiss cannot be proved, and that the attempt to reconcile the two statements on this basis breaks down (cf. also Wright, *Problems*, p. 149 ff.).

The ancient solution of the difficulty was to suppose a corruption (F for Γ, or *vice versâ*) of the text, more often in John than in Mark; and rightly, because in Mark there are three several notes of time (Mk 15^1 $\parallel$ $^{25.}$ $^{33}\parallel$) which hang together. So Eus. *ad Marinum*, with a group of MSS *scholia* (*vid.* Tisch. on Jn 19^{14}), etc. This solution is accepted by Mr. Wright (*op. cit.* p. 156 ff.), and it may conceivably hold good.

Prof. Ramsay lays stress rather on the rough and approximate way in which the ancients used the reckoning by hours. It must be remembered that an 'hour' with them was a twelfth part of daylight, and not a fixed space of 60 measured minutes, as with us. If the two statements had been inverted—if Mk 15^{25} had described the end of the trial and Jn 19^{14} the raising of the cross —this elasticity might have amply covered both. As the two passages stand, it hardly does so.

We may ask ourselves whether, supposing that the slaughter of the Paschal lambs began at 3 p.m. (the time of slaughter is given at 3–5 p.m. by Jos. *BJ* VI. ix. 3), there would not be a rather strong temptation on typological grounds to fix the moment of the death of the Messiah at that hour. The other notes of time would naturally be conformed to this. But, on the other hand, St. John's 'sixth hour' seems inconveniently late for the events which have to be compressed between it and the evening. The whole question must be left open. There is a choice of possibilities, but nothing more.

Can we get beyond a similar choice on the last and most important point (3), the discrepancy as to the day of the month of the Crucifixion and of the Last Supper? Perhaps not.

It is the Last Supper which the Synoptists appear to fix by identifying it with the Passover. They say expressly that on the morning of the 'first day of

unleavened bread, when they sacrificed the Passover'
(Mk 14[12]||), the disciples asked where the Passover was
to be eaten. This would be on the morning of Nisan
14. In the evening, which from twilight onwards
would belong to Nisan 15, would follow the Last
Supper, and on the next afternoon (still, on the Jewish
reckoning, Nisan 15) the Crucifixion. St. John, on the
other hand, by a number of clear indications (Jn 13[1]
18[28] 19[14, 31]) implies that the Last Supper was eaten
before the time of the regular Passover, and that the
Lord suffered on the afternoon of Nisan 14, about the
time of the slaying of the Paschal lambs.

We are thus left with a conflict of testimony; and
the question is, on which side the evidence is strongest?
Now, if we are to believe a very competent Jewish
archæologist, Dr. Chwolson, the Synoptists begin with
an error. 'From the Mosaic writings down to the
Book of Jubilees (cap. 49), Philo, Josephus, the Palestinian Targum ascribed to Jonathan ben Uziel, the
Mishnah, the Talmud, the Rabbinical writings of the
Middle Ages, indeed down to the present day, the Jews
have always understood by the phrase יוֹם רִאשׁוֹן לְחַג
הַמַּצּוֹת "the first day of the feast of unleavened bread,"
only the 15th, and not the 14th' (*Das letzte Passamahl
Christi u. der Tag seines Todes*, p. 3 f.); so that it
would be a contradiction in terms to say with Mk 14[12]||
'on the first day of unleavened bread, when they sacrificed the Passover.' It is, however, only right to add
that Chwolson's assertion is denied by another very
good authority, Dr. Schürer, *ThL*, 1893, col. 182.
[Schürer does not directly meet the statement that
where the feast of Unleavened Bread is represented as

extending over eight days, the days intended are Nisan 15–22, not 14–21.*]

Waiving this point, however, for the present, we observe (after Chwolson, but cf. *Authorship of the Fourth Gospel*, 1872, p. 206 f. etc.) that the Synoptists make the Sanhedrin say beforehand that they will not arrest Jesus 'on the feast day,' and then actually arrest Him on that day; that not only the guards, but one of the disciples (Mk 14^{47}‖) carries arms, which on the feast day was not allowed; that the trial was also held on the feast day, which would be unlawful (on these points see Chwolson, *op. cit.* p. 6 ff.); that the feast day would not be called simply 'Preparation'; that the phrase 'coming from the field' (Mk 15^{21}‖) means properly 'coming from work'; that Joseph of Arimathæa is represented as buying a linen cloth (Mk 15^{46}), and the women as preparing spices and ointments (Lk 23^{56}), all of which would be contrary to law and custom.

It follows that the Synoptists are really inconsistent with themselves, and bear unwilling witness to the chronology of St. John. We may be still reluctant to think that the contradiction is final. The Synoptists, so far as they identify the Last Supper with the Passover, look as if they were telling the truth. It is possible that there may be some way of reconciling the two accounts, which we do not know enough of the circumstances to specify.

* It is worth noting that the Gospel of Peter agrees with the Johannean rather than the Synoptic tradition, placing the Crucifixion not on, but before, the first day of unleavened bread (πρὸ μιᾶς τῶν ἀζύμων, *Ev. Pet.* 3).

One hypothesis, which the writer was at one time tempted to entertain, — very tentatively, — that the 'Passover' which lay before the disciples and the Sanhedrin was not the Passover proper, but the eating of the *Chăgîgāh* (so Edersheim, M'Clellan, Nösgen), he now believes to be untenable (see *Expos.* 1892, i. 17 ff., 182 f., and Wright, *Problems*, p. 173 ff.). It is more likely that, for some reason or other, the regular Passover was anticipated.

Dr. Chwolson, writing as an archæologist, and a Jewish archæologist, would account for such anticipation by the fact that in the year of the Passion, Nisan 15 (not 14) fell upon a Sabbath. But it must be confessed that his argument seems strained (cf. also Schürer in *ThL, ut sup.*).

Mr. Wright thinks that the Synoptists have combined the narrative of the Last Supper with that of some previous Paschal meal partaken of by our Lord (*Problems*, p. 179 ff.). But even if this hypothesis held good, it would hardly meet the case; because it is just the details of the Last Supper, belonging to it *qua* Last Supper (*e.g.* the 'cup of blessing'), which remind us of the Passover. And, in any case, the hypothesis deserts the documents too far to be at all capable of proof.

As the question at present stands, we can only acknowledge our ignorance. [The literature will have been sufficiently given in the course of this section; cf. esp. Mr. A. Wright's *Some New Testament Problems*, London, 1898, p. 147 ff.]

§ **61.** (iii.) *The Prophetic Teaching of the Last Week.* Prophetic Oracle of the last week

—This, too, has raised difficulties which are not only apparent but real. It is important to bear in mind that no less than six distinct kinds of prediction are ascribed to our Lord during this week or in the period preceding. There is (1) the prediction of His own death and resurrection. There is (2) the prediction of the siege and destruction of Jerusalem. With this in the great passage (Mk 13‖) is directly connected (3) the prediction of the end of the world and the last judgment. (4) The discourses in Jn clearly predict the coming of the Paraclete as the substitute for Christ Himself. (5) In another leading passage (Mk 9¹) a phrase is used which may be explained, though it is not usually explained, of the remarkable spread of the Christian Church from the Day of Pentecost onwards. Lastly (6), there is the explanation which is frequently given of the 'Coming of the Son of Man' as a so-called 'historical coming,' a coming not exhausted by a single occasion, but repeated in the great events of history.

The first three of these classes of predictions are, in any case, authentic and certain. To the believer in the genuineness of the Fourth Gospel the prophecy of the Paraclete is equally certain, and there is much which goes to confirm it in the Acts and Epistles independently of its direct attestation. The other two forms of prediction are more hypothetical. They have been introduced more or less in order to meet the difficulties, although they may have substantial grounds of their own. We will not as yet beg the question either way.

The great difficulty is that, as our documents stand, the second and third predictions are intimately connected with each other, and in at least one other passage it would seem as if it were expressly stated that the coming of the Son of Man (*i.e.* the final Coming, the Coming to Judgment) would take place within the lifetime of that generation. We know that it has not so taken place, and the great question is what we are to say to this. Is it an error in One who has never been convicted of error in anything else? We must not endeavour to explain away facts; but we may interrogate them, and interrogate them somewhat strictly, to see whether they are facts or no.

We cannot disguise from ourselves that, whatever the precise language used by our Lord, the disciples would be exceedingly prone to attribute to Him the prediction of His own return as near at hand. The connexion of the Messiah with a world-wide judgment was no new doctrine, but was a common feature in the Jewish apocalypses. But this return would seem to them, as applied to our Lord, the necessary complement of the life of humiliation which He had led upon earth. For it was reserved the full triumph over His enemies which so far must have seemed very imperfect. Resurrection and Ascension would seem to be only foretastes of the great coming in glory on the clouds of heaven. They were steps, but only steps, towards the goal.

We might have been sure, even if we had not been told, that the disciples would naturally fix their thoughts on this Second Coming, and that it would be a natural inference for them to suppose that it was near at hand. Instances like the comparison of Mt 24^{29} = Mk 13^{24} = Lk 21^{25} show that the expectation as to time was not fixed but variable.

On the other side, no doubt, must be set the fact that in the apostolic circle the belief in the nearness of the Second Coming was almost universal (1 Th $4^{14ff.}$, 1 Co $7^{29ff.}$ 16^{23}, 2 Co 5^3, Ro $13^{11.\ 12}$, Ph 4^5, 1 P 4^7, 1 Jn 2^{18}, Rev 1^3 22^{10} etc.). The obvious conclusion to draw from this would be, that the belief had a common root in the teaching of Christ Himself.

And in favour of that conclusion might be quoted the language of 1 Th 4^{15}, though it may be questioned how much of this is a 'word of the Lord,' and how much the construction put upon it by St. Paul. The ease with which the apostles postponed their expectation under the teaching of events, would tell against the supposition that the words of Christ had been precise on the subject; and when we come to look into the Gospels, there are many hints that the time of the Second Coming could not be fixed precisely and might be distant (Mt 24^{37-51}‖ $25^{10-13.\ 14}$). These passages are indeed so clear that they may be fairly said to neutralize those which are quoted on the other side, and to heighten the probability that the apparent definiteness of these other passages is due to the disciples rather than to the Master.

But another hypothesis has been put forward to remove the difficulty. It has been supposed that the Coming of the Son of Man in the places where it is spoken of as near at hand, refers not to the final coming, but to another kind of coming in the great events of history. The prologue of St. John's Gospel appears to point to such repeated comings (Jn 1^9); and if any event deserves the name, it might well be given to the Destruction of Jerusalem, which was certainly one of the turning-points of history, and had a momentous influence upon the fortunes of Christianity. There is no doubt that our Lord directly predicted this catastrophe; and it might well seem that the passages which apparently speak of the final coming as near were due to a confusion in the minds of the disciples between the two events regarded as 'Comings.'

It is, however, a question whether this idea of repeated coming can be made good. Most recent writers are inclined to set it down as a modernism (Schwartzkopff, *Weissagungen Jesu Christi*, etc. p. 155; Holtzmann, *Neutest. Theol.* i. 315). It is also very doubtful whether it has any real support in OT. What the prophets looked forward to was '*the* day of the Lord'—a single great intervention of God—not *a* day or succession of days.

On this point the writer is glad to be able to refer to a note which he has received from Dr. Driver: 'The usual expression is "*the* day of Jehovah": in Is 2^{12}, however, it is indef. (" for there is a day for," etc., or "Jehovah hath a day"; Zec 14^1 has also "a day"; Ezk 30^3 is lit. "For near is a day, and near is a day for Jehovah"; Is 34^8 "For there is a day of vengeance for Jehovah (or "Jehovah hath"), a year of recompense for," etc.; also "his days" in apparently the same sense, Job 24^1. But these hardly differ except formally from the usual "day of Jehovah." I do not think that a succession of judgments is represented under this figure—except, of course, in so far as what the prophet pictured as taking place in a single day was in reality effected gradually.'

Another hypothesis, however, also appears deserving of consideration. The strongest of all the passages which would make our Lord expressly predict His own Second Coming within the apostolic age itself, is Mt 16^{28} 'Verily I say unto you, There be some of them that

stand here which shall in no wise taste of death, till
they see the Son of Man coming in his kingdom.'   But
when we compare this with the parallels, Mk 9^1 =
Lk 9^{27} it is clear that the words Son of Man are
intrusive, and that the clause really runs, 'till they see
the kingdom of God come with power' (om. 'with
power,' Luke).   It is not the 'Son of Man coming in
his kingdom,' but the 'kingdom' itself which comes.

What is meant by the kingdom here?   Is it not a
very natural interpretation to explain it of that great
intervention of the Spirit of God in the world, that
great influx of Divine powers and energies which dates
from Pentecost?   In other words, is it not natural to
equate it with the promise of the Paraclete in the
Fourth Gospel, where it is implied that the coming of
the Paraclete is equivalent to the coming of Christ
Himself? (Jn 14^{16-18}).

The teaching of the Fourth Gospel respecting the
Paraclete is already strongly confirmed by the part
assigned to the Holy Spirit by St. Paul; and if the
explanation just suggested * holds good, it would be
also confirmed from another and unexpected quarter.

There was at one time a strong tendency in the advanced liberal
camp to get rid entirely of the apocalyptic and eschatological
element in the teaching of our Lord.   The chief means through
which this is done has been the supposed discovery that in the
discourse of Mk 13‖ there is incorporated a 'Little Apocalypse'
of Jewish (Weizsäcker) or Jewish-Christian (Colani, Pfleiderer,
Weiffenbach) origin, usually regarded as a 'fly-sheet' composed
in A.D. 67–68 during the troubles which immediately preceded the
siege of Jerusalem, and identified with the 'oracle' which led to

---

* A similar view is taken by Haupt, p. 133 f., and Bruston
(Holtzmann, *Neutest. Theol.* i. 315 n.), but commended itself to the
writer of this independently.   Cf. also Swete, *ad loc.*

the flight of the Christians to Pella (Eus. *HE* III. v. 3). The first to hit upon this idea was Colani (*Jésus Christ et les Croyances Messianiques de son Temps*, ed. 2, 1864, p. 201 ff.), who was followed by Weizsäcker, Pfleiderer, and on an elaborate scale by Weiffenbach, *Der Wiederkunftsgedanke Jesu*, Leipzig, 1873. This last-named work is usually referred to as having established the position. In the final form of the theory the 'fly-sheet' in question is supposed to consist of Mk 13[7-9a]‖ [14-20]‖ [24-27]‖ [30-31]‖. And it is true that these verses are fairly detachable from the rest and make a fairly compact whole.

By thus eliminating the central passage on which the eschatological teaching of Jesus seemed to rest, it became not very difficult to explain away that teaching altogether. Weiffenbach did so by the hypothesis that the critically verified allusions to the Second Coming of the Messiah all originally referred to *His Resurrection,* the predictions of which formed the genuine nucleus out of which the rest had grown, through misunderstanding of the words of Jesus and the blending with them of current apocalyptic doctrines. By this expedient, Weiffenbach, whose object was less radical than that of most of those who went with him, escaped some real difficulties; but just in this it may be doubted whether he has found any follower. It will be seen that the critical analysis of Mk 13‖ is the starting-point of the whole construction; and that has not perhaps as yet been brought to any final solution.

§ 62. iv. The Last Supper.—The part of the Last Supper of which it is most incumbent upon us to speak here is its culmination in the solemn acts and words which institute the second of the two great Sacraments. Besides the debates of centuries which have gathered round this subject, a number of questions have been raised in recent years which require discussion. In particular, new light has been thrown upon the text of one of our leading authorities. And our first step must be to determine as nearly as we can its exact bearing.

§ 63. (1) *The Text of Lk* 22[14-20].—The importance of

this section is such, and it is so desirable that the evidence should be given with completeness and precision, that we may be forgiven if in this instance we print the full text of the original (after Greek RV), and then proceed to give the more crucial variants in technical fashion.

The evidence of the leading Latin MSS is given in full; that of the two oldest forms of the Syriac Version in a retranslation, based for the Sinai MS on Mrs. Lewis and Merx, and for the Curetonian on Baethgen. For the Coptic Version the new critical edition is used (Oxford, 1898).

Lk 22$^{14-20}$. ^{14} Καὶ ὅτε ἐγένετο ἡ ὥρα, ἀνέπεσε, καὶ οἱ ἀπόστολοι σὺν αὐτῷ. ^{15} καὶ εἶπε πρὸς αὐτούς, Ἐπιθυμίᾳ ἐπεθύμησα τοῦτο τὸ πάσχα φαγεῖν μεθ' ὑμῶν πρὸ τοῦ με παθεῖν· ^{16} λέγω γὰρ ὑμῖν, ὅτι οὐ μὴ φάγω αὐτό, ἕως ὅτου πληρωθῇ ἐν τῇ βασιλείᾳ τοῦ Θεοῦ. ^{17} καὶ δεξάμενος ποτήριον εὐχαριστήσας εἶπε, Λάβετε τοῦτο, καὶ διαμερίσατε εἰς ἑαυτούς· ^{18} λέγω γὰρ ὑμῖν, ὅτι οὐ μὴ πίω ἀπὸ τοῦ νῦν ἀπὸ τοῦ γεννήματος τῆς ἀμπέλου ἕως ὅτου ἡ βασιλεία τοῦ Θεοῦ ἔλθῃ. ^{19} καὶ λαβὼν ἄρτον εὐχαριστήσας ἔκλασε, καὶ ἔδωκεν αὐτοῖς λέγων, Τοῦτό ἐστι τὸ σῶμά μου τὸ ὑπὲρ ὑμῶν διδόμενον· τοῦτο ποιεῖτε εἰς τὴν ἐμὴν ἀνάμνησιν. ^{20} καὶ τὸ ποτήριον ὡσαύτως μετὰ τὸ δειπνῆσαι λέγων, Τοῦτο τὸ ποτήριον ἡ καινὴ διαθήκη ἐν τῷ αἵματί μου, τὸ ὑπὲρ ὑμῶν ἐκχυνόμενον.

Locum integrum habent Codd. Græc. et Verss. omn., iis tantum testibus exceptis qui infra nominantur; item Latt. c f q Vulg.; *agnoscunt,* Tert. *adv. Marc.* iv. 40; Eus. *Can.*; Bas. *quæ feruntur Ethica*; Cyril. Alex. *Comm. in Luc.*

Om. vv.$^{16.17.18}$ Cod. Copt. ℵ (*Catena Curzoniana, excerpto ut videtur Tito [Bostrensi]*).

Om. vv.$^{17.18}$ Lect. 32, Pesh. *codd.*

Om. vv.$^{19b.20}$ τὸ ὑπὲρ ὑμῶν διδόμ.—ἐκχυνόμενον, D a ff^2 i l.

Iisdem omissis transp. vv.$^{17.18}$ *ita ut partem* v.^{19} *priorem sequantur* b e. [^{16} Dico enim vobis, quia ex hoc non manducabo illud, donec . . . in regno dei. ^{19} Et, accepto pane, gratias egit, et fregit, et dedit illis, ^{17} dicens: Hoc est corpus meum. Et accepto calice, gratias egit; et dixit: Accipite hoc et dividite inter vos. ^{18} dico enim vobis, quod non bibam de generatione hac vitis hujus, donec regnum dei veniat.

[21] Verumtamen ecce manus, etc. b [16] Dico enim vobis quia
jam non manducabo illud doneque adimplear in regno d̄i. [19] et
accepit panem et gratias egit et fregit et dedit eis [17] dicens hoc
est corpus meū. Et accepit calicē et gratias egit et dixit
accipite vivite inter vos. dico enim vobis amodo non vivam
(*sic*) amodo de potione vitis quoadusque regnum d̄i veniat
verum ecce manus, etc. e.]

Item transp. vv. [17.18] *omisso* (Cur.) *vel partim interjecto* (Sin.) v.[20]
Syrr. (Sin.-Cur.). [[16] . . . ἕως ὅτου πληρωθῇ ἐν τῇ βασ. τοῦ Θεοῦ.
[19] καὶ λαβὼν ἄρτον εὐχαριστήσας ἔκλασεν καὶ ἔδωκεν αὐτοῖς λέγων·
τοῦτό ἐστι τὸ σῶμά μου τὸ ὑπὲρ ὑμῶν διδόμενον (*om.* Cur.)· τοῦτο
ποιεῖτε εἰς τὴν ἐμὴν ἀνάμνησιν. [17] καὶ (ὡσαύτως μετὰ τὸ δειπνῆσαι
ins. ex v.[20] Sin.) δεξάμενος ποτήριον (*vel* τὸ ποτ.) εὐχαριστήσας εἶπε·
λάβετε τοῦτο διαμερίσατε εἰς ἑαυτούς (τοῦτό ἐστι τὸ αἷμα μου [ἡ]
καινὴ διαθήκη *add.* Sin.). λέγω (*ins.* γάρ Sin.) ὑμῖν ὅτι ἀπὸ τοῦ
νῦν οὐ μὴ πίω ἀπὸ τοῦ γεννήματος τούτου τῆς ἀμπέλου (*vel om.* ?)
ἕως ὅτου ἡ βασ. τοῦ θεοῦ ἔλθῃ.]

To the textual critic these phenomena are fairly clear.
The omission of vv.[19b–20] (D aff[2] il) belongs to the oldest
form of the Western text. The next step (b e) was to
transpose the order of vv.[17. 18] and [19a], so as to make
the sequence of the Bread and the Cup correspond to
that in the other authorities. The next (Cur.) was
to supplement the words relating to the Bread from
1 Co 11[24]. The next (Sin.) was to supplement in like
manner the part relating to the Cup by somewhat free
interpolations partly suggested by Matthew, Mark, but
mainly from 1 Co 11[25]. In this instance Syr.-Sin.
represents a later stage than Syr.-Cur., though it is
more often earlier. The omissions of vv. [[16]] [17. 18] are
probably not important.

We have then confronting each other the primitive
form of the Western text, which is shorter, makes
Luke transpose the order of the Bread and the Cup,

and omits all mention of a second Cup, and the great mass of Greek MSS and other authorities, which introduce a second Cup, or second mention of the Cup, and fill out the whole mainly from St. Paul. We cannot doubt that both these types of text existed early in the second century. Either may be original. And this is just one of those cases where internal evidence is strongly in favour of the text which we call Western. The temptation to expand was much stronger than to contract; and the double mention of the Cup raises real difficulties of the kind which suggest interpolation.

§ 64. (2) *Relation of the Texts to each other.*—The adoption of the Western text of Luke greatly diminishes the coincidences between St. Luke and St. Paul. Indeed, it reduces them to the practically equivalent εὐχαριστήσας for εὐλογήσας (in reference to the Bread; Matthew, Mark use it of the Cup). The greatest loss is that of the apparent confirmation by St. Luke of the command to repeat the rite in memory of its Founder. It may be doubted, however, whether the introduction of this into the text of Luke, which—to obtain the circulation it had—must have taken place exceedingly early, and must have been carried out at the headquarters of the Church, is not even stronger testimony to the current practice of the Church than that of a single writer could be, even though that writer was an evangelist.

As to the main lines of the rite, all the authorities are agreed. All note the taking of the Bread, the blessing (or 'giving thanks'), the breaking, the words, 'This is my Body.' All note the Cup, which both in the

Synoptic (Matthew, Mark) and Pauline tradition is related to the [new] Covenant inaugurated by the shedding of the Blood of the Messiah. In the Synoptics (Matthew, Mark, Luke) there is an express mention of the giving of the Bread to the disciples, with the further command, 'Take' (Matthew, Mark), 'eat' (Matthew), and a like communication of the Cup (Synoptics, though with some difference of phrase). And whereas St. Paul emphasizes the redemptive value of the sacrificed Body (τὸ ὑπὲρ ὑμῶν *lectio vera*), Matthew, Mark do the same for the shedding of the Blood (τὸ περὶ [ὑπὲρ] πολλῶν ἐκχυννόμενον Matthew, Mark, and εἰς ἄφεσιν ἁμαρτιῶν Matthew). St. Paul not only doubles the command for repetition, but also adds, 'For as often as ye eat this bread and drink this cup, ye proclaim the Lord's death till he come.'

§ 65. (3) *Other NT Evidence.*—We thus have the institution of the Sacrament fully set before us. But if we look at one of the documents upon which we have been drawing, the first in order of writing, though it is only incidentally historical, 1 Co 11, we find there that the Sacrament proper is associated with something else—the common meal or *agape* (Jude [12], 2 P 2[13] *var. lect.*). We ask ourselves what can be the origin of this association? It can hardly go back to the original institution. It is more probable that the association arose out of the state of κοινωνία described in Ac 2[42. 44–46] 4[32–35] 6[1. 2].

Perhaps it goes back further still, at least to the very beginning of the period. For one of the characteristic expressions is ἡ κλάσις τοῦ ἄρτου, κλᾶν

II

ἄρτον (Ac 2⁴²·⁴⁶), of which Blass says, 'est autem
κλᾶν τὸν ἄρτον sollemnis designatio cenæ dominicæ.'
It must, however, be somewhat wider than that, for
in the immediate context we have κλῶντες τε κατ'
οἶκον ἄρτον μετελάμβανον τροφῆς, κ.τ.λ., where τροφή
would seem to embrace the common meal as well as
the Eucharist.

We are reminded further that the same phrase κλᾶν
(κατακλᾶν) ἄρτον is repeatedly used of a solemn act of
our Lord independently of the Eucharist (Mk 6⁴¹ ‖ 8⁶ ‖ ¹⁹,
Lk 24³⁰).   And we gather from the context of the last
passage that there was something distinctive in this particular act by which our Lord was recognized (Lk 24³⁵).
We are reminded also of the many instances in which
attention is specially called to the 'blessing' (εὐλογεῖν
or εὐχαριστεῖν) of food by our Lord.   They are the
same words which are used in connection with the
sacramental Bread and the sacramental Cup.

There is something in these facts which is not quite
fully explained.   There are *lacunæ* in our knowledge
which we would fain fill up if we could.   The institution
of the Eucharist appears to have connexions both backwards and forwards—backwards with other meals which
our Lord ate together with His disciples, forwards with
those common meals which very early came into existence in the Apostolic Church.   But the exact nature
and method of these connexions our materials are not
sufficient to make clear to us.

§ 66. (4) *Significance of the Eucharist.* — We feel
these gaps in our knowledge when we pass on to
consider the significance of the Sacrament.   Certainly

Harnack was not wholly wrong, however far we may think him from being wholly right, when he held that the primary object of Christ's blessing was the *meal as such*, in its simplest elements, not specifically bread and wine (cf. *TU* VII. ii. 137).

The prominence given to the meal and to the natural products of the earth which contribute to it, finds some support in the eucharistic prayers of the *Didaché*. 'First, as regards the cup : We give thee thanks, O our Father, for the holy vine of thy son David which thou madest known unto us through thy Son Jesus ; thine is the glory for ever and ever. Then as regards the broken bread : We give thee thanks, O our Father, for the life and knowledge which thou didst make known to us through thy Son Jesus ; thine is the glory for ever and ever. As this broken bread was scattered upon the mountains, and being gathered together became one, so may thy Church be gathered together from the ends of the earth into thy kingdom ; for thine is the glory and the power through Jesus Christ, for ever and ever. . . . Thou, Almighty Master, didst create all things for thy name's sake, and didst give food and drink unto men for enjoyment, that they might render thanks to thee ; but didst bestow upon us spiritual food and drink and eternal life through thy Son' (Did. ix. 2–4, x. 3).

It would, however, be doing an injustice both to the ancient and to the modern writer if we supposed that they had in view only the gifts of God in nature. Harnack writes : 'The Lord instituted a meal in commemoration of His death, or rather He described the food of the body as His Flesh and Blood, *i.e.* as the food of the soul (through the forgiveness of sins), when it was partaken of with thanksgiving, in memory of His death' (*op. cit.* p. 139). And the *Didaché* looks beyond the physical eating and drinking to the 'spiritual food and drink,' and to the 'eternal life' bestowed through the Son ; and when it speaks of the 'holy vine of David,' there is at least an allusion to the Jewish doctrine of the Messiah, if not directly to the Johannean allegory of the Vine.

We thus come round to an aspect of the Supper which has been emphasized and illustrated, especially by Spitta. There are allusions not only in the immediate context of the words of institution (Mk 14^{25} ||), but also elsewhere (Lk 14^{15} 'Blessed is he that shall eat bread in the kingdom of God'; cf. Mt 8^{11} 22$^{2ff.}$ 25^{10}), to the language in use among the Jews respecting the great Messianic banquet. This took its start from the teaching of the Prophets (*e.g.* Is 25^6), and has points of contact with prominent passages in the Wisdom literature. Thus in Pr 9^5 Wisdom issues her invitation, 'Come, eat ye of my bread, and drink of the wine which I have mingled'; which is taken up in Sir 24$^{19-21}$ 'They that eat me shall yet be hungry, and they that drink me shall yet be thirsty.' And in a like connexion the idea of the manna is applied in Wis 16$^{20f.}$ 'Thou gavest thy people angels' food to eat, and bread ready for their use didst thou provide from heaven without their toil. . . . For thy nature ($\dot{\eta}$ $\dot{\upsilon}\pi\acute{o}\sigma\tau\alpha\sigma\acute{\iota}\varsigma$ σov) manifested thy sweetness toward thy children.'

We are clearly upon the line of thought which links on to the discourse in the synagogue at Capernaum. Indeed, we meet here with the same phenomenon that has already come before us on other sides of our Lord's teaching. The current ideas are not discarded, but taken up on to a higher plane and filled with a new content. We have seen that Wisdom was regarded as giving herself to be 'eaten' (*i.e.* spiritually appropriated and assimilated). Philo repeatedly identifies the manna with the Logos (Spitta refers to ed. Mangey, i. 120,

²14, 484, 564). Hence we are not surprised to find that St. Paul speaks of the πνευματικὸν βρῶμα and πνευματικὸν πόμα, the miraculously-given meat and drink which nourished the Israelites in the wilderness being treated as typical of the Christian Sacrament. In 1 Co 10⁴ it is not the water but the stricken rock as the source of the water, which St. Paul identifies with Christ Himself. But a little further he says plainly, 'The cup of blessing which we bless, is it not a communion of the blood of Christ? The bread which we break, is it not a communion of the body of Christ?' (*ib.* v.¹⁶). And in Jn 6⁴⁸⁻⁵¹ our Lord is made to describe Himself as the 'living bread which came down out of heaven,' and it is explained that the bread which He will give is His flesh, for the life of the world.

We take the view that the discourse in question does not relate directly to the Eucharist. But it does not do so only because it expresses the larger idea of which the Eucharist is a particular concrete embodiment, the one leading embodiment which Christ has bequeathed to His Church. As there is a communion with Him which is wider than—though it culminates in—that which we call κατ᾽ ἐξοχήν, the Holy Communion, so is there a sense in which He is the Bread from heaven, which is wider than that in which He is given through the sacramental Bread, but it is that bread of which He said, 'This is my Body, which is for you.'

The parallelism between Jn 6⁵¹ and 1 Co 11²⁴ (cf. Mk 14²⁴ ||) is so close, that we are certainly justified in interpreting the words of institution in the manner in which the Sacrament itself is interpreted by both St. Paul and St. John.

No writer has brought out this aspect of the Supper as signifying primarily the spiritual assimilation of Christ more forcibly than Spitta. But when he goes on to maintain that the Eucharist has no relation to His death, it is sheer paradox, which can be maintained only by the most arbitrary methods.

The assimilation of Christ does not exhaust the meaning of the Sacrament. If we take the words of institution as they stand, another idea is even more prominent. We have seen that there is considerable doubt as to how far the Last Supper is to be identified with the Paschal meal. St. Paul describes the Death of Christ as the Christian Passover (1 Co 5[7]), and not only he but other NT writers apply to that Death the language of Sacrifice. But the particular sacrifice with which our Lord's own words most directly connect it is the sacrifice, or group of sacrifices, which inaugurated the Covenant (Ex 24[4-8]). As the sprinkling of the blood upon the altar of God and upon the people ratified the covenant between Israel and Israel's God, so (it was implied) by partaking of the consecrated symbol of the Blood of Christ the Christian had brought home to him his share in the new Covenant—a covenant which had at once its inestimable privileges and its obligations. It was the means of admission to the state of Divine favour, and it bound over those who were admitted to that favour to a life of loyal service. Here, too, if we want a comment on the words of institution, we may seek it rightly in the later NT writings. For words could not well be more strongly attested than those which accompany the giving of the bread and of the cup, and together they converge upon a root-idea which is expanded most directly in He 9^{18-28}, but is also illustrated by Ro $3^{24f.}$ $5^{1f.}$ $8^{1ff.}$, Eph 1^7, 1 P 1^{19}, 1 Jn 1^7 2^2, Rev 1^5.

If we start from the idea of the Death of Christ as a Sacrifice, then it lies near at hand to conceive of the Sacrament as the sacred meal which follows the sacrifice. In this there would be combined the universal and immemorial significance of such meals as an act of communion at once with the Deity worshipped and of the worshippers with each other. This double communion, under this aspect of the sacrificial meal, seems clearly indicated in 1 Co $10^{16f.\ 21}$, but it is also suggested by the words of institution, taken with the distribution of the elements of bread and wine, and the stress which is laid upon the general participation ('Drink ye *all*,' 'they *all* drank').

§ 67. (5) *Critical Theories.* — A common feature in recent critical theories respecting the Last Supper is the denial that the command, 'This do in remembrance of me,' formed part of the original institution; or, in other words, that the particular circumstances which marked this solemn parting meal were meant to be repeated in the form of a permanent Sacrament. This view was put forward about the same time, and, it is probable, independently, in England by Dr. P. Gardner (*The Origin of the Lord's Supper*, London, 1893), and in Germany by Jülicher in the volume of essays in honour of Weizsäcker (*Theol. Abhandl.* etc., Freiburg i. B. 1892), and by Spitta (*Zur Gesch. u. Lit. d. Urchristentums*, Göttingen, 1893). The English writer is the most thoroughgoing. Assuming the correctness of the WH text of Lk 22[19. 20], St. Paul is left as the sole authority for the express command of repetition.   It is then argued from the phrasing of 1 Co 11[23] 'I received of the Lord,' that the whole account belongs to one of St. Paul's ecstatic revelations, and has not a solid historical foundation.   In default of this, it is thought that the apostle had been influenced during his stay in Corinth by the near proximity of the Eleusinian mysteries, the central point in which 'appears to have been a sacred repast of which the initiated partook, and by means of which they had communion with the gods' (p. 18).

How St. Paul could confuse such subtle external influences with a revelation 'from the Lord,' and how he came to deliver as authoritative instructions to the Corinthians what he had (upon the theory) only himself acquired during his stay at Corinth, are only incidental questions.   We cannot tell precisely how St. Paul received his knowledge in such a sense that he could refer it to the Lord.   But the solemn simplicity of phrase reads like history, and, so far as other authorities exist, it is completely verified.   In any case, it is incredible that a usage which is thus treated as practically the invention of St. Paul could have spread from an outlying Gentile Church over the whole of Christendom. We cannot doubt that not only the Synoptic version of the Supper, but its repetition as a Sacrament, had their origin in the Mother Church.   The $\kappa\lambda\acute{a}\sigma\iota\varsigma$ $\tau o\hat{v}$ $\mathring{a}\rho\tau o\upsilon$ of Ac 2[42. 46] is an indication of this, which is confirmed by the evidence of Ignatius, Justin, and the *Didaché*. Spitta's theory, that the repeated Sacrament was due, not to a command of Christ Himself, but to the spontaneous instinct of affectionate recollection among His

disciples, is more possible, but still gratuitous and
hypercritical. We may not allege the witness of St.
Luke himself in confirmation of St. Paul, but, as we
have already seen (p. 160 *sup.*), the familiar text of his
Gospel is no less valid evidence of the common belief
and practice.

Of the critical theories respecting the origin of the
Eucharist, that which we have just mentioned is the
most important. Harnack's contention, that it was
sometimes administered with water instead of wine,
not only here and there among the sects but in
the main body of the Church, belongs rather to the
history of the Early Church than to the Life of our
Lord. It turns, however, upon a somewhat cavalier
treatment of the text of Justin, and has met with
strong opposition and (it is believed) practically no
acceptance.

LITERATURE.—A summary may be given of the more recent
special literature to most of which reference has been made.
Lobstein, *La Doctrine de la Cène*, Lausanne, 1889; a lucid exposi-
tion dating from the time before the rise of the newer theories. A
reasonable criticism may go back to it with advantage. Harnack,
TU VII. ii., 1891 (replies by Zahn, *Brot u. Wein*, Leipzig, 1892;
Jülicher, as below; Headlam, *Class. Rev.* 1893, p. 63); Jülicher in
Theol. Abhandlungen C. von Weizsäcker gewidmet, Freiburg i.
B. 1892; Spitta, *Zur Gesch. u. Lit. d. Urchristentums*, Göttingen;
P. Gardner, *The Origin of the Lord's Supper*, London, 1893 (comp.
also a criticism by Mr. Wright, *NT Problems*, p. 134 ff.); Grafe in
Z. f. Theol. u. Kirche, 1895 (said to be an excellent summary of the
controversy); Schultzen, *Das Abendmahl im NT*, Göttingen, 1859
(also a full review and examination); Schaefer, *Das Herrenmahl*,
Gütersloh, 1897. Bishop Wordsworth's Visitation Addresses on
The Holy Communion (2nd ed. 1892), though written before the
controversy and dealing largely with the liturgical aspect of the
question, may be specially commended to English readers.

Resurrection

§ 68. v. **The Resurrection.**—For our present purpose the discussion of the Resurrection of our Lord will resolve itself into a consideration of (1) the evidence attesting the fact ; (2) the sequence of the events, or the appearances which followed the Resurrection ; (3) the explanations which have been put forward to account for the Resurrection without miracle ; (4) its doctrinal significance.

testation

§ 69. (1) *The Attestation.*—A fact so stupendous as the Resurrection needs to be supported by strong evidence, and very strong evidence both as regards quantity and quality is forthcoming ; but all parts of it are not of equal value, and it is well that the authorities should be compared with each other and critically estimated.

When this is done, one piece of evidence drops almost entirely to the rear—the concluding verses of St. Mark. This is not invalidated merely by the fact that the verses were probably not part of the original Gospel.   Since Mr. Conybeare's discovery of the Armenian MS, which appears to refer them to the 'presbyter Ariston' or 'Ariston,' it is fair to attach that name to them, because, although the authority is but slender, there is nothing at all to compete with it ; and the Aristion mentioned by Eusebius (*HE* iii. 39) as one of the 'elders' consulted by Papias, would suit the conditions as well as any one else belonging to the same generation (say A.D. 100–125).   Such an authority cannot be wholly without weight ; if it represented a distinct line of tradition, its weight would be considerable.   But when the verses Mk 16⁹⁻²⁰ are examined, it seems pretty clear that the earlier portion of them is really a summary of the narratives in the extant Gospels of St. Luke and St. John, and therefore adds nothing to these Gospels beyond such further sanction as the name of Aristion may give to them. It is proof that the statements in those Gospels were accepted as satisfactory by a prominent Church teacher, himself a depositary of tradition, in the region where St. John had been active. So much the verses contribute, but not more.

There is still some mystery hanging over the close of the Second Gospel. The most probable view appears to be that its original conclusion has been lost—it is more likely than not—by some purely mechanical accident. The fragment that remains, Mk 16^{1-8}, is insufficient to enable us to trace it to its source. If we could be sure that it was complete, we should have to say that St. Mark was *not* here drawing upon the Petrine tradition, because that tradition could not have failed to speak of the appearance to Peter himself. It is, however, possible that that was contained in the missing portion.

This may detract somewhat from the weight of the common Synoptic narrative, which is here disappointingly meagre. And yet, if we are to throw the absence of any mark of Petrine origin into the one scale, there is a little bit of confirmatory evidence which it is fair to throw into the other. All through the history of the Passion St. Luke has access to a special source, which we may well believe to have been oral, but which gave him some items of good information. This information relates especially to the court of Herod Antipas (Lk 23^{7-12}), and it is natural to connect it with the particular mention of 'Joanna the wife of Chuza, Herod's steward,' in Lk 8³. Now this very same Joanna appears again in St. Luke's account of the visit of the women to the sepulchre (Lk 24¹⁰). The rest of the paragraph appears to be based as usual upon St. Mark. But the renewed mention of Joanna is an indication of the special source, which at least goes to show that there was nothing in that source which conflicted with the Marcan document. In other words, it confirms that document by a distinct line of testimony (cf. Lk 23²¹⁻²⁴).

Is it not possible that the story of the Walk to Emmaus has a like origin? The name Cleopas (= Cleopatros) is just such as we should expect to find in the same Herodian circle. In any case, the source bears other marks of being a good one. It gives a graphic picture of the dejection through which the disciples passed; and the phrase 'we hoped that it was he which should redeem Israel' points back to a time before the dreams of national triumph had been purified of the grosser element in them. But most striking of all is the direct confirmation by St. Paul (1 Co 15⁵) of another very incidental reference, the appearance to Peter (Lk 23³⁴). Not only does St. Paul confirm the fact, but he puts it practically in the same place in the series.

We have, then, every reason to think both that the special source used by St. Luke was excellent in itself, and also that it agreed in substance with the fragmentary record of St. Mark.

If St. Luke thus reaches a hand in one direction towards St. Mark, he does so in another direction

towards St. John.   For the appearance of Lk 24$^{36ff.}$
corresponds to that of Jn 20$^{19ff.}$; and both alike receive
the seal of authentication from St. Paul (1 Co 15^5).
We may not, for the reason given above, use Mk 16^9
in ratification of Jn 20$^{11ff.}$.   We note, however, that the
incident of St. Thomas is a striking concrete illustration of the disbelief on which so many of our authorities
lay stress.*   For the rest, the narrative in the Fourth
Gospel must go with the problem as to that Gospel
generally.   It has found a vigorous recent defender in
Dr. Loofs (*Die Auferstehungsberichte und ihr Wert*,
Leipzig, 1898).

The peculiar element in Matthew might have seemed
to possess the lowest claim to acceptance, were it not
for the singular convergence of proof that something
like the injunction of Mt 28^{19} must have been given,
or most probably was given, by our Lord Himself (see
p. 100 *sup.*; also p. 231 ff.).   We believe that for this
paragraph, too, there is solid foundation.

And yet the Resurrection is a part of the evangelical
narrative for which the leading witness is, after all,
not the Gospels, but St. Paul—the double witness
of what St. Paul says and what he implies.   It is
hardly possible for testimony to be stronger than this
is.   In the same precise and deliberate manner in

* This trait is not less authentic because it passed over from
primary documents into secondary (such as the Coptic work
discovered by Carl Schmidt and commented upon by Harnack
in *Theol. Studien B. Weiss dargebracht*).   It really does throw
into relief, and the early disciples saw that it threw into relief,
the revulsion of feeling on the part of the witnesses to the
Resurrection and the strength of their conviction.   Otherwise
Harnack, p. 8, and Loofs, p. 21.

which he had rehearsed the particulars of the Last Supper, St. Paul enumerates one by one the leading appearances of the Lord after the Resurrection: (1) to Peter, (2) to the Twelve (as a body), (3) to an assembly of more than five hundred, (4) to James, (5) to all the apostles (1 Co 15$^{5-7}$).

We have spoken of these as the 'leading' appearances, because St. Paul doubtless has in view, not all who under any circumstances 'saw the Lord,' but those who were specially chosen and commissioned to be witnesses of the Resurrection (Ac 1^{22} 4^{33}, cf. 1 Co 15^{15}), *i.e.* as we should say, to assert and preach it publicly. For this reason there would be nothing in St. Paul's list to exclude such an appearance as that to Mary Magdalene (Jn 20$^{11-18}$). It may have been on this ground—because the two disciples involved were not otherwise conspicuous as active preachers or prominent leaders—that St. Paul does not mention the scene on the road to Emmaus. But it is equally possible that the story of this had not reached him.

We have seen by what a striking coincidence this story confirms, from a wholly independent quarter, the first appearance to Peter. The next in order, that to the Twelve, may well be identical with that which is more exactly described in Lk 24$^{33ff.}$, Jn 20$^{19-24}$. The appearance to James is attested by another line of tradition embodied in the Gospel according to the Hebrews. Beyond this identifications are uncertain.

St. Paul contents himself with a bare enumeration, not from lack of knowledge, but because he assumes knowledge in his readers. He reminds the Corinthians of what he had delivered unto them first of all (ἐν πρώτοις, *i.e.* at the very beginning of his ministry among them). This throws back the date of the evidence some four years—we may say from the year 55 to 51, possibly earlier, but at the latest from 57 to 53.

We are thus brought to much the same date as that of another piece of evidence, not so detailed as that in 1 Co, but quite as explicit, so far as the fact of the Resurrection is concerned, the evidence of the first extant NT writing, 1 Th 1¹⁰ 4¹⁴. The assured tone of these passages shows, not only that the apostle is speaking from the very strongest personal conviction, but that he is confident of carrying his readers with him; we may go further, and say that the belief to which he gives this expression was unquestioned, the universal belief of Christians. We might infer this from the attitude of St. Paul in regard to it. Unfortunately, we have no evidence equally early from the Church of Palestine; but as soon as evidence begins to appear it is all to the same effect. The early chapters of Acts no doubt represent a Palestinian tradition, perhaps a written tradition; and they take the same line as St. Paul in making it the chief function of the apostles to bear witness to the Resurrection (Ac 1⁸· ²² etc.). We need not pursue this evidence further.

It is noticeable that although there were doubts in the Apostolic Age on the subject of resurrection (1 Co 15¹², 2 Ti 2¹⁷ᶠ·), it is not as to the resurrection of Christ, but as to that of Christians. St. Paul argues on the assumption that Christ was really raised as from a premiss common to himself and his opponents.

And it is no less noticeable that even the most

rationalistic of Christian sects, those (*e.g.*) which denied the Virgin-Birth, nevertheless shared the belief in the Resurrection (Irenæus, *adv. Hær.* i. xxvi. 1, 2 [where *non* before *similiter* should be expunged]; Hippolytus, *Ref. Hær.* vii. 35).

§ 70. (2) *The Sequence and Scene of the Events.*—It is not an exaggeration—it is only putting in words the impression left by the facts—to say that the conviction among Christians that Christ was really raised, dates from the very morrow of the Resurrection itself. It was not a growth spread over a long period and receiving gradual accretions of strength; but it sprang suddenly into existence, and it swept irresistibly over the whole body of disciples. Of the force and universality of the belief there can be no doubt, but when we come to details it would seem that from the first there was a certain amount of confusion, which was never wholly cleared up. We have records of a number of appearances, not all contained in a single authority, but scattered over several distinct authorities; and it is probable enough that even when all the recorded appearances are put together they would not exhaust all those that were experienced. Different traditions must have circulated in different quarters, and specimens of these traditions have come down to us without being digested into accordance with a single type. The list which approaches most nearly to this character, that which is given by St. Paul in 1 Co, is, as we have seen, not so much a digest as a selection. It is a selection made for purposes of preaching, and consisting of items which had already been used for

this purpose. Compared with this, a story like the
Walk to Emmaus is such as might have come out of
private memoirs. The brief record in St. Mark is more
central, but in its present condition it is too mutilated
to satisfy curiosity. The narrative of St. John is no
less authoritative than that of St. Paul, but it is
authority of a rather different kind. St. Paul writes
as the active practical missionary, who seeks to com-
municate the fire of his own conviction to others.
St. John also wishes to spread conviction (Jn 20[31]),
but he does so by bringing forth the stores of long
and intense recollections from his own breast. He too
selects what had taken the most personal hold upon
him, and does not try to cover the whole ground.

It is as a consequence of these conditions that when
we come to look into the narratives of the Resurrection
we find them unassimilated and unharmonised. It is
not exactly easy to fit them into each other. The
most important difference is as to the chief scene of
the appearances. Was it Jerusalem and the neighbourhood, or was it Galilee? The authorities are
divided. St. Paul and the Gospel according to the
Hebrews make no mention of locality. Matthew and
Mark throw the stress upon Galilee. The latter Gospel
does not indeed (in the genuine portion) record a
Galilean appearance, but the women are bidden to say
that the risen Lord would meet the disciples in Galilee
(Mk 16[7]). This is in fulfilment of a promise to the
same effect given in the course of the Last Supper, and
recorded in the same two Gospels (Mk 14[28], Mt 26[32]).
The express mention of prediction and fulfilment in
both Gospels not only proves their presence in the

12

common original, but also shows that they were no accidental feature in that original, but an essential part of the whole conception. We have besides a Galilean appearance described in Jn 21, and clearly implied at the point where the fragment of the Gospel of Peter breaks off (*Ev. Pet.* § 12 [60]).

On the other hand, all the scenes of Jn 20 are laid in Jerusalem; and Jerusalem or the neighbourhood is the only locality recognised in Lk 24, which ends with a command to the disciples to wait in the city for the outpouring of the Holy Spirit (Lk 24[49]).

It is not unnatural that the critical school should regard these two versions as alternatives, one of which only can be taken. The more usual course has been to follow that of Mark and Matthew, with or without the supposition that the grave was really found empty (Loofs, p. 18 ff.). According as this assumption was made or not, several constructions were possible, but all equally speculative.

Dr. Loofs has, however, recently argued in favour of the other tradition represented by Lk–Jn 20. And he has certainly succeeded in showing that there is as much intrinsic probability on this side as on the other. But, in order to carry out this theory, he is obliged to treat Jn 21 as having a different origin from the rest of the Gospel, and as falling into two parts, one of which (the fishing scene = Lk 5[1-11]) has got misplaced, not having originally belonged to the period after the Resurrection, while the other (the dialogue of Jn 21[15-23]) had originally nothing to connect it with Galilee. These are strong measures, which, however high our estimate of the tradition, Luke–John, are obviously not open to one who thinks that the identity of style between Jn 21 and the rest of the Gospel is too great to permit of their separation (the argument in *Expos.* 1892, i. 380 ff., may easily be extended to ch. 21).

The only remaining course is to combine the traditions, much as they seem to be combined in the Fourth Gospel and the Gospel of Peter. We must not disguise from ourselves the difficulties which this solution leaves. The most serious of these are caused by the command of Lk 24[49], and the contracted space within which we shall have to compress the events in Galilee. We have only forty days to dispose of, in all, if we accept the traditional date of the Ascension,—and even if we regarded this as a round number, the nearness of the Day of Pentecost would allow us very little more margin. From these Forty Days we should have to take off a week at the beginning on account of Jn 20[26]. And if, as we reasonably may, we suppose that there has been some *foreshortening* in Lk 24[36-53], and that two or three distinct occasions are treated as if they were continuous, we should still, to find a place for the injunction to wait in Jerusalem, have to cut off another like period at the end. That would leave not much more than three weeks for the retirement to Galilee and return to Jerusalem—a length of time which cannot be pronounced wholly insufficient, but which does not fit in quite naturally with the way in which the apostles are described in Jn 21[3] as returning to their ordinary occupations. These difficulties would be avoided if we could regard *the* Day of Pentecost as that of the following year; but any such hypothesis would conflict directly with Ac 1³, and the interval implied in Jn 21¹⁴* is also a short one.

Whichever way we turn, difficulties meet us, which the documents to which we have access do not enable us to remove. We have said enough as to the nature of these documents, and of the lines of tradition to which they give expression. It is not what we could wish, but what we have. And no difficulty of weaving the separate incidents into an orderly well-compacted narrative can impugn the unanimous belief of the Church which lies behind them, that the Lord Jesus Christ rose from the dead on the third day and appeared to the disciples.

§ **71.** (3) *Attempted Explanations.* —This universal belief is the root fact which has to be accounted for. It would be the natural product of a real event such as the Epistles assume and the Gospels describe. But what if the event were not real? In that case the widely held and deeply planted belief in it must needs constitute a very serious problem.

In the last century a succession of efforts was made to account for the belief in the Resurrection without accepting it as a fact. Many of the hypotheses put forward with this object may be regarded as practically obsolete and abandoned. No one now

---

* The numbering of this Galilean appearance as the 'third' might seem to be at variance with St. Paul's list in 1 Co 15; but it is clear that the appearances which St. John enumerates were those to the body of 'the disciples' (*i.e.* primarily, to a group including the apostles). He himself does not count that to Mary Magdalene; nor would he have counted those to St. Peter or the Emmaus travellers.

believes that the supposed death was really only a swoon, and that the body laid in the tomb afterwards revived, and was seen more than once by the disciples (on this see a trenchant sentence by Strauss, *Leben Jesu*, 1863, p. 298, end of paragraph).   Equally inadmissible is the hypothesis of fraud—that the body was really taken away by Joseph of Arimathæa or Nicodemus, and that the rumour was allowed to grow that Jesus was risen. The lingering trace of this which survives in Renan, *Les Apôtres*, ed. 13, p. 16 ('ceux qui savaient le secret de la disposition du corps'), is thrown in quite by the way as a subordinate detail.

More persistent is the theory of 'visions.' This has been presented in different forms, assigning the leading part now to one and now to another of the disciples. Renan, who goes his own way among critics, sees in this part of the narrative a marked superiority of the Fourth Gospel (*Les Apôtres*, p. 9).   In accordance with it, he refers the beginning of the series to Mary Magdalene (cf. Strauss, *Leben Jesu*, 1863, p. 309). A woman out of whom had been cast 'seven devils' might well, he thinks, have been thrown into a state of nervous tension and excitement which would give form and substance to the creations of fancy.   And when once the report had got abroad that the Lord had been seen, it would be natural for others to suppose that they saw Him.   Strauss and Pfleiderer (*Giff. Lect.* pp. 112, 149) start rather from the case of St. Paul.   Both lay stress upon the fact that he places the appearance to himself on a level with those to the older disciples. His own vision they would agree in explaining as due to a species of epileptic seizure, and the others they would regard as equally subjective, though led up to by different trains of psychological preparation.

It is at this point that some of the best attested details of the Resurrection interpose difficulties. To carry through a consistent theory of visions, two conditions are necessary. (*a*) If they arose, as Strauss supposes, from affectionate dwelling upon the personality of Jesus, combined with reflection upon certain passages of OT (Ps 16^{10}, Is 53^{10-12}), it follows, almost of necessity, that we must also with Strauss throw over the tradition of the 'third day,' and regard the belief as the outcome of a somewhat prolonged process—a process spread over weeks and months rather than days. (*b*) On the other hand, if we must discard the tradition as to the beginning of the appearances, we must equally discard that as to their end. The wave of feverish enthusiasm to which on this hypothesis they owed their origin, certainly would not have subsided in the interval between Passover and Pentecost. We note, as it is, an ascending scale in the appearances— they occur first to individuals (Mary Magdalene, Peter, the Emmaus disciples), then to the Ten and the Eleven, then to the Five Hundred. We can see how one appearance prepares the way for another. St. Peter (*e.g.*) must have been present at three or four. With this increasing weight of testimony, and increasing predisposition in the minds of the disciples, we should naturally expect that the appearance to the Five Hundred would contain within itself the germs of an indefinite series. We should not have been surprised if the whole body alike of Christians and of half Christians had caught the contagion. But that is not the

case. There is just the single appearance to James;
and then—the vision of St. Paul standing rather by
itself—with one more appearance to the assembled
apostles, the list comes to what seems an abrupt
end.

This description of the facts rests on excellent evidence. The 'third day' is hardly less firmly rooted in
the tradition of the Church than the Resurrection itself.
We have it not only in the speech ascribed to St. Peter
(Ac 10[40]), but in the central testimony of St. Paul, and
then in the oldest form of the Apostles' Creed. It is
strange that so slight a detail should have been preserved at all, and still stranger that it should hold the
place it does in the standard of the Church's faith.
We must needs regard it as original. And for the
circumscribed area of the appearances, we have at
once the positive evidence of the canonical documents,
and a remarkable silence on the part of the extra-
canonical.

These phenomena are difficult to reconcile with a
theory of purely subjective visions. An honest inquirer like Keim felt the difficulty so strongly, that,
while regarding the appearances as essentially of the
nature of visions, he held them to be not merely subjective, but divinely caused for the express purpose of
creating the belief in which they issued.

This is the least that must be asserted. A belief
that has had such incalculably momentous results must
have had an adequate cause. No apparition, no mere
hallucination of the senses, ever yet moved the world.
But we may doubt whether the theory, even as Keim
presents it, is adequate or really called for. It belongs

to the process of so trimming down the elements that we call supernatural in the Gospel narratives, as to bring them within the limits of everyday experience. But that process, we must needs think, has failed. The facts are too obstinate, the evidence for them is too strong; and the measures which we apply are too narrow and bounded. It is better to keep substantially the form which a sound tradition has handed down to us, even though its contents in some degree pass our comprehension.

§ **72.** (4) *The Permanent Significance of the Resurrection.*—The innermost nature of the Resurrection is hidden from us. And if we ask why the supreme proof that God had visited His people took this particular form, the answer we can give is but partial. Some things, however, seem to stand out clearly.

(*a*) In the first place, it is obvious that the idea of a resurrection was present to men's minds. Herod thought that the works of Jesus were works of the Baptist restored to life (Mk $6^{14, 16}$||). Men were quite prepared to see Elijah or some other of the ancient prophets reappear upon the scene (Mk 9^{11-13}||, Jn 1^{21}). In Palestine and among the circles in which Christianity arose, no mark of special divine indwelling seemed at the time so natural. The belief had not been allowed to grow up without a reason.

For (*b*) from the very first the ideas of bodily and spiritual resurrection were closely intertwined together. Perhaps the oldest passage in which there is a hint of such an idea is the vision of Ezekiel (ch. 37); and there the revivification of the body is the symbol of a spiritual revival. This intimate connexion of bodily and spiritual is never lost sight of in Christianity.

(c) 'Die to live' is one of the most fundamental of Christian principles, and this principle is embodied once for all in the Resurrection. If the one side was 'placarded' before the eyes of the world (Gal 3¹) in the Crucifixion, the Resurrection was a no less signal manifestation of the other. There is a double strain of inference and application.

(d) On the one hand, the Resurrection of Christ was the pledge and earnest of physical resurrection and the life beyond the grave. St. Paul founds upon it the hope of immortality (1 Th 4¹⁴, Ro 8³⁴, 1 Co 6¹⁴ 15¹²ff., 2 Co 4¹⁴ etc.).

(e) But he equally founds upon it the most earnest exhortations to holiness of life. It is not only that this follows for the Christian as a duty: if his relation to Christ is a right relation, it is included in it as a necessity (Ro 6³⁻⁶). St. Paul can hardly think of the physical Resurrection apart from the spiritual. And there is a very similar vein in the teaching of St. John (Jn 5²⁴, 1 Jn 3¹⁴). The Resurrection is the corner-stone of Christian mysticism.

(f) In another aspect, as a divine act, the crowning mark of divine approval, it is a necessary complement of the Crucifixion. It supplies the proof, which the world might desiderate, that the Sacrifice of the Cross was accepted. If the death of the Cross was a dying for human sin, the rising again from the tomb was the seal of forgiveness and justification (Ro 4²⁵, cf. 6⁷). St. Paul saw in it an assurance that the doors of the divine mercy were thrown open wide ; and to St. Peter in like manner it was through it that mankind was begotten again to a 'lively hope' (1 P 1³).

All this mass of biblical teaching hangs together. If the Resurrection was a reality, it has a solid nucleus, which would be wanting even to the theory of objective visions. The economy which begins with a physical Incarnation, naturally and appropriately ends with a physical Resurrection. Thus much we can see, though we may feel that this is not all.

LITERATURE. — Besides the recent literature mentioned above (among which the paper by Dr. Loofs deserves rather special attention), and besides the treatment of the subject in numerous works on the Gospel History and on Apologetics, it is well to remember two monographs in English—Dr. Westcott's *Gospel of the Resurrection* (first pub. in 1866), and the late Dr. Milligan's *The Resurrection of Our Lord* (first pub. in 1881).

§ 73. (vi.) **The Ascension.** — The Resurrection in itself was incomplete. It was not the goal, but the way to the goal. The goal was the return of the Son to the Father, with His mission accomplished, His work done.

§ 74. (1) The apostolic writers unanimously represent this return as a triumph. The keynote is struck in the speech which is put into the mouth of St. Peter on the day of Pentecost * (Ac 2³³⁻³⁶). It would seem

---

* When we ask how these early discourses were transmitted to the writer of the Acts, there is a natural reluctance to use them too strictly as representing the exact words spoken. And yet, taken as a whole, they fit in singularly well to the order of development and the thought of the primitive community, which has an antecedent verisimilitude and accords well with indications in the Pauline Epistles.

that the form of expression which the conception assumed was influenced largely by Ps 110¹, a passage to which attention had been drawn by our Lord Himself shortly before His departure, and which spontaneously recurred to the mind as soon as the nature of His return to the Father had declared itself. Along with this would be recalled the saying with which our Lord had answered the challenge of the high priest (Mk 14⁶²‖). Psalm and saying alike represented the Messiah as seated ' at the right hand ' of the Most High. This phrase appears to have at once (in the forms ἐκ δεξιῶν and ἐν δεξιᾷ) established itself in the language of the primitive Church; it occurs repeatedly, not only in the Acts (7⁵⁵ᶠ·) and in the Pauline Epistles, but in Hebrews, 1 Peter, and Revelation; and, like the detail of the ' third day,' it occupies a fixed place in the Apostles' Creed.

The speech of St. Peter culminates in the declaration, ' Let all the house of Israel know assuredly, that God hath made him, whom ye crucified, both Lord and Christ' (Ac 2³⁶); and it is substantially a paraphrase of this when in a famous passage St. Paul, after speaking of the humiliation of the Christ, adds, ' Wherefore also God highly exalted him, and gave unto him the name which is above every name, that in the name of Jesus every knee should bow,' etc. (Ph. 2⁹ᶠ·). The return of the Son to the Father was not merely the resumption of a previous state of glory (Jn 6⁶² 17⁵ etc.), it was the resumption of it with the added approval and recognition which His obedience unto death had called forth. We speak of these things κατὰ ἄνθρωπον; or rather, we are content to echo in regard to them the language of the apostles and of the first Christians, who themselves spoke κατὰ ἄνθρωπον. The reality lies behind the veil.

§ 75. (2) How did our Lord Jesus Christ enter upon this state of exaltation? Now that we have before us corrected texts of the Gospels, it would seem to be probable that they did not give an answer to this question. The answer was reserved for the second volume which St. Luke addressed to Theophilus; it forms the opening section of the Acts of the Apostles.

Mk 16[19] belongs to the Appendix to the Gospel, which we have seen (p. 170 f. *sup.*) to have been probably composed, not by St. Mark himself, but by the presbyter Aristion in the early years of the second century. The reading of Lk 24[51] stands thus—

Καὶ ἀνεφέρετο εἰς τὸν οὐρανόν, ℵ° ABCLXΔΛΠ, etc., c f q Vulg. Syrr. (Pesh.-Harcl.-Hier.) *rell.*, Cyr-Alex. Aug. 1/2.

Om. ℵ*D, a b e ff₂ Syr.-Sin., Aug. 1/2.

This means that the omission of the words is a primitive Western reading, which in this case is probably right: it was a natural gloss to explain the parting of the Lord from the disciples of the Ascension; there was no similar temptation to omit the words if genuine.

In Ac 1[1-11] the final separation is described as an 'ascent unto heaven.' When the last instructions had been given, the disciples saw their Lord 'taken up (ἐπήρθη), and a cloud received him out of their sight.' The over-arching sky is a standing symbol for the abode of God; and the return of the Son to the Father was naturally represented as a retreat within its blue recess, the ethereal home of light and glory. It is sometimes necessary that a symbol should be acted as well as written or spoken. The disciples were aware of a vanishing, and they knew that their Lord must be where His Father was.

That the narrative in the Acts is not a myth, seems proved by an authentic little touch which it contains, a veritable reminiscence of what we may be sure was their real attitude at the moment, though it soon ceased to be. When they asked, 'Lord, dost thou at this time restore the kingdom to Israel?' their thoughts were still running in the groove of the old Jewish expectation. It is the last trace of them that we have in this naïve form.

§ 76. (3) From the point of view of Christian doctrine, for those who not only accept the facts of the life of Christ but the construction put on those facts by the writers of NT, the main stress of the Ascension lies upon the state to which it forms the entrance. (*a*) It is the guarantee for the continued existence of Him who became incarnate for our sakes. (*b*) It not only guarantees His continued existence, but the continued effect of His work. It puts the seal of the divine approval upon all that the incarnation accomplished. It is the final confirmation of the lessons of the Baptism and of the Transfiguration, 'This is my beloved Son, in whom I am well pleased.' (*c*) The primitive phrase 'at the right hand of God' describes as nearly and as simply as human language can describe the double truth that Christ still is and that His work still is, that the Incarnation was no transient episode, but a permanent and decisive factor in the dealing of God with man. (*d*) This truth is stated in other words in the doctrine of the High Priesthood of Christ, a doctrine implicitly contained in many places in the writings of St. Paul, and worked out with great clearness and fulness in the Epistle to the Hebrews. There is something in the relation of the exalted Son to the Father and to His Church corresponding to and that may be expressed in terms of the functions of the earthly high priest in relation to God and to Israel. The great High Priest presents the prayers of His people; He intercedes for them; He 'pleads' or 'presents' His own sacrifice. Only, when we use this language, it should be remembered that we are not speaking of 'specific acts done or words spoken by Christ in His glory. His glorified presence is an eternal presentation; He pleads by what He is' (Moberly, *Ministerial Priesthood*, p. 246 n.).

LITERATURE.—Dr. Milligan left a volume on the Ascension as a pendant to that on the Resurrection (*Baird Lectures* for 1891), which is the most comprehensive treatment of the subject in English.

CHAPTER VII.

SUPPLEMENTAL MATTER: THE NATIVITY AND INFANCY.

§ 77. Throughout His public ministry Jesus passed for the son of Joseph and Mary, two peasants of Nazareth. Some of those who were present at the long discourse in the synagogue at Capernaum expressed their astonishment at the high pretensions which it seemed to contain, by asking, 'Is not this Jesus, the son of Joseph, whose father and mother we know?' (Jn 6⁴; cf. 1⁴⁵). The inhabitants of Nazareth appear to have put a similar question when He came and preached there. The exact words are somewhat differently transmitted. Mk 6³ has (in the better attested text), 'Is not this the carpenter?' Mt 13⁵⁵ 'Is not this the carpenter's son?' Lk 4²³ a passage which, although divergent, contains reminiscences of the same original, has still more directly, 'Is not this Joseph's son?' In the preliminary chapters the same evangelist speaks repeatedly of 'his parents' (γονεῖς, Lk 2²⁷· ⁴¹· ⁴³). And not only does he himself resolve this into 'his father and his mother' (2³³), but he makes the mother of Jesus say, 'Thy father and I sought thee sorrowing' (2⁴⁸).

2 Gospels trace
ealogies of Jesus
Joseph.

It is in keeping with this language that both the First and the Third Gospels place in their forefront genealogies of Jesus, which, in spite of many attempts to prove the contrary, must be admitted to trace His descent through Joseph and not through Mary.

Yet, on the other hand, the same two Gospels, though differing widely in the details of the narrative, assert unequivocally that Joseph had no share in the parentage of Jesus, and that the place of a human father was taken by the direct action of the Spirit of God. The differences show that the two traditions are independent of each other; and yet both converge upon this one point. They agree not only in representing Jesus as born of a virgin, but also in representing this fact as supernaturally announced beforehand,—in the one case to Joseph, in the other case to Mary.

What account is to be given of these seeming inconsistencies? We cannot get rid of them by assigning the opposed statements to different sources. In St. Matthew the genealogy which ends in Joseph is followed immediately by the narrative of the Annunciation and Virgin-Birth. In St. Luke the successive sections of ch. 2, which begins with the Nativity and ends with the scene of the boy Jesus in the Temple, where we have seen that such expressions as 'his parents,' 'his father and mother,' occur so freely, are linked together by the recurrent note, 'Mary kept all these sayings, pondering them in her heart,' 'his mother kept all these sayings in her heart' (Lk $2^{19.51}$; cf. also the argument which Professor Ramsay skilfully draws from 1^{80} $2^{40.52}$ *). And when we turn to St. John we cannot but

* *Was Christ born at Bethlehem?* p. 87.

remember that the Gospel which records so frankly the Jews' question, 'Is not this Jesus, the son of Joseph, whose father and mother we know?' if it nowhere refers directly to the Virgin-Birth, yet goes further than any other Gospel in asserting the pre-existence of the Son as God with God.

What we regard as inconsistent will clear itself up best if we consider the order of events and the way in which these preliminary stages of the history were gradually brought to the consciousness of the Church.

The sources from which the knowledge of them was derived were, without doubt, private.* We shall consider presently the character of these sources. We know more about that of which use was made by St. Luke than of that used by St. Matthew, and we can rely upon it as a historical authority with greater confidence. We shall see that it is ultimately traceable to the Virgin herself, in all probability through the little circle of women who were for some time in her company.

We are told expressly that the Virgin Mary 'kept all these sayings (or things) in her heart.' She, if any one, might well say, μυστήριον ἐμὸν ἐμοί. It was only by slow degrees in the intimacy of confidential inter-

* 'Luke gives, from knowledge gained within the family, an account of facts known only to the family, and in part to the Mother alone' (Ramsay, op. cit. p. 79). Professor Ramsay, however, seems to go too far in contrasting Matthew with Luke when he says, 'Matthew gives the public account, that which was generally known during the Saviour's life and after His death.' We do not think that any account was known during the Saviour's life, and we prefer to think of the Matthæan version as parallel to rather than contrasted with the Lucan.

13

course that she allowed her secret to pass beyond herself, and to become known. Even if committed to writing before it came into the hands of St. Luke, it probably did not reach any wide public until it was embodied in his Gospel. The place which the Virgin-Birth occupies in Ignatius and in the Creed seems to show that it cannot have been much later than the middle of the century before the knowledge of it made its way to the headquarters of Christianity. But before some such date as that there is no reason to think that it was generally known. It was no part of our Lord's own teaching. The neighbours among whom His early life was passed, the changing crowds who witnessed His miracles or gathered round Him to hear Him, had never had it proclaimed to them. 'Jesus son of Joseph, the prophet of Nazareth,' was the common name by which He was known. And it is a great presumption of the historical truth of the Gospels, that they so simply and naturally reflect this language. We may well believe that the language was shared, as the ignorance which caused it was shared, even by the Twelve themselves. It would be very fitting if the channel through which these sacred things first came to the ears of the Church was a little group of women.*

---

* 'If we are right in this view as to Luke's authority, and as to the way in which that authority reached him, viz. by oral communication, it appears that either the Virgin was still living when Luke was in Palestine during the years 57 and 58 . . . or Luke had conversed with some one very intimate with her, who knew her heart and could give him what was almost as good as first-hand information. Beyond that we cannot safely go; but yet one may venture to state the impression—though it may be

§ **78. i.** *The Sources of the Narrative.*—It has often been observed that whereas the first two chapters of St. Matthew appear to be written from the point of view of Joseph, the first two chapters of St. Luke are written from the point of view of Mary. In Matthew the Annunciation is made to Joseph; it is Joseph who is bidden in a dream not to fear to take to him his wife; Joseph who is told what the Son whom she is to bear is to be called. It is Joseph, again, who is warned to take the young Child and His mother into Egypt, and who, when the danger is past, receives the command to return; and it is Joseph also whose anxious care is the cause that the family settle in Galilee and not in Judæa. On the other hand, when we turn to St. Luke the prominent figures at first are the two kinswomen, Elisabeth the mother of John the Baptist, and Mary. Mary herself receives the announcement of

generally considered fanciful — that the intermediary, if one existed, is more likely to have been a woman than a man. There is a womanly spirit in the whole narrative, which seems inconsistent with the transmission from man to man, and which, moreover, is an indication of Luke's character; he had a marked sympathy with women' (Ramsay, *op. cit.* p. 88). In view of the close resemblance between much that appears in the text and Professor Ramsay's admirable chapter, it is perhaps right to explain that this had not been read at the time when the text was written, and that it represents an opinion formed long ago. The question as to whether the source was written or oral is left open, because there is reason to think that St. Luke used a special (written) source which may have been connected with the women mentioned below, and through them with the Virgin Mary. The writer could not speak quite so confidently as Professor Ramsay as to the nearness of this source to the Virgin, but he does not think that it could be more than two or three degrees removed from her. It must have been near enough to retain the fine touches which Professor Ramsay so well brings out.

the holy thing that is to be born of her. The *Magnificat* is her song of thanksgiving. She treasures in her heart the sayings of the shepherds and of her Divine Son. The aged Simeon points his prophecy to her, and foretells that a sword should pierce through her soul.

In regard to the Matthæan document we are in the dark. The curious gravitation of statement towards Joseph has a reason; but beyond this there is not much that we can say. It would not follow that the immediate source of the narrative was very near his person. In the case of St. Luke we can see farther down the vista. We have already had grounds for connecting the source from which he draws ultimately with the Mother of Jesus. Through what channel did it reach the evangelist? Probably through one of the women mentioned in Lk 8^3 24^{10}; and as Joanna is the least known of the group, and therefore the most likely to drop out for any one not personally acquainted with her, perhaps we may say, by preference, through her (cf. p. 172 *sup.*). We learn from Jn 19^{25} (cf. Ac 1^{14}) that the Mother of Jesus was thrown into contact with this group,—perhaps not for any great length of time, but yet for a time that may well have been sufficiently long for the purpose. And we believe that thus the secret of what had passed came to be disclosed to a sympathetic ear.

Such an inference, if sound, would invest the contents of these chapters with high authority. Without enlarging more on this, we may perhaps be allowed to refer in confirmation to what has been already said as to the appropriateness of the picture given of the kind of circle in which Christ was born, and in which His birth was most spontaneously greeted (see p. 22 ff.). It was just the Simeons and Annas, the Elisabeths and Zachariahs, who were the natural adherents of such a Messiah as Jesus. And the phrases used to describe them are beautifully appropriate to the time and circumstances, 'looking for the consolation of Israel,' 'looking for the redemption of Jerusalem' (Lk 2$^{25, 38}$).

The elaborate and courageous attempt of Resch (*TU* iv. Heft 3, 1897) to reconstruct, even to the point of restoring the Hebrew original, a *Kindheits-evangelium*, which shall embrace the whole of the first two chapters of Luke and Matthew with some extra-canonical parallels, is on the face of it a paradox, and although no doubt containing useful matter, has not made converts.

§ 79. ii. *The Text of Mt* 1^{16}.—Within recent years certain phenomena have come to light in the text of the first chapter of St. Matthew which demand consideration in their bearing upon this part of our subject.

The peculiarities of the Curetonian Syriac, the (so-called) Ferrar group, and some MSS of the Old Latin, had been known for some time, but in themselves they did not seem of very great importance. A new and somewhat startling element was introduced by the publication of the Sinai-Syriac in 1894. More recently still a further authority has appeared, which contains the eccentric reading. This is the curious dialogue published by Mr. F. C. Conybeare under the names of *Timothy and Aquila* (Oxford, 1898). It professes to be a public debate between a Christian and a Jew held in the time of Cyril of Alexandria (A.D. 412–444), and it is in the main a string of *testimonia* commonly adduced in the Jewish controversy. It is a question how far some of this material comes from a work older than the date assigned. The criticism of the dialogue has been acutely treated by Mr. Conybeare, but the subject needs further examination. We will set forth the evidence at length, and then make some remarks upon it.

Mt 1[16] Ἰακὼβ δὲ ἐγέννησεν τὸν Ἰωσὴφ τὸν ἄνδρα Μαρίας, ἐξ ἧς ἐγεννήθη Ἰησοῦς ὁ λεγόμενος Χριστός, *Codd. Græc. unc. qui exstant omn. minusc. quamplur. Verss.* (*incl.* f ff₂, *def.* l), *cf. Dial. Tim. et Aq.* fol. 113 r°.

Ἰακὼβ δὲ ἐγέννησε τὸν Ἰωσήφ, ᾧ μνηστευθεῖσα παρθένος Μαριὰμ ἐγέννησεν Ἰησοῦν τὸν λεγόμενον Χριστόν, 346–826–828 (*auctore* K. Lake, *def.* 13–69); cui desponsata virgo (*om.* q) Maria genuit Jesum qui dicitur (vocatur g_1 q), Christus a g_1 q, *cf. Dial. Tim. et Aq.* fol. 93 v°.

Similiter, cui desponsata virgo Maria genuit (peperit d) Jesum Christum (*om.* τὸν λεγόμ., Christum Jesum d) d k Syr.-Cur.

Jacob autem genuit Joseph, cui desponsata erat virgo Maria : virgo autem Maria genuit Jesum b (*cf.* c).

Ἰακὼβ ἐγέννησεν τὸν Ἰωσὴφ τὸν ἄνδρα Μαρίας, ἐξ ἧς ἐγεννήθη Ἰησοῦς ὁ λεγόμενος Χριστός· καὶ Ἰωσὴφ ἐγέννησεν τὸν Ἰησοῦν τὸν λεγόμενον Χριστόν, *Dial. Tim. et Aq.* fol. 93 r°.

Ἰακὼβ ἐγενν. τὸν Ἰωσήφ· Ἰωσήφ, ᾧ ἐμνηστεύθη παρθένος Μαριάμ, ἐγέννησεν Ἰησοῦν τὸν λεγόμενον Χριστόν, Syr.-Sin.

The eccentric readings all occur within the range of the so-called Western text, and there is no doubt that they belong to a very early stage in the history of that text. Two opposite tendencies appear to have been at work, which are most conspicuously represented in ancient forms of the Syriac Version, though the original in each case was probably Greek.

On the one hand, there was a tendency to emphasize the virginity of Mary, and to remove expressions which seemed in any way to conflict with this. For the blunt phrase, 'Joseph her husband,' the Curetonian Syriac with the oldest Latin authorities substitutes, 'Joseph to whom was espoused'—not only 'Mary,' but 'the Virgin Mary.' A little lower down (with Tatian's *Diatessaron*), for 'Joseph her husband being a just man' (ὁ ἀνὴρ αὐτῆς δίκαιος ὤν) it reads 'Joseph being a just man' (ἀνὴρ δίκ. ὤν). In v.[20] for 'thy wife' it has 'thine espoused.' In v.[24], again with Tatian, it has some such softened phrase as 'he dwelt chastely with her,' and for 'took his wife' it has 'took Mary'; and in v.[25] (but here in agreement with אBZ *al.*) it has simply 'brought forth a son,'—not 'her firstborn son.'

In some of these readings, or parts of them, the Sinai-Syriac agrees, but along with them it has others which seem to be of a directly opposite tendency. The most prominent is, of course, 'Joseph begat Jesus,' in v.[16]. We might have thought that this was an accident due to the influence on the mind of the scribe of the repeated ἐγέννησεν of the previous verses ; but in v.[21] the same MS has 'bear thee a son,' and in v.[25] 'she bore him a son' ; and in Lk 2[5] there is a counter change to that of the Curetonian in v.[20] ('with Mary his wife' for 'Mary his espoused') ; all which readings hang together, and appear to be distinctly anti-ascetic. And now the singular reading in v.[16] has found a coincidence in the conflate text of one of the quotations in the *Dialogue of Timothy and Aquila*.

It is of course true that both these authorities—the Sinai-Syriac and the *Dialogue*—are very far from thoroughgoing. The Syriac text has not tampered in any way with the explicit language of vv.[18. 20] ; and, what is especially strange—in the very act of combining Ἰωσήφ with ἐγέννησεν it inserts a large fragment of the Curetonian reading (ᾧ ἐμνηστεύθη παρθένος Μαριάμ) substituted for τὸν ἄνδρα Μαρίας. On the other hand, the peculiar reading occurs in one only out of three quotations in the dialogue, and there in the form of a conflation with the common text. But is it the case that these authorities point to some form of reading older than any of those now extant, which made Joseph the father of Jesus ? There would be a further question, whether, supposing that such a reading existed, it formed any part of the text of our present Gospel?

There would seem to be three main possibilities. (*a*) The genealogy may in the first instance have had an existence independently of the Gospel, and it may have been incorporated with it by the editor of the whole. In that case it is quite conceivable that the genealogy may have ended Ἰωσήφ δὲ ἐγέννησεν τὸν Ἰησοῦν. Unless it were composed by someone very intimate indeed with the Holy Family, it might well reflect the current state of popular opinion in the first half of the apostolic age. (*b*) The reading might be the result of textual corruption. There would always be a natural tendency in the minds of scribes to assimilate

mechanically the last links in the genealogy to preceding links. A further confusion might easily arise
from the ambiguous sense of the word γεννᾶν, which
was used of the mother as well as of the father (cf. Gal
4²⁴). If we suppose that the original text ran, Ἰωσὴφ
τὸν ἄνδρα Μαρίας ἡ ἐγέννησεν Ἰησοῦν τὸν λεγόμενον
Χριστόν, that would perhaps account for the two
divergent lines of variants better than any other. A
reading like this appears to lie behind the Coptic (Bo-
hairic) Version. (c) It is conceivable that the reading
(or group of readings) in Syr.-Sin. may be of definitely
Ebionite origin. That which we call 'heresy' existed
in so many shades, and was often so little consistent
with itself, that it would be no decisive argument
against this hypothesis that the sense of the readings is
contradicted by the immediate context. It would be
enough for the scribe to have had Ebionite leanings,
and he may have thought of natural and supernatural
generation as not mutually exclusive. We can only
note these possibilities; the data do not allow us to
decide absolutely between them.

LITERATURE.—The fullest discussion of this subject took place
in a lengthy correspondence in *The Academy*, towards the end of
1894 and beginning of 1895.

§ 80. iii. The Genealogies.—At the time when it
was thought necessary at all costs to bring one biblical
statement into visible harmony with another, two hypotheses were in favour for reconciling the genealogy of
our Lord preserved in Mt 1¹⁻¹⁷ with that in Lk 3²³⁻³⁸.
These were (a) the hypothesis of adoption or levirate
marriage, according to which the actual descent might

differ at several points from the legal descent, so that there might be two equally valid genealogies running side by side; and (*b*) the hypothesis that the one genealogy might be that of Joseph, as the reputed father of Jesus, and the other genealogy (preferably St. Luke's) that of Mary. A certain handle seemed to be given for this latter supposition, by the tradition which was said to be found in the Talmud (tr. *Chagig.* 77, col. 4, Meyer-Weiss), that Mary was the daughter of Eli. [This statement appears to be founded on a mistake, and should be given up; see G. A. Cooke in Gore, *Dissertations*, p. 39 f.] It was felt, however, that this view could only be maintained by straining the text of the Gospel; and it is now generally (though not quite universally) agreed that both genealogies belong to Joseph. On the other hand, the theory of levirate marriage or adoption, though no doubt a possible explanation, left too much the impression of being coined to meet the difficulty. The criticism of to-day prefers to leave the two genealogies side by side as independent attempts to supply the desiderated proof of Davidic descent. Were they the work of our present evangelists, or do they go back beyond them? Both genealogies appear to have in common a characteristic which may point to opposite conclusions as to their origin. That in the First Gospel bears upon its face its artificial structure. The evangelist himself points out (Mt 1^{17}) that it is arranged on three groups of fourteen generations, though these groups are obtained by certain deliberate omissions. That would be, in his case, consistent with other peculiarities of his Gospel: he evidently shared the Jewish fondness **for** artificial arrangements of numbers (Sir John Hawkins, *Horæ Synopticæ*, p. 131 ff.). From this fact we might infer that the stem of descent had been drawn up by himself from the OT and perhaps some local tradition. If such tradition came to him in writing, the list might still conceivably have ended in some such way as that which is found in the Sinai-Syriac, though, if the list was first committed to writing in the Gospel, the probability that it did so would be considerably diminished.

It would seem that a like artificial arrangement (77 generations = 7 × 11) underlies the genealogy in Luke. But as this is not in the manner of the Third Evangelist, and as he does not appear to be conscious of this feature in his list, it would be more probable that he found it ready to his hand. In that case it would be natural that it should come from the same source as chs. 1. 2, which would invest the genealogy with the high authority of those chapters. We cannot speak too confidently, but the conclusion is at least spontaneously suggested by the facts.

§ 81. iv. **The Census of Quirinius.**—Until a very short time ago the best review of the whole question of the Census of Quirinius (Lk 2^{1-5}) was that by Schürer in *NTZG* § 17, Anhang 1 (*HJP* i. ii. 105 ff.). This was based upon a survey of the whole previous literature of the subject, and was really judicial, if somewhat severely critical, in its tone. As distinct from the school of Baur, which was always ready to sacrifice the Christian tradition to its own reconstruction of the history, Dr. Schürer is an excellent representative of that more cautious method of inquiry which carefully collects the data and draws its conclusions with no prepossession in favour of the biblical writers, if also without prejudice against them. In the present instance he summed up rather adversely to the statements in St. Luke; and in the state of historical knowledge at the time when he wrote (1890?), that he should do so was upon his principles not surprising.

According to St. Luke, our Lord was born at Bethlehem on the occasion of a general 'enrolment' ($\dot{a}\pi o$-$\gamma\rho a\phi\acute{\eta}$) ordered by the Emperor Augustus, and carried out in Palestine under Quirinius as governor of Syria. The date was fixed as being before the death of Herod, which took place in B.C. 4; and it was explained that Joseph and Mary, as belonging to the lineage of David, had gone up to enter their names at Bethlehem, David's city.

There were several points in this statement which seemed to invite criticism. (i.) In the first place, there was no other evidence that Augustus ever ordered a general census of the empire, although there was good reason to think that he took pains to collect statistics in regard to it. (ii.) Even if he had ordered such a census, it seemed doubtful whether it would be carried out in a kingdom which possessed such a degree of independence as Judæa. And (iii.) if it had been conducted in the Roman manner, there would have been no necessity for Joseph and Mary to leave their usual place of residence. Further, (iv.) while it was allowed, on the strength of a well-known inscription, that Quirinius probably twice held office in Syria, yet, as it was known that Sentius Saturninus was governor B.C. 9–7, and Quinctilius Varus at least B.C. 7–4, it was argued that Quirinius'

first term of office could not be before B.C. 3–1, *i.e.* after
the death of Herod.   (v.) As there was, in any case, a
census of Judæa conducted by Quirinius after its
annexation by the Romans in A.D. 6, it was thought
that St. Luke had a confused recollection of this, and
antedated it (in the Gospel, though not in Ac 5³⁷) to the
lifetime of Herod.

The chief authority for the census of A.D. 6 is Josephus ; and an
eminent German scholar, Dr. Th. Zahn, put forward in 1893 the
view that it was Josephus who was at fault in dating from this
year an event which really fell in B.C. 4–3 (*Neue Kirchliche Zeitschrift*, pp. 633–654). This brought the data more nearly, though
still not entirely, into agreement with St. Luke. The theory need
not, however, be more fully considered as it has not met with
acceptance, and there can be little doubt that it seeks a solution
of the difficulties in the wrong direction.

There was one little expression which might have
given pause to the critics of St. Luke, viz. his careful
insertion of the word 'first' ('the first enrolment made
when Q. was governor of Syria').   It might have
shown that he was in possession of special knowledge
which would not permit him to confuse the earlier
census with that of A.D. 6.   And yet the existence of
the earlier census remained without confirmation, until
it suddenly received it from a quarter which might
have been described as unexpected, if experience did not
show that there is hardly anything that may not be
found there—the rubbish heaps of papyrus fragments in
Egypt.

Almost at the same time, in the year when Dr. Zahn
made his ingenious but unsuccessful attempt (1893),
three scholars, one English and two German, made
the discovery that periodical enrolments (ἀπογραφαί)

were held in Egypt under the Roman empire, and that they came round in a fourteen-year cycle. The proof of this was at first produced for the enrolments of A.D. 90, 104, 118, 132, and onwards; but in rapid succession the list was carried back to A.D. 76, 62, and 20.

This gave the clue, which was almost at once seized, and the whole problem worked out afresh in masterly fashion by Prof. W. M. Ramsay, first in two articles in *Exp.* 1897, and then in his volume, *Was Christ born at Bethlehem? A Study in the Credibility of St. Luke* (London, 1898). It was not too much to say that every detail is absolutely verified. The age of Augustus as compared with that which precedes and with that which follows is strangely obscure, and the authorities for it defective. But considering this, the sequence of argu-ment which Prof. Ramsay unfolds is remarkably clear and attractive. (i.) He shows it to be very probable that there was a series of periodical enrolments initiated by Augustus at the time when he first received the tribunician power, and his reign formally began in B.C. 23 (this is the official date usual in inscriptions, p. 140). (ii.) He also makes it probable that this was part of a deliberate and general policy—that the census-takings were not confined to Egypt, but extended to other parts of the empire, and more particularly to Syria. Here, too, there was a tendency to periodic recurrence, though the evidence is not, and is not likely to be, so complete as in the case of Egypt. (iii.) He has shown that Palestine was regarded as part of the 'Roman world,' *i.e.* of the empire. Though Herod had the liberty of a *rex socius*, the Roman power and the

emperor's will were always in the background; he had
to see that the whole Jewish people took an oath of
allegiance to the emperor; he could not make war
without being called to account; he could not determine
his own successor or put to death his own son without
an appeal to Rome; in a moment of anger Augustus
threatened that whereas he had hitherto treated him
(Herod) as a friend, he would henceforth treat him as a
subject (Jos. *Ant*. XVI. ix. 3). It was therefore likely
enough that Herod would wish, if he was not positively
ordered, to fall in with the imperial policy by taking a
census of his people, as another subject king did in
Cilicia in A.D. 35. (iv.) But although Herod held a
census at the instance of Augustus, it would be in keeping with his whole character and conduct to temper it
to Jewish tastes as much as possible; and he would do
this by following the national custom of numbering the
people by their tribes and families. This was the broad
distinction between this enrolment of Herod's and the
subsequent census of A.D. 6 or 7. The latter was
carried out by Roman officials and in the Roman
manner, which was the real cause of the offence which
it gave, and of the armed resistance which it excited.
(v.) Some uncertainty still hangs over the mention of
Quirinius. Mommsen thought that he was the acting
legatus of Syria in B.C. 3–1. Prof. Ramsay inclines to
the view that he held an extraordinary command by the
side of Varus some years earlier, as Corbulo did by the
side of Ummidius Quadratus, and Vespasian by the
side of Mucianus. Such a command might carry with
it the control of foreign relations, and be included
under the title ἡγεμών.

§ 82. *The Meaning of the Virgin-Birth.*—It is but a very few years since there arose in Germany (the date was 1892) a rather sharp controversy, in which many leading theologians took part, over the clause of the Apostles' Creed, 'Conceived by the Holy Ghost, born of the Virgin Mary.' The echoes of that controversy reached this country, and although not much was said in public, it is probable that some impression was made upon public opinion. This impression was strengthened by the publication soon afterwards of the Sinai-Syriac with its peculiar reading, which was not unnaturally caught at as representing a more ancient and truer text than that to which we are accustomed. But if what has been written in the preceding sections has been followed, it will have been seen that for some time afterwards there was a certain reaction. The eccentric reading has found its level. As it stands, it cannot possibly be original; and however it arose, it cannot really affect the belief of the Church, as it introduces no factor which had not been already allowed for. And at the same time the historical value of the documents, especially Lk 1. 2, has been gradually rising in the estimation of scholars, until the climax has been reached in the recent treatise of Prof. Ramsay. Even those who desire to see things severely as they are, must feel that the opening chapters of St. Luke are full of small indications of authenticity, that they are really not behind the rest of the Gospel, and that they form no exception to the claim made at the outset that the facts recorded have been derived from 'eye-witnesses and ministers of the word.' [The most recent period (1901–1904) would have to be differently characterized.]

Along with this process there has been growing up a better and fuller philosophy of the Incarnation. This has been due especially to some of the contributors to *Lux Mundi*, and may be seen in Bishop Gore's *Bampton Lectures* (1891) and *Dissertations* (1895), in Dr. Moberly's *Lux Mundi* essay, and in Mr. Illingworth's *Bampton Lectures* (1894) and *Divine Immanence* (1898).

To those who regard primitive ideas as compounded of nothing but idle imagination, ignorance, and superstition, the evidence in folk-lore of stories of supernatural birth (such as are collected in Mr. Sidney Hartland's *Legend of Perseus*, vol. i., 1894) seems to discredit all accounts of such birth, even the Christian. They do not sufficiently consider the entire difference of the conditions under which the Christian tradition was promulgated from those which surrounded the creations of mythopoeic fancy. The Christian tradition belongs to the sphere, not of myth but of history. It is enshrined in documents near in date to the facts, and in which the line of connexion between the record and the fact is still traceable.

But, apart from this, if we believe that the course of human ideas, however mixed in their character—as all human things are mixed—is yet part of a single development, and that development presided over by a Providence which at once imparts to it unity and prescribes its goal,—those who believe this may well see in the fantastic outgrowth of myth and legend something not wholly undesigned or wholly unconnected with the Great Event which was to be, but rather a dim unconscious preparation for that Event, a groping towards it of the human spirit, a prophetic instinct gradually moulding the forms of thought in which it was to find expression.

And if we ask further what it all means,—why the Son of Man was destined to have this exceptional kind of birth, the answer is, because His appearance upon earth—His Incarnation, as we call it—was to be in its innermost nature exceptional; He was to live and move amongst men, and was to be made in all points like His brethren, with the one difference that He was to be—unlike them—without sin.   But how was a sinless human nature possible?   To speak of a sinless human nature is to speak of something essentially outside the continuity of the species.   The growth of self-conscious experience, expressed at its finest and best in the formulæ of advancing science, has emphasized the strength of heredity.   Each generation is bound to the last by indissoluble ties.   To sever the bond, in any one of its colligated strands, involves a break in descent.   It involves the introduction of a new factor, to which the taint of sin does not attach. If like produces like, the element of unlikeness must come from that to which it has itself affinity.   Our names for the process do but largely cover our ignorance, but we may be sure that there is essential truth contained in the scriptural phrase, 'The Holy Ghost shall come upon thee, and the power of the Most High shall overshadow thee; wherefore also that which is to be born shall be called holy, the Son of God.'

[The most important literature has been mentioned in the course of this section.]

14

CHAPTER VIII.

CONCLUDING SURVEY: THE VERDICT OF HISTORY.

A. CHRIST IN HISTORY.

§ 83. So far we have been involved in the study of the details of the Life of Christ, mainly on the basis of the Gospels. But the Gospels alone, though the fragments which they have preserved for us of that Life are beyond all price, would yet convey an incomplete idea of the total impression left by it even upon contemporaries, still less of all that it has been in the history of the world. Especially would this be the case if, as some would have us do, we were to follow the first three Gospels only, to the exclusion of the fourth. To that point we shall return for a moment presently. But the time has now come to enlarge our view, to look back upon our subject from the vantage-ground which we occupy at the beginning of the twentieth century, and to endeavour to see it no longer as an episode affecting a small portion of an 'unimportant branch of the Semitic peoples,' but as it enters into the course of the great world-movement of the centuries.

If we would appreciate this, we must once more go back to the Origins, not now so much in search of details, as in order, if possible, to catch rather more of the total impression. We cannot, of course, attempt to interrogate the whole of history. For our present purpose it may be enough to consider (i.) the net result, if we may so speak, of the portraiture of Christ in the Gospels; (ii.) the impression left by a similar reading of other parts of the New Testament, especially the Epistles; (iii.) the testimony borne by the Early Church, both formulated and informal; (iv.) the appeal that may be made to the religious experience of Christians.

The last of these heads is not really so disparate as it may seem from the rest. The ultimate object that we have in view is to bring home—or to suggest lines on which it may be possible to bring home—what Christ really was and is to the individual believer. In order to do this, we endeavour to collect (i.) what He was to those among whom He moved during His life on earth; (ii.) what He was to His disciples, and primarily to the apostles after His departure; (iii.) what the still undivided Church apprehended Him as being. It will thus be seen that there is no real antithesis, as though the appeal were in the one case to history and in the other to experience. For our present purpose history may be regarded as the collective experience of the past, which we are seeking to put into line with the individual or collective experience of the present. Our historical survey, so far as it goes, simply embodies so many superimposed strata of experience.

§ 84. i. *The Christ of the Gospels.*—We should thus be inclined to deprecate the attempts which are from time to time made to set in contrast some one or other branch of the appeal that we are making as against the rest. In this country we are accustomed to the opposition between the Christ of the (Synoptic) Gospels and the Christ of 'Dogma' or of the Church. And in Germany of late there has been a tendency to oppose the Christ conceived and preached by the apostles to the biographical Christ of the Gospels, and the experience of faith to any external and objective standards. (See especially the works of Kähler and Hermann mentioned below.)

The disparagement of the Gospels as biographies seems to us, so far as it goes,—and neither writer is really very clear on the subject,—to rest upon a somewhat undue degree of scepticism as to the critical use that can be made of the Gospels. It does not follow that all that is doubted is really doubtful. For a more detailed testing of the historical character of the Gospels we must content ourselves with referring to the previous part of this article, only adding to it the two points which will be more appropriately introduced at the end of the next section,—the peculiar kind of confirmation which the two pictures (the evangelic and the apostolic) supply to each other, the difference between them showing that the teaching of the Epistles has not encroached upon the historical truth of the Gospels, while the less obvious likeness shows that they are in strict continuity. We shall also have to state once more in that context our reasons for believing the Fourth Gospel to be really the work of an eye-witness.

But the point that concerns us most at the present moment is that, even if we make to negative criticism larger concessions than we have any right to make, there will still remain in the Gospel picture ineffaceable features which presuppose and demand that estimate of the Person of Christ which we can alone call in the strict sense Christian.

Take, for instance, that central passage Mt 11$^{28-38}$ 'Come unto me, all ye that labour and are heavy laden, and I will give you rest. Take my yoke upon you, and learn of me; for I am meek and lowly in heart: and ye shall find rest unto your souls. For my yoke is easy, and my burden is light.' Could we conceive such words put into any other lips, even the loftiest that the history of mankind has produced? They are full of delicate self-portraiture. They present to us a character which we may say certainly *was*, because it has been so described. No mere artist in words ever painted such a canvas without a living model before him. The portrait is of One who is 'meek and lowly in heart,' whose yoke is easy and His burden light; and yet He speaks of both yoke and burden as 'His' in the sense of being imposed by Him; He invites men to 'come' to Him, evidently with a deep significance read into the phrase; He addresses His invitation to weary souls wherever such are to be found; and (climax of all!) He promises what no Alexander or Napoleon ever dreamt of promising to his followers, that He would give them the truly supernatural gift of rest—the tranquillity and serenity of inward peace in spite of the friction of the world; that all this should be theirs by 'coming' to Him.

And then how easy is it to group round such a passage a multitude of others! 'I say unto you, Resist not him that is evil: but whosoever smiteth thee on thy right cheek, turn to him the other also' (Mt 5^{39}). 'The Son of Man came not to be ministered unto, but to minister' (Mk 10^{45}||). 'Suffer the little children to come unto me; forbid them not: for of such is the kingdom of God' (*ib.* v.^{14}||). 'Whosoever would save his life shall lose it: and whosoever shall lose his life for my sake and the gospel's shall save it' (Mk 8^{35}). 'The Son of Man came to seek and to save that which was lost' (Lk 19^{10}, comp. the three parables of Lk 15). 'Inasmuch as ye did it unto one of these my brethren, even these least, ye did it unto me' (Mt 25^{40}).

Sayings like these, it is needless to add, could be multiplied almost indefinitely. Through all of them there runs, indirectly, if not directly, the same self-portraitures. And it is a self-portraiture that has the same two sides. On the one hand there is the human side, the note of meekness or lowliness, condescension that is not (though it really is!) condescension but infinite sympathy, patience, tenderness; and, on the other hand, no less firmly drawn, for all the lightness and restraint of touch, an absolute range of command and authority; all things delivered to the Son in heaven and on earth (cf. Mt 11^{27} 28^{18}).

That which we have called the 'human side' fills most of the foreground in the Gospels; the other, the transcendental side, is somewhat shaded by it; and we can see that it was deliberately shaded, that the proportions were such as mainly (though, as we shall see, not entirely) corresponded to the facts, or, in other words, to the divine method and order of presentation. But when we turn from the Gospels to the rest of the NT, we shall find these proportions inverted.

We only pause upon this Gospel picture a moment more to say that, apart from any question of criticism of documents or of details in the narrative, it seems to us to be utterly beyond the reach of invention. The evangelists themselves were too near to the events to see them in all their significance. They set down, like honest men, the details one after another as they were told them. But it was not their doing that these details work in together to a singular and unsought harmony.

LITERATURE.—The fullest account of recent discussions as to the adequacy and trustworthiness of the presentation of Christ in the Gospels will be found in the second enlarged edition of Kähler's *Der sogenannte historische Jesus und der geschichtliche, biblische Christus*, Leipzig, 1896. Another work, which lays the stress rather on personal experience of the life of Christ, and is written with great earnestness from that point of view, but seems to us too restricted in its historical basis, is Herrmann's *Der Verkehr des Christen mit Gott*, ed. 2, Stuttgart, 1892 (Eng. tr. 1895).

§ 85. ii. *The Christ of the Apostles.*—In passing over from the Gospels to the rest of the NT, we find ourselves hampered by critical questions. What we should most wish to ascertain is the conception of Christ held by the mass of the first disciples. And to some extent we can get at this; but, so far as we can do so, it is nearly always indirectly. The writings that have come down to us are those of the leaders, not of the followers; and many even of these are encumbered with questions as to date and origin. Some of these do not so much matter, because in any case they belong to the end rather than the beginning of the apostolic age. The one book which we should most like to use more freely than we can is the Acts, the earlier chapters of which we quite agree with the author of the article in Dr. Hastings' Dictionary in estimating highly.

We will, however, cut the knot by not attempting to summarize the teaching of all the undisputed books, but by taking a single typical example of manageable compass, the first extant NT writing, 1 Thessalonians, written probably about A.D. 51—in any case not later than 53, or within the first quarter of a century after the Ascension.

Let us suppose for a moment, with the more extreme critics, that a thick curtain falls over the Church after this event. The curtain is lifted, and what do we find? We turn to the opening verse of the Epistle (emended reading). St. Paul and his companions give solemn greeting to the 'Church of the Thessalonians (which is) in God the Father and the Lord Jesus Christ.' An elaborate process of reflexion, almost a system of theology, lies behind those familiar terms. First we note that the human name 'Jesus' is closely associated with the title 'Christ' or 'Messiah,' which in the Gospels had been claimed with such quiet reticence and unobtrusiveness. From this time onwards the two names are almost inseparable, or the second supersedes the first : in other words, Jesus is hardly ever thought of apart from His high Messianic dignity. This effect is pressed home by the further title 'Lord' ($K\acute{v}\rho\iota\sigma$). The disciples had been in the habit of addressing their Master as 'Lord' during His lifetime, in a sense not very different from that in which any Rabbi might be addressed by his pupils (Jn 13$^{13f.}$). But that sense is no longer adequate ; the word has been filled with a deeper meaning. That 'Jesus is Lord' has become the distinctive confession of Christians (1 Co 12^3, Ro 10^9), where 'Lord' certainly='the exalted Lord' of the Resurrection and Ascension (cf. Ac 2^{36}).

What is still more remarkable, the glorified Jesus is, as it were, bracketed with 'God the Father.' Let us think what this would mean to a strict Jewish monotheist; yet St. Paul evidently holds the juxtaposition, not as something to which he is tentatively feeling his way, but as a fundamental axiom of faith. In the appellation 'Father' we have already the first beginning—may we not say the first decisive step, which potentially contains the rest?—of the Christian doctrine of the Trinity. And we observe, further, that the Thessalonian Church is said to have its being 'in Christ' as well as 'in God.' This is a characteristic touch of Pauline mysticism. The striking thing about it is that in this, too, the Son already holds a place beside the Father (cf. 2^{14} 4^{16}).

There is another passage in the Epistle (1 Th 3^{11}) in which there is the same intimate combination of 'our God and Father' and 'our Lord Jesus.' Here the context is not exactly mystical, but the two names are mentioned in connexion with the divine prerogative of ordering events. The apostle prays that God and Christ will together 'direct' (κατευθύναι, 'make straight and unimpeded') his way to them (the Thessalonians).

It is not by accident that the Holy Spirit is in a similar manner implicated in divine action ($1^{5,\ 6}$ 4^8 5^{19}), though it would be too much to say that the Spirit is spoken of distinctly as a Person.

The historical events of the life of Christ are hardly alluded to, except His death and resurrection (1^{10} 4^{14} 5^{10}). In the last of these verses Christ is said to have died 'for us'; and in the preceding verse 'salvation,' which is contrasted with 'death,' is said to come 'through' Him. In 1^{10} He is also spoken of as delivering Christians 'from the wrath to come.' It is assumed that Christ is in heaven, from whence He is expected to come again with impressive manifestations of power (1^{10} $4^{15f.}$; cf. also the frequent allusions to ἡ παρουσία τοῦ Κυρίου).

The Second Coming is the only point on which the Epistle can be said to contain direct and formal teaching. The other points mentioned are all assumed as something already known, not as imparted for the first time.

Not only may we say that they are known, but it is also fair to infer that they are undisputed. There is a hint of controversy with the unbelieving Jews, but no hint of controversy with the Judæan Churches, which stand in the same relation to Christ (2^{14-16}). This is important; and it is fully borne out by the other Epistles, which show just how far the disputed ground between St. Paul and the other apostles extended. There was a good deal of sharp debate about the terms on which Gentiles should be admitted. There is no trace of any debate as to the estimate of the Person of Christ.

We have referred to the Pauline mysticism and to the hints, slight but significant, of what is known as the doctrine of the Atonement. It is clear that St. Paul ascribed to Christ not only divine attributes but divine activities — activities in the supersensual sphere, what he elsewhere calls 'heavenly places' (τὰ ἐπουράνια). We know how these activities are enlarged upon in the Epistles to Corinthians, Galatians, and Romans. It would, of course, be wrong to suppose that all Christians, or indeed any great number, had an intelligent grasp of these 'mysteries'; but we can see from the Epistle to Hebrews, 1 Peter, Epistles of John, and Revelation, that conceptions quite as transcendental had a wide diffusion. And a verse like 2 Co 13^{14} shows that there must have been large tracts of important teaching which are imperfectly represented in our extant documents. When we consider how occasional these documents are in their origin, the wonder is not that they have conveyed to us so little of the apostolic teaching, but that they have conveyed so much.

The summary impression that we receive is indeed that the revolution foreshadowed at the end of the last section has been accomplished. The historical facts of the Lord's life were not neglected; for Gospels were being written, of which those which we now possess are only surviving specimens. But in the whole epistolary literature of NT they have receded very much into the background, as compared with those transcendental conceptions of the Person and Work of Christ, to which the Gospels pointed forward, but which (with one exception) they did not directly expound.

No doubt this was in the main only what was to

be expected. The narrative of the Gospels goes back to the period before the Resurrection; the epistolary literature dates altogether after it. Still it is remarkable how we seem to be plunged all at once into the midst of a developed theology. Nor is the wonder lessened, it is rather increased, when we remark that this theology is only in part set before us deliberately as teaching. The fact that it is more often presupposed shows how deep a hold it must have taken alike of the writer and of his readers.

Impressive contrasts are sometimes drawn (*e.g.* at the beginning of Dr. Hatch's *Hibbert Lectures*) between the Sermon on the Mount and the Nicene Creed; and the contrast certainly is there. But it goes back far beyond the period of the Arian controversy. It is hardly less marked between the Sermon on the Mount and the writings which have come down to us under the names of St. Peter and St. Paul. And yet these writings are practically contemporary with the composition of the Gospels. The two streams, of historical narrative on the one hand and theological inference on the other, really run side by side. They do not exclude but rather supplement, and indeed critically confirm, each other. For if the Gospels had been really not genuine histories of the words and acts of Christ, but coloured products of the age succeeding His death, we may be sure that they would have reflected the characteristic attitude of that age far more than they do. They do not reflect it, but they do account for it by those delicate hints and subtly inwoven intimations that He who called Himself so persistently Son of Man was also Son of God.

The one Gospel which bridges the gap more unmistakably than the others is the Fourth. And the reason is obvious, if St. John was its author. He had a foot in both worlds. As the disciple whom Jesus loved, he vividly remembered His incomings and outgoings. And in the same capacity, as a disciple who was also an apostle, it fell to him to build up that theology which was the deliberate expression of what Jesus was to His Church, not in a section only of His being, the short three years which He had spent among His followers, but in His being as He had revealed it to them as a whole. It is difficult to think of either function as merely assumed by the writer at second-hand. On the contrary, we acquire a fresh understanding of the weight and solemnity of his words when we think of these as springing from direct personal contact with Christ, and intense personal conviction of what Christ really was, not to himself only, but to the world. In this respect the Fourth Gospel is unique; and the very expansion which it gives of the divine claims of Christ prepares us more completely than the other Gospels alone might have done for the transition from them to the Epistles.

It is an especial satisfaction to be able to quote, in support of this view of the first-hand character of the Fourth Gospel, Dr. Loofs in *PRE*[3] iv. 29.

§ **86.** iii. *The Christ of the Undivided Church.*—For the purpose which we have before us we must examine the evidence of the Undivided Church on three distinct points. (*a*) What was the estimate of the Person of Christ in the age immediately succeeding that of the

Apostles? (*b*) Are there any traces of a tradition different from this? (*c*) What is the bearing upon the subject of the creeds and conciliar decisions?

(*a*) On the first head we may say broadly that the mass of Christian opinion was in strict continuity with the NT, rarely (as we might expect) rising to an apprehension of its heights and depths, and keeping rather at the average level, but steadily loyal in intention, and showing no signs of recalcitrance.

Ignatius of Antioch has the strongest grip of distinctive features of NT teaching (Virgin-Birth, pre-existence, incarnation, Logos, Trinitarian language). Clemens Romanus, though much less theological, also has pre-existence and a clearly implied Trinity (lviii. 2). In the former point Barnabas and Hermas agree, though the latter shows some confusion, not uncommon at this date, between Son and Spirit. And then we have the opening words of 2 Clement, which exactly describe the general temper, 'Brethren, we ought so to think of Jesus Christ as of God, as of the Judge of quick and dead.'

These, with Polycarp and Aristides, who adopt a similar tone, are the writers. And then, when we look for evidence as to popular feeling and practice, we have the wide prevalence of baptism in the Threefold Name (*Didaché* and Justin), and the hymns sung 'to Christ as God' (Pliny, *Ep. ad Trajan.* xcvi.; cf. Eus. *HE* v. xxviii. 5). It is clear that prayer was generally offered to Christ. Origen's objection to this was a theological refinement, as he held that the proper formula was εὐχαριστεῖν τῷ θεῷ διὰ Χ. 'Ι. (*de Orat.* 15).

The group of Apologists which stands out so clearly in the middle of the second century is characterized chiefly by the use that is made of the Logos doctrine, which was identified with the Logos of philosophy. With them begins a more active spirit of reflexion and speculation. The relation of the Son to the Father, and indeed the whole problem of unity and distinctions in the Godhead (Justin and Athenagoras), is beginning to be keenly canvassed. And at the same time it is clear that the question of what were afterwards called the 'Two Natures' was causing much perplexity. It was this difficulty which really lies behind the experiments of Gnosticism.   When we come to the latter half and last quarter of the century, with the theologians of Asia Minor, Irenæus, and Clement of Alexandria, the foundations have been laid of a Christian theology, which already bears the stamp that marks it throughout succeeding centuries, viz. that it is not free speculation, but reflexion upon *data* given by the Bible.

(*b*) It was natural, and could not well have been otherwise, that there was in this reflexion at first a considerable tentative element. There was no break, and no conscious divergence between it and the canonical writings.   But are there no signs of such divergence? Are there no signs of a tradition differing from that embodied in these writings?   Perhaps we ought to say that there are.

The Gnostics began by inventing traditions of their own, but they soon fell into the groove, and professed to base their views like the rest on the canonical Scriptures.   A conspicuous example of this is Heracleon's commentary on St. John.   But in these circles there was what we might call recalcitrance, as when Cerinthus and Carpocrates rejected the Virgin-Birth as impossible (Iren. *adv. Hær.* I. xxvi. I, xxv. I).   The Gnostics, however, are outside the true development of Christianity, and their systems had a different origin.

In closer contact with Christianity proper are the heretical Ebionites.   For them a better claim might be made out to represent a real divergence of tradition.   It is possible that their denial of the Virgin-Birth was derived from the state of things when the canonical narratives had not yet obtained any wide circulation. And yet we should have to pass upon these Ebionites a verdict similar to that already passed upon the Gnostics.   They were really Jews imperfectly Christianized.   If they regarded Christ as ψιλὸς ἄνθρωπος, it was doubtless because the Jews did not expect their Messiah to have any other origin.   This is a different thing from, though it may have some subordinate connexion with, the views (*e.g.*) of Paul of Samosata, whose difficulty was caused by the union of the two natures.   The human nature he regarded as having an ordinary human birth, though it came to be united to the Divine Logos.

A like account would hold good of Theodotus of Byzantium and the Rationalists described in Eus. *HE* v. xxviii. At last the reader may think that he is upon the track of a genuine Rationalism; but this did not go very deep. It was consistent with belief in the Virgin-Birth and in the Resurrection (Hippolytus, *Ref. Hær.* vii. 35); in fact it probably amounted to little more than a dry literal exegesis.

The *Clementine Homilies* point out that Christ did not call Himself 'God' but the 'Son of God,' and they emphasize this distinction somewhat after the manner of the later Arians (xvi. 15, 16). When we have said this, we shall have touched (it is believed) on all the main types of what might be thought to be a denial of Christ's full Godhead.

The more pressing danger of primitive Christianity lay in an opposite direction. Loyalty to Christ was so strong that the simpler sort of Christians were apt to look upon the humanity as swallowed up in the divinity. This is the true account of the early prevalence of Docetism (which made the deity of Christ real, the humanity phantasmal or unreal), and of the later prevalence of what is known to students as Modalistic Monarchianism, and to the general reader as Sabellianism (the doctrine that the Son and the Spirit were not distinct Persons in the Godhead, but modes or aspects of the One God). The answer of Noetus was typical of the frame of mind that gave rise to this, 'What harm do I do in glorifying Christ?' (Hippol. *c. Noet.* 1) : it seemed meritorious to identify Christ with God. Both these tendencies were far stronger and more widely spread than anything that savoured of Rationalism. Docetism entered largely into the Apocryphal Gospels and Acts, which were very popular; and both Tertullian (*Prax.* 1, 3) and Hippolytus (*Ref. Hær.* ix. 6, μέγιστος ἀγών) imply that the struggle against Monarchianism was severe.

It is evident from this to which side the scales inclined. The traces of anything like Rationalism in the modern sense are extremely few and slight. For the most part, what looks like it is not pure Rationalism (or Humanitarianism) at all. More formidable was the excess of zeal which exalted the divine in Christ at the expense of the human. But the main body of the Church held an even way between both extremes,—

held it at least in intention, though there were no doubt
a certain number of unsuccessful experiments in the
construction of reasoned theory.

(*c*) It was inevitable that in the early centuries there
should be a great amount of tentative thinking. But
little by little this was sifted out ; and by the middle
of the fifth century the ancient Church had practically
made up its mind. It formulated its belief in the
Chalcedonian definition (ὅρος τῆς ἐν Χαλκηδόνι τετάρτης
συνόδου) of the year 451 (which counts as Ecumenical,
though the only Westerns present were the two legates
of Pope Leo and two fugitive bishops from Africa), and
in the *Quicumque vult*, a liturgical creed composed,
according to a tradition which may be sound, by
Dionysius [of Milan] and Eusebius [of Vercelli], (cf. the
remarkable preface in the Irish *Liber Hymnorum*, i. 203,
ii. 92, ed. Bernard and Atkinson, Lond. 1898).

This creed and the definitions of Chalcedon represent the end
of the process ; the beginning is marked by the creed known as
the Apostles'. Criticism has of late been active upon this creed as
well as upon the so-called Nicene and Athanasian, with a result
which tends, it may be generally said, to heighten the value of all
three. The date of the Apostles' Creed (in its oldest and shortest
form) has been reduced within the limits A.D. 100–150 ; Kattenbusch,
the author of the most elaborate monograph on the subject, leans
to the beginning of that period, Harnack to the end. It is agreed
that it was in the first instance the local baptismal creed of the
Church of Rome, and that it was the parent of all the leading
provincial creeds of the West. The principal open question at
the present time (1899, 1904) is as to its relation to the Eastern
creeds. Kattenbusch and Harnack both think that it was carried
to the East under Aurelian (*circa* 270), and that it became the
parent of a number of Eastern creeds, including that which we
know as the Nicene ; but this is conjecture. Harnack thinks that
the Roman creed coalesced with floating formulæ, to which he
gives the name of *Kerygmata*, already circulating in the East.

But these also are more or less hypothetical. And the question is, whether the Eastern creeds, which resemble the Roman, were not rather offshoots, parallel to it, of a single primitive creed, perhaps originating in Asia Minor? This is substantially the view of Dr. Loofs. The main argument in favour of it is that characteristic features of the Eastern type of creed already appear in Irenæus and in a less degree in Justin. Harnack would explain these features as due to his *Kerygmata*; and from the point of view of the history of doctrine the difference is not very great, because the *Kerygmata* were in any case in harmony with the creed.

It would be difficult to overestimate the value of the existence of this fixed traditional standard of teaching at so early a date. It was the rallying and steadying centre of Catholic Christianity, which kept it straight in the midst of Gnostic extravagances and among the perils of philosophical speculation. Our so-called Nicene Creed is only the Apostles' Creed in one of its more florid Oriental forms, with clauses engrafted into it to meet the rising heresies of Arius and Macedonius ; while the Chalcedonian formula and the *Quicumque* take further account of the controversies connected with the names of Apollinaris, Nestorius, and Eutyches.

The decisions in question were thus the outcome of a long evolution, every step in which was keenly debated by minds of great acumen and power, really far better equipped for such discussions than the average Anglo-American mind of to-day. If we can see that their premises were often erroneous (especially in such matters as the exegesis of the OT), we can also see that they possessed extraordinary fertility and subtlety in the handling of metaphysical problems. The disparaging estimates of the Fathers, which are often heard and seen in print, are very largely based upon the most superficial acquaintance with their writings. There are many things in these which may provoke a smile, but as a whole they certainly will not do so in any really open mind. There exists at the present time in Germany a movement, which bears the name of its

author, Albrecht Ritschl (1822–1889), directed against
metaphysics in theology generally. No doubt Ritschl
also was a thinker and writer of great ability; and the
stress that he lays upon religious experience is by no
means without justification. But it has not yet been
proved that the negative side of his argument is equally
valid, or that metaphysics can be wholly dispensed
with. And so long as this is the case, we certainly
cannot afford to ignore these ancient decisions. Every
word in them represents a battle, or succession of
battles, in which the combatants were, many of them,
giants.

LITERATURE.—The subject of this section brings up the whole
history of 'Christology,' which may be studied in well-known
works of Baur, Dorner, and Thomasius, or in Harnack's *History
of Dogma*. There is an excellent survey by Loofs in *PRE*³ iv.
16 ff., art. 'Christologie, Kirchenlehre,' marked by much independent judgment and research. In English may be mentioned
Gore, *Bampton Lectures* (1891); Fairbairn, *Christ in Modern
Theology* (1893); R. L. Ottley, *Doctrine of the Incarnation* (1896).

The later phases of the critical discussions on the creeds are
set forth in Kattenbusch, *Das Apost. Symbol* (Leipzig, 1894, 1897,
1900); Harnack's art. 'Apost. Symb.' in *PRE*³ i. 741 ff. (this is
the author's most complete and latest utterance; the Eng. reader
may consult *Hist. of Dogma*, i. 157 ff.), and an important art. by
Loofs in *Gött. gel. Anzeigen*, 1895.

For Ritschl's attitude it may be enough to refer to his tract,
Theologie u. Metaphysik, Bonn, 1881. We had an English version
of the opposition to metaphysics in the writings of Matthew
Arnold.

§ 87. iv. *The Christ of Personal Experience.*—In the
case of Ritschl the religious experience of the individual
or of communities is directly pitted against metaphysics
as the criterion of theological truth. But apart from
philosophical theory, it is the criterion which is practi-

cally applied by hundreds of thousands of plain men—
we will not say in search of a creed, but in support of
the creed which they have found or inherited.   And
there is an immense volume of evidence derived from
this source in corroboration of the truth of Christianity,
or of what amounts to the same thing, the Christian
estimate of the Person of Christ.   The singular attrac-
tion of this Person, the sense of what Christ has done,
not only for mankind at large but for the individual
believer, the sense of the love of God manifested in
Him, have been so overpowering as to sweep away
all need for other kinds of evidence.   They create a
passionate conviction that the religion which has had
these effects cannot be wrong in its fundamental doctrine, the pivot of the whole.

This personal experience operates in two ways.   It
makes the individual believer cling to his belief in spite
of all the objections that can be brought against it.
But it also possesses a formative power which so
fashions men in the likeness of Christ, that they in
turn become a standing witness to those who have not
come under the same influence.   St. Paul expresses this
by a forcible metaphor when he speaks of himself as in
travail for his Galatian converts ' until Christ be formed '
in them, as the embryo is formed in the womb (Gal 4^{19}).
The image thus formed shines through the man, like
a light through glass, and so He who came to be
the Light of the world has His radiance transmitted
downwards through the centuries and outwards to the
remotest corners of the earth.

This that we speak of is, of course, matter of common knowledge and of everyday experience.   The note

of the true Christian cannot help being seen wherever there is genuine Christianity. It is, however, an inestimable advantage that the process should have found expression in such classics of literature as the *Confessions of St. Augustine* and the *De Imitatione*. In these it can not only be seen but studied.

B. The Person of Christ.

§ 88. It is necessary that these outlines should be brought to a close, and the close may seem rather abrupt. And yet the design which the writer set before himself is very nearly accomplished. It will be his duty at a later date to return to his subject on a somewhat larger scale; and for the present he would conclude, not so much by stating results as by stating problems.

§ 89. i. *The Problem as it stands.*—We have seen that there are four different ways of attempting to grasp what we can of the significance of the Person of Christ. Towards these four ways the attitude of different minds will be different. For some the decisions of the undivided Church will be absolutely authoritative and final. They will not seek to go either behind them or beyond them. Others will set the comparative simplicity of the Gospel picture against the more transcendental and metaphysical conceptions of the age that followed. To others, again, the picture traced in the Gospels will seem meagre and uncertain by the side of the exalted Christ preached by the apostles.* Yet others will take

* 'We know, literally speaking, with much greater certainty what Paul wrote than what Jesus spoke.' 'The centre of gravity

refuge in the appeal to individual experience, which will seem to give a more immediate hold on Christ and to avoid the necessity and perplexities of criticism. Others, still more radical in their procedure, will begin with the assumption that Christ was only man, and will treat all the subsequent development as reflecting the growth of the delusion by which He came to be regarded as God.

This last is a drastic method of levelling down the indications of the divine in history, against which human nature protests and will continue to protest. But, short of this, the other milder alternatives seem to us to put asunder what ought rather to be combined. They seem to us to propound antitheses, where they ought rather to find harmony. As the phases in question, distinctly as they stand out from each other, are so many phases in the history of Christianity, they ought to contribute to the elucidation of the Christianity which they have in common.

They ought to contribute to it, and we believe that they do contribute to it. There is, however, room still left for closer study, especially of the *transitions*. We have been so much in the habit of studying the Gospels by themselves and the Epistles by themselves, that we have not paid sufficient attention to the transition from the one to the other. If we follow this clue, it will, we believe, show that the first three Gospels in particular need supplementing, that features which in them appear subordinate will bear greater emphasis, and that the

for the understanding of the Person (of Christ) and of its significance falls upon what we are in the habit of calling His Work' (Kähler, *Jesus u. das AT*, pp. 37, 60).

resulting whole is more like that portrayed in the Fourth Gospel than is often supposed.

For instance, we are of opinion that much of the teaching of Jn 14–16 is *required by* the verse 2 Co 13[14] and other allusive passages in the early Epistles of St. Paul; that the command of Mt 28[19] (or something like it) is required by *Didaché* vii. 1, 3; Just. *Apol.* i. 61; that the teaching respecting the Paraclete is required by the whole Pauline doctrine of the Spirit; that the allegory of the Vine is required by the Pauline doctrines of the Head and the Members, and of the Mystical Union; that the full sense of Mk 10[45]‖ is required by such passages as Ro 3[24. 25] 4[25] 5[6–8] etc., and the full sense of Mk 14[24]‖ by He 9[18–22]. And observations of this kind may be very largely extended.

In like manner, while it is certainly right that the conceptions current in the early Church as to the Person and Work of Christ should be rigorously analyzed and traced to their origin, full weight should be given to the analogues for them that are to be found in NT; and where they have their roots outside the Bible, even there the efforts of the human mind to express its deepest ideas may deserve a more sympathetic judgment than they sometimes receive.

And throughout, it is highly important that the doctrinal conceptions, whether of the apostolic age or of subsequent ages, should be brought to the test of living experience, and as far as possible expressed in the language of such experience. The mind and heart of to-day demands before all things reality. It is a right and a healthy demand; and the Churches should try with all their power to satisfy it. If they fail, the fault will not lie in their subject-matter, but in themselves.

§ **90.** ii. *A pressing Portion of the Problem.*—There is one portion of the problem as to the Person of our Lord Jesus Christ which, both in this country and in Germany, has excited special interest in recent years. In its most concrete form this is the question as to our Lord's Human Knowledge, which, however, runs up directly into what is generally known as the question of the *Kenosis.* And that, again, when thoroughly examined, will be found to raise the whole question of the Two Natures. In regard to this series of connected questions there is still abroad an active spirit of inquiry.

It was started in the first instance by the argument from our Lord's use of the OT in its bearing upon the question of OT criticism. This led to a closer examination of the text, Mk 13[32] || *var. lect.* That, again, expanded into a discussion of the technical doctrine of the *Kenosis* (see *DB, s.v.*), an episode in which was a renewed study of the exegesis of Ph 2[5-11]. And that, in turn, in its later phase (H. C. Powell's *Principle of the Incarnation,* 1896), has opened up the whole question of the Two Natures, which in Germany for some time past has been far more freely handled than in Great Britain.

These discussions have produced one little work of classical value, Dr. E. H. Gifford's study of Ph 2[5-11], entitled the *Incarnation,* a model of careful and scientific exegesis, which appears to leave hardly anything more to be said on that head. It is also right to note the special activity on this subject of the diocese of Salisbury, largely due to the initiative and encouragement of its bishop (Mr. W. S. Swayne's *Our Lord's Knowledge as Man,* with a preface by the Bishop of Salisbury, 1891, and Mr. Powell's elaborate work mentioned above). Weighty contributions have been made to the subject by Dr. Bright in *Waymarks of Church History* (1894), Canon [now Bishop] Gore (*Dissertations,* 1898), and in arts. in the *Ch. Quarterly,* Oct. 1891, and July 1897.

On the Continent special views of the *Kenosis* are connected with the names of Dorner, Thomasius, Gess, Godet, and others rather more incidentally.   Tracts upon the smaller questions appeared not long ago by Schwartzkopff (*Konnte Jesus irren?* 1896), and Kähler (*Jesus u. das AT*, 1896).

In spite of all this varied activity, it may be doubted whether the last word has yet quite been said (Dr. Gifford's treatment of the exegetical question seems to us to come nearest to this).   The first concern of the historian is that the facts shall be taken candidly as they are.   It is more probable that our inferences will be wrong than the data from which they are drawn. And for the rest, we should not be surprised if a yet further examination of the subject should result rather in a list of *tacenda* than of *prædicanda*.

C. THE WORK OF CHRIST.

§ 91. In regard to the work of Christ, also, it is best for us to state problems.   Of these the most important are the two that meet us first; they have not been much discussed; and complete agreement upon them has not yet been attained.

§ 92. i. *The Place in the Cosmical Order of the Ethical Teaching of Christ.*—It is almost a question of names when it is asked whether Christ brought into the world a new ethical ideal.   The question would be what constituted a new ideal.   The Christian ideal, properly so called, is a direct development of what is found in OT, esp. in Psalms and the Second Part of Isaiah.   But it receives a finish and an enrichment beyond what it ever possessed before, and it is placed on deeper foundations.

The chief outstanding question in regard to it would be the relation in which it stood to the older ideals of the best pagan life and philosophy in regard to the civic virtues, and to the newer ideals put forward in modern times in the name of science, art, and industry. The Christian ideal, it must be confessed, rather leaves these on one side. That it should do so would be quite as explicable if we adopt the Christian estimate of the Person of Christ as if we do not. If we do not adopt it, then the omission (so far as there is an omission) would be one of the limitations for which we were prepared. But if we take St. John's view of the relation of the Son to the Father, and see in His action the action willed by the Father, we shall see it as part of the great world-movement, presupposing so much of that movement as had proved itself to be of permanent value in the past, and leaving room for further developments, corresponding to altered states of society, in the future. The teaching of Christ was not intended to make a *tabula rasa* of all that had gone before in Greece or Rome any more than in Judæa; nor was it intended to absorb into itself absolutely all the threads of subsequent evolution, where those threads work back to antecedents other than its own. It was intended so to work into the course of the world-movement as ultimately to recast and reform it. Its action has about it nothing violent or revolutionary, but it is none the less searching and effective. It is a force 'gentle yet prevailing.'

Some remarks have been made above (p. 89 f.) on

the way in which the Christian ethical ideal operates and has operated. It is not thought that they are really sufficient; but they represent such degree of insight as the writer has attained to at present, and he would welcome warmly any new light on the subject.

§ **93.** ii. *The Significance of the Personal Example of Christ in regard to His Ethical Teaching.*—When once it is realized that the root principle of the ethics of Jesus is *Life through Death*, the death of the lower self with a view to the more assured triumph of the higher, it must needs break in upon us that the Life of Christ bears to His teaching a wholly different relation from that which the lives of ordinary teachers bear to theirs. An honest man will no doubt try to practise what he preaches, but that will be just a matter of maxims of conduct. The Life of Christ, we can see, was something very much more than this. It was a systematic working out of the Christian principle on a conspicuous and transcendent scale. The Death and Resurrection of Jesus were the visible embodiment of the law of all spiritual being that death is the true road to the higher life.

When we reflect further who it was that was thus exhibiting in His own Person the working out of this law to the utmost extremity, we become aware that Christians have it indeed 'placarded' before their eyes (Gal 3¹) in a sense in which no moral law ever was set forth before.

Add that Christ had Himself predicted, and that His followers generally believed, that after His Ascension

He was again visiting His people through His Spirit;
that Divine forces were at work in the world, all radi-
ating from Himself—Himself at once crucified and
risen; add this to the previous beliefs of which we
have just spoken,—remember that Christians supposed
themselves to be actually conscious of these forces
impressing and moulding their own hearts and lives,
and we may come gradually to understand what St.
Paul meant when He spoke of 'dying' or 'being crucified' with 'Christ' and 'rising again with Him.' It
seems to be a similar idea to that which St. John expresses when he puts into the mouth of Christ the
claim, 'I am the Way.' Rather, perhaps, we should
not narrow down this phrase to anything less than the
whole content of the Life of Christ on earth. 'He
supplied in Himself the fixed plan, according to which
all right human action must be framed: the Spirit
working with their spirit supplied the ever-varying
shapes in which the one plan had to be embodied'
(Hort, *Huls. Lect.* p. 30).

§ **94.** iii. *The Work of Christ as Redemptive.*—Here
we come on to more settled ground. At a very
early date Christian tradition gave to Christ the title
'Saviour' (Lk 2^{11}, Ac 5^{31} 13^{23} etc.; cf. Mt 1^{21}, Lk 19^{10}),
'Saviour of the world' (Jn 4^{42}; cf. 3^{17} 12^{47}). What
does this title 'Saviour' include? It doubtless includes
every sense in which Christ rescued and rescues men
from the power and the guilt of sin. He does this, as
we have seen, both by teaching and by example—by
inimitable teaching and by a consummate example.
But if we follow the method indicated above (p. 230 f.),

if we take the hints in the Gospels, with the fuller light thrown upon them by the Epistles, we shall be led to the conclusion that there was something yet more in the Life and Death and Resurrection of our Lord Jesus Christ than this, that there was something in these connected acts of His which had its counterpart in the sacrifices of OT; and that the deepest meaning and purpose of sacrifice was fulfilled in Him. This is a belief which Christians have held from the first days onwards; and it is a belief which does not and will not lack careful restatement at the present time.

§ 95. iv. *The Work of Christ as Revelation.*—On a similar footing is the belief that Christ came not only to give, but to be a revelation of the inmost mind and character of the Father. Such a revelation was needed. It is not contained in the 'cosmic process.' If we had that process alone before us, we could not infer that God was a Being absolutely righteous and absolutely loving. The idea that He might be so could not rise above a hypothesis. But at this point the Incarnation intervenes. And here again the Synoptic Gospels present us with one central passage (Mt 11^{27}‖) with other scattered hints which are taken up and made more explicit in the Fourth Gospel, while that again does but give the fuller ground for a belief which was certainly held in the apostolic circle (comp. *e.g.* the central passage Jn 14^{7-10} with $10^{14f.}$ 3^{16}, 1 Jn $4^{8.\ 16}$, Ro 5^8 etc.). So we get the broad doctrine led up to by St. Paul and Epistle to the Hebrews (2 Co $4^{4.\ 6}$, Col 1^{15}, He 1^3), and finally formulated by St. John, that the Son was the Logos or Word (which might be paraphrased 'mouthpiece,' or 'vehicle of utterance of the mind') of the Father.

§ **96.** v. *The Founding of the Church.*—Conventional language is too often heard as though the immediate object of the Incarnation was the founding of the full hierarchical system as it existed in the Middle Ages. This language is based on the complete identification of the Church with the 'kingdom of heaven' (see p. 83 f. *sup.*).   On the other hand, there is a school of critics, both in Germany and in England, who deny that 'Jesus ever created, or thought of creating, an organized society.'   The main ground for this latter view is the doubt that rests over the two instances— one of them ambiguous — of the use of the word 'Church' which are confined to the peculiar element of the First Gospel (Mt 16^{18} 18^{17}), and the certainty that there are some senses in which the 'kingdom' and the Church cannot be identified.   In some (though not in all) of those who adopt this line of reasoning there is the further tendency to minimize or restrict all that would imply an extended outlook of Jesus over the ages.

It seems to us, however, to be going too far to say that the 'kingdom of heaven is without organization and incapable of being organized.'   The two parables of the Tares and the Draw-net distinctly imply the existence of a society; and that the divine laws and influences which constitute the kingdom should express themselves in a society as the vehicle for their realization is antecedently probable.   But when Jesus gathered round Him the Twelve, He was practically forming the nucleus of a society; and that society has had a continuous existence ever since, so that it is difficult to think that it was not contemplated. Moreover, when we turn to the writings of St. Paul, we find that even in his earlier Epistles he seems to think of Christians as forming a single body with differentiation of function (Ro 12^{4-8}, 1 Co 12^{4-30}), and in his later Epistles (Ephesians, Colossians, Pastoral Epistles) the unity of the Church with its regular forms of ministry is brought out still more emphatically.

We also find that the Day of Pentecost is described in Acts as inaugurating a state of things which agrees well with the indications in the Epistles of St. Paul, while it confirms the promise of Lk 24^{49}, Jn $14^{16.\ 26}$.

On the assumptions made in these *Outlines*, it would be extremely improbable that this series of phenomena was not fully foreseen and deliberately designed by Christ. It would seem, however, that, after the manner of the divine operations in nature, He was rather content to plant a germ with indefinite capacities of growth, than thought it necessary Himself to fix in advance the details of organization.

The exact nature of the powers conferred upon the apostles is still a subject of much discussion as these concluding lines are written (1899).

§ 97. LIVES OF CHRIST.—To write the Life of Christ ideally is impossible. And even to write such a *Life* as should justify itself either for popular use or for study, is a task of extreme difficulty. After all the learning, ability, and even genius devoted to the subject, it is a relief to turn back from the very best of modern *Lives* to the Gospels. And great as are the merits of many of these modern works, there is none (at least none known to the writer—and there are several that he ought to know but does not) which possess such a balance and combination of qualities as to rise quite to the level of a classic. What is wanted is a Newman, with science and adequate knowledge. No one has ever touched the Gospels with so much innate kinship of spirit as he. It should be needless to say that the Life of Christ can be written only by a believer. Renan had all the literary gifts—a *curiosa felicitas* of style, an æsthetic appreciation of his subject, and a saving common-sense which tempered his criticism; but even as literature his work is spoilt by self-consciousness and condescension, and his science was not of the best.

It will be well here only to name a select list of books which may be used more or less systematically. The minor works are legion.

Among the older works that would still most repay study would probably be those of Neander (ed. 7, 1873), Hase (*Leben Jesu*, ed. 5, 1865; *Geschichte Jesu*, 1876), Ewald (vol. vi. in Eng. tr. of *Gesch. d. Volkes Israel*, 1883), Andrews (American; revised ed. Edinburgh: T. & T. Clark, 1892).

In this country the books most generally current are Farrar's *Life of Christ* (since 1874); Edersheim's *Life and Times of Jesus the Messiah* (since 1883, revised editions from 1886, abridged ed. 1890); to which should perhaps be added Cunningham Geikie, *Life and Words of Christ* (1877). Of these the best is probably Dr. Edersheim's (with very ample illustrations from Jewish sources); but none of the three can quite be said to grapple with the deeper underlying problems, critical or other. A striking attempt was made by the late Professor J. R. Seeley to realize in modern forms the ethical and social aspect of the Life of Christ in *Ecce Homo* (ed. 6, 1866). And the imaginative works, Dr. Edwin A. Abbott's *Philochristus* (ed. 3, 1878), and the anonymous *As Others Saw Him* (1895, see p. 145 *sup.*), may be consulted with advantage. [Dr. Abbott's later works have been mentioned above (p. 117).]

In French, besides Renan, E. de Pressensé (1866, Eng. tr. same date and later; Protestant) may still be read. Père Didon (1891, also translated; Roman Catholic) represents with dignity the older orthodoxy; and A. Réville (1897) the newer criticism.

The most thoughtful and searching, as well as (if we except Dr. Edersheim) the most learned work, has been done in Germany. The two writers who have tried most earnestly to combine the old with the new are Bernhard Weiss and Beyschlag. Of these we prefer Weiss. His *Leben Jesu* (1882, Eng. tr. 1883,

1884) is a conscientious and thorough piece of work, which, however, has to be studied rather than read. Beyschlag's (1885 and later) is more flowingly written, but also exhibits rather more markedly the weaker side of a mediating theology. Keim's *Jesu von Nazara* (1867–1882, abridged ed. 1873–1883) is impressive from the evident sincerity of its author, his intellectual force and command of his materials, but the critical premisses are unfortunate. A concise *Life* which has just appeared by Dr. P. W. Schmidt of Basel (*Gesch. Jesu*, 1899) seems, if a glance may be trusted, to come under the head of minor works. It gains its conciseness by omitting debatable matter. [This work is now complete : vol. ii. contains elaborate Notes on the text of vol. i. There is also, now translated into English, a larger *Life* by Oscar Holtzmann, which may be said to represent (with a few individualisms of no very great importance) the average opinion of German critical circles.]

The student may be advised to take Weiss for his principal commentary, referring to Schürer (p. 28 *sup.*) or Edersheim for surroundings, and using along with it Tischendorf's *Synopsis Evangelica*, or a Harmony like Stevens and Burton's. He should read *Ecce Homo*.

APPENDIX I.

The Position in 1903.

A Paper read at the Church Congress, Bristol, October 1903.

MY subject is somewhat narrowed down. It deals, not with the New Testament as a whole, but only with the Gospels. At the same time, the Gospels are so very much the most vital part of the whole New Testament, that what applies to them will *a fortiori* apply to the rest, and will even affect the whole Christian position.

From the point of view of the subject assigned to me it may be said that we here in England have entered upon a new period, roughly speaking, with the beginning of the new century. We may take as a landmark the publication in English of Harnack's lectures, known to us under the title, *What is Christianity?* in 1901. The same year saw the appearance of Vol. II. of *Encyclopædia Biblica* (through the accident of the alphabet there had been nothing of great importance for our subject in Vol. I.); and that work has now, as you know, been completed. With the present year we have a new volume of the 'Theological Translation Library,' Wernle's *Beginnings of Christianity*; and we have also had translations of two rather noticeable pamphlets on the Virgin Birth, by Lobstein and Soltau.

The general effect of these publications may be said to be that the English public has been placed more completely on a level with the more advanced criticism on the Continent than it has ever been before. And this applies especially to the particular subject on which I am asked to speak. I have little doubt that the ablest of all the articles on New Testament subjects in the *Encyclopædia Biblica* are those by Professor P. W. Schmiedel, of Zürich. To him have fallen the articles, 'Gospels,' 'John, son of Zebedee,' 'Mary,' 'Resurrection-and-Ascension-Narratives'; and he has treated these crucial subjects with great fulness and thoroughness. The article, 'Nativity,' has fallen to another distinguished German scholar, Professor Hermann Usener, of Bonn. All these articles are significant; they are significant in the history of German as well as of English theology, for I do not think that the views expressed had ever been stated in quite so trenchant a manner. Since the great works of Keim and Weizsäcker there had been rather a lull in the more penetrating criticism of the Gospels. Here in Great Britain I may point to Dr. Hastings' *Dictionary of the Bible*, Dr. Swete's *St. Mark*, Dr. Plummer's *St. Luke*, Sir John C. Hawkins' *Horæ Synopticæ*, and other works as proof that British scholars have not been idle. But it would be true to say that their efforts have been directed primarily to the literary criticism and analysis of the Gospels rather than to the criticism of their subject - matter; it was generally felt that analysis of the documents ought to go further before

the greater and more fundamental questions were
raised

Perhaps the time had come for the next step to be
taken.   But, whether that is so or not, in any case it
has been taken; we are directly face to face with the
whole problem, or series of problems, that the Gospels
raise for us.

It should not be supposed that the writers I have
mentioned, or their English and Scotch sympathizers,
are in all respects simply radical and destructive.
The erratic fancies of the Dutch school (represented
in *Encyclopædia Biblica* by Professor Van Manen) find
no favour in their eyes.   Harnack, in particular, is on
most points of literary criticism decidedly conservative.
Apart from a certain difference of tone in his latest
utterances about the Fourth Gospel, there would not
be a wide interval between his views and those that
are largely held in this country.   Neither is Schmiedel
nor Wernle extreme in literary criticism, strictly as
such.   But in the treatment of the subject-matter of
the Gospels there are some common characteristics
that run through all this recent literature.   I will try
to state these briefly.

I. There is a great tendency to narrow down the
Gospel to the actual teaching of our Lord.   Hitherto
we have most of us been in the habit of describing
by that name the sum of the teaching of the whole
New Testament.   In the hands of the critics it is
reduced to something less than the whole teaching
of the Gospels; the Fourth Gospel is practically put
aside, and considerable deductions are made from the
other three.

II. It is another aspect of the same thing, that the apostolic writers outside the Gospels are criticised with the utmost freedom. For instance, Wernle says in his preface: 'Fidelity to the Christian conscience implies the clearest and most unflinching criticism of all that contradicts it, even though it be received upon the authority of a St. Paul or a St. John, *i.e.* the Gospel is to be employed practically as the canon and standard for all its later historical accretions.' At the outset of his lectures Harnack promised to make use of the apostolic writings to supplement the data supplied by the Gospels; but he never adequately made good this promise.

III. In particular, he did not use these writings as the Christian Church has been in the habit of using them, to complete his estimate of the Person of Christ. The distaste for dogma characteristic of the school reaches its highest under this head. Full value is given to the recognition of our Lord as Son of Man, but it could not be said that equally full value is given to the recognition of Him as Son of God.

IV. In the treatment of the Gospel narrative we observe a general tendency (1) to the denial of the Virgin Birth; (2) to the restriction of miracles to the miracles of healing; (3) to the adoption of some form of the vision-theory of the Resurrection.

On the whole, it must be said that the Christianity of these writers is greatly reduced in its contents; and we are not surprised to find that the criticism which is so freely exercised on the more outlying portions of the New Testament does not spare even that central nucleus from which it takes its start—the teaching of our Lord Himself.

Now the question that will be asked is, How far are these results the natural and logical outcome of the 'newer historical methods'? Are they really so scientific as they claim to be, and are very often supposed to be? I venture to think that they are not. It seems to me that they rest on too narrow a basis. The assumption with which they start—that essential Christianity is confined to the teaching of Christ—is, after all, only an assumption, and, I believe, not a valid assumption.

No great movement can rightly be judged only by its initial stages, or apart from the impression left by it upon the highest contemporary minds.

It is a peculiar advantage that we have in the New Testament the impression made by Christ upon minds endowed with an extraordinary genius for religion. There may be in the writings (*e.g.*) of St. Paul and St. John a certain element that is derived from the current ideas of the time, but behind and beneath this element we can see a fresh and vivid impression that comes straight from the facts.

Hitherto Christians have thought that they could not do better than try to reproduce in themselves an attitude of mind like that which they observe in these great Apostles. And there is much reason to doubt whether any other attitude—and in particular the attitude of the modern critics—can have equal value from the point of view of religion.

Further, we have the advantage of being able to study the experience of other eminent Christians all down the centuries. I conceive that this double study, in the first place of the experience embodied in the New Testament, and in the second place of the like experience carried through eighteen additional centuries of Christian history, is a real induction, and an induction that rests on the widest basis possible.

If we ask ourselves which describes most adequately the total effect of all this experience—the language hitherto held by the whole Christian Church and expressed in its Creeds, or the language now used by a group of critics—we cannot hesitate a moment for the answer.

The critics of whom I have been speaking seem to me to be in too great haste to rationalize the Gospel history. They are too eager to make the narrative of the Gospels conform to the conditions of other narratives, and to make the Life described in it conform to the standard of other lives. I do not think that there is anything, at least in the sounder part of modern historical methods, that compels us to do this. It is one thing 'to read the Bible like any other book,' and another thing to assume that we shall only find in it what is found in other books. Unique spiritual effects require a unique spiritual cause, and we shall never understand the full significance of that cause if we begin by denying or minimizing its uniqueness.

I have always considered the ideal temper to be one that renders to Cæsar the things that are Cæsar's, and to God the things that are God's; in other words, that gives to criticism all that properly belongs to it, and yet leaves room for the full impression of that which is

Divine. What we want to do is to keep a perfectly
open mind towards that which transcends our experience
as well as towards that which falls within it. I am
well aware that this is not an easy thing—that to
determine the exact relations of human and Divine in
the Gospels is a task at once difficult, delicate, and
responsible. I am far from thinking that the last
word has yet been said by anyone ; and I distinctly
recognize that writers from whom I differ very widely
may yet be really suggestive and helpful. But at the
same time I very much hope that we shall hold our
ground in reference to them ; I very much hope that
we shall not model our beliefs on the pattern of
Encyclopædia Biblica.

There is an important warning of Dr. Hort's :
'Criticism is not dangerous except when, as in so
much Christian criticism, it is merely the tool for
reaching a result not itself believed on that ground
but on the ground of speculative postulates' (*Hulsean
Lectures*, p. 177). It is these 'speculative postulates'
that really need to be closely cross-examined. We all
have our postulates ; and for all of us they affect the
whole course of our reasoning ; but it is important that
we should see exactly what they are and where they are
leading us.

In the case of the writers to whom I have been
referring, the postulates are not only speculative or
philosophical ; there are postulates of another kind
that have exercised a deeper influence over their work
than the writers perhaps themselves are aware. They
all start with the same kind of religious ideal, an ideal
which is the more powerful because it is latent rather

than expressed, taken for granted rather than explicitly argued. And this ideal is rather peculiar; it is certainly not common to all Christians; I do not think that it would be very largely shared in the Church of England.

A short time ago, in writing of Harnack's lectures, I could not help remarking that 'there are three things of which he rarely speaks without some disparaging epithet. They are Church, Doctrine, and Worship.' We might say the same thing with yet greater emphasis of Wernle, and I suspect also in a more latent form of Schmiedel. The religious ideal of all three appears to reduce those three things—Church, Doctrine, and Worship—to an absolute minimum. I sometimes wonder what the ideal would be like carried out in practice. It could hardly be that of ordinary Lutheranism. One is almost inclined to suppose that there must be in Germany a sort of professorial religion which exists rather in the air, in a religious Cloud-Cuckoo-Town, and does not correspond to that of any actual religious body.

I have said that this ideal is taken for granted and not explicitly argued. And that is the serious part of it; because the ideal is constantly being invoked, and is constantly affecting the judgment, though it is nowhere distinctly stated and compelled to give an account of itself.

I should not be surprised if Harnack and Wernle (I would rather not speak so definitely of Schmiedel) were under the impression that their own views reflect the teaching of the Gospels, and were even taken from them. But if they do think this, I feel sure that they are very much mistaken. The inference is not sound. It is, I believe, far too roughly and inconsiderately drawn. But in any case, I have little doubt that this is where the weak point in the argument lies—in the region of pre-suppositions. It is the pre-suppositions which need a far more serious testing than they have ever received.

The truth is that all these writers represent a reaction—and, as I am convinced, an excess of reaction —against the historical tradition of the Church. The true solution, I feel sure, is to be sought more on Church lines, *i.e.*, with more regard for historical continuity, with a firmer faith that the Divine guidance of the Church throughout all these centuries has not been really, and even fundamentally, wrong.

APPENDIX II.

The Position in 1905.

A Paper read at the Diocesan Conferences at Chichester and Taunton, November 1905.

I UNDERSTAND that I am invited to give a sort of report on the present position of New Testament criticism, more especially in its bearing upon the clergy and their outlook for themselves and for their people. And I understand also that, to do this at all adequately, I ought not to confine myself to this country, but to look abroad to the Continent and America, and to see what clouds there are on the horizon.

There are clouds upon the horizon—clouds that may be fertilizing though they are, perhaps, at first sight, disquieting. And it may be well for us to look at them a little in the distance before they come nearer. The present state of things is one that was sure to come sooner or later; and, when it came, it could not but have a certain gravity. There are three stages in the history of criticism—not necessarily succeeding each other in order of time—to some extent going on concurrently, but yet with a tendency to follow each other in succession. The first may be called the stage of literary criticism—the stage at which the principal

252

questions discussed have to do with the authorship, structure and composition, and date of the New Testament writings. This stage may be said to be drawing to its close. No doubt it will go on more or less actively for some time; but the period of greatest pressure is in all probability past. The second stage is *2* that of <u>historical criticism</u>. This is at present in full course; and it has advanced to a point at which it is really passing into the third stage, which may be described as that of <u>ultimate problems</u>. It is because these *3* questions are coming to the front with some insistence that I have characterized the situation as presenting a certain gravity.

<u>The group of literary questions</u> relating to the New Testament has had the greatest amount of work done upon it, and it <u>would seem to be coming to at least a provisional conclusion</u>. Some of my hearers may remember Harnack's famous preface to his elaborate work on the *Chronology of Early Christian Literature*, written (*i.e.* the preface) in 1896. The main point in that preface was that the interest in purely literary questions affecting the New Testament might be expected to decline, because it was coming to be agreed that—broadly speaking and upon the whole—Christian tradition was right. The attitude of suspicion which had marked so much New Testament criticism since Baur, was seen to be unreasonable. <u>On the whole, the early Christian writings had stood the tests applied to them.</u> It is interesting to think that probably the turning-point in this long controversy was the searching examination by our own Bishop Lightfoot, and by Zahn in Germany, of the genuineness of the Ignatian Letters.

Harnack himself considered only one of the New Testament Books to be in the strict sense 'pseudonymous' (*i.e.* put forward under an assumed name), the Second Epistle of St. Peter. It is right to say that, in giving this general verdict, there were other books the genuineness of which Harnack took with some qualification— the Fourth Gospel, the Pastoral Epistles, the Catholic Epistles, and the Apocalypse. But his point was that there was no book (except 2 St. Peter) the tradition as to which had not some substantial ground. I am not, of course, quoting Harnack's opinion as final; I only take it as summing up what an eminent scholar believed to be the general tendency of expert opinion at the time.

Nine years have elapsed since Harnack wrote to this effect, and in the main his forecast has been made good. There has been some rather sharp controversy, not as yet brought to an end, about the Fourth Gospel. The points that Harnack treated as somewhat doubtful remain somewhat doubtful still. But on the whole the tendency, as he described it, has been maintained. Extravagant theories — I am speaking, be it remembered, of literary theories—are on all hands being discarded. The extreme Dutch school is losing its hold in Holland itself, and sober views generally prevail. The experience of the past has by this time taught so much that I do not anticipate that this state of things will be greatly altered.

Perhaps I ought at this point to say something about two novelties of method recently advocated by Professor Cheyne (*Bible Problems*, 1904). He bids us be prepared for a new textual criticism of the New Testament, for

which he appeals especially to the writings of Mr. F. C.
Conybeare.   As yet this criticism has been put forward
tentatively and sporadically, rather in regard to particular readings than upon a general survey of principles.
A typical example was examined by Dr. Chase in the
July number of the *Journal of Theological Studies*
('The Lord's command to Baptize,' Mt 28^{19}).   The
familiar reading of this verse is questioned on grounds
which Dr. Chase shows to be wholly insufficient, and
I quite agree with him.   I ought to warn you that
this newer textual criticism does not at all correspond
to that which is at the present time most in favour
among our classical scholars.   It does not turn upon
the weighing of external authorities.   The external
authorities, rich and abundant as they are, are not
really weighed.   There is no attempt to reconstruct the
history of readings.   A very slight amount of external
evidence is held to be enough, if the reading which it
attests, or seems to attest, deviates from the current
tradition.   Some of the more important readings con-
tended for have no MS authority at all, but rest entirely
upon patristic quotations, perhaps only in a single writer.
I must needs think that this kind of foundation is
most precarious.

   It is not surprising that Dr. Cheyne, coming to the
New Testament from the Old, should find himself
attracted by this method.   I do not wish to express
any opinion as to his own treatment of the text of the
Old Testament.   I am no Hebraist; and to form an
estimate of Hebrew readings is beyond my competence.
I know that there have been scholars, like Bentley, endowed with a gift which almost amounts to divination.

Of course, the vast majority, even of Bentley's readings, were uncalled for, and certainly wrong. We are told that 'it was his forte to make rough places smooth, his foible to make smooth places rough' (Jebb, *Bentley*, p. 190). His *Paradise Lost* is a warning. I have often wondered how far the readings advocated in the Old Testament are really Bentleyan, in the good sense. But I cannot help seeing that there is a strongly defined difference between the Old Testament and the New. In the case of the Old Testament there is an interval of many centuries between the oldest extant Hebrew MSS and the dates at which the books were composed. Granting that we can push back the beginnings of the Massoretic text to the first half of the second century, and granting that the transmission of the text has been comparatively uniform from that time onwards, the interval still remains wide; and we know that within this interval the texts were exposed to great vicissitudes and were copied with great freedom. A comparison of the Septuagint with the Hebrew, or such facts as the state of the Alphabetical Psalms, for instance, are proof that the text has undergone considerable depravation. I can, therefore, entirely follow such a cautious treatment of the text as that in Dr. Driver's *Parallel Psalter*. I can even go further, and see that beyond this there is room for a certain amount of conjecture; though it is important that we should know when we are guessing, and still more when we are building up one guess on the top of another.[1]

[1] Dr. F. G. Kenyon, at the end of an interesting paper on the bearing upon textual criticism of recent discoveries of early Greek papyri, writes as follows: 'It cannot be denied that in general

But the difference is great when we pass over to the New Testament. There we have MSS, both Greek and Latin, going back to the fourth century; we have versions, like the Latin and Syriac, going back to the second; we have patristic quotations which begin to be copious by the end of the second century. The lines of descent that are drawn to readings attested by these various authorities take us up very near to the autographs themselves. In these conditions the place left for conjecture must be very small, and, as a matter of fact, in the New Testament the textual critic hardly feels the need of conjecture, and if he exercises at all, does so very sparingly. I have no doubt that in this he is right, and that the attempts that are being made to draw him into other paths are at once superfluous and misleading.

The other method which Dr. Cheyne commends is based upon a comparison of the mythology of non-Christian religions. The examples given under this head fall into two classes.

1. It is doubtless true that the figures of speech employed both in the Old and New Testaments have their history, and that history carries us back sometimes into the field of mythology. A verse like Is 52^9 'Art thou not it that cut Rahab in pieces, that pierced the dragon?' has its connections both forwards

the papyri do not support the conjectures of modern scholars. When they do the variations have generally been quite small; in no case, it may safely be said, has any sweeping change been justified by the papyri. . . . The chances against successful divination are great; and, even if a critic should chance to be right, it is hardly possible to demonstrate his success' (*Proceedings of the British Academy*, i. 166).

17

and backwards. I can well believe that the 'dragon' of Rev. 12$^{3, 4, 7}$ may belong to the same group of conceptions, and I would not deny that it may ultimately have affinities with the Babylonian *Tiâmat* (the chaos-dragon). My feeling about such things is very much as when one looks out the etymology of a word in the dictionary. If one goes back far enough, one may find that it is connected with a Sanscrit root; the connection is real, and the history may be continuous, though it will not throw very much light upon the modern use. In like manner these mythological parallels may help us a little, but not much. At most they only affect the embroidery, so to speak, of the Biblical conception.

2. There are other examples which are of more importance than this—such, for instance, as those which are brought to bear upon the Virgin Birth. Dr. Cheyne, I observe, treats some of these as relevant and others as not relevant. And it is, no doubt, desirable that each should be examined upon its own merits. What I would chiefly deprecate is the assumption that the existence of these analogies justifies us in dismissing at once the whole class of phenomena to which they belong. We are learning by degrees to think of Christianity, not as something entirely isolated in the history of the world, but as the climax and crown of other religions. We are indeed coming round by a strange circuit, and with a different set of categories, to a view which presents many points of contact with that of such ancient Christian thinkers as Justin and Clement of Alexandria. Justin held that there were seeds of the Divine Word diffused among the pagan religions. These religions contained elements of truth

which had been corrupted and perverted by the activity
of demons.   We, too, recognize that there have been
evil influences at work as well as good.   We must
think of the whole system of things as adapted to
imperfect, and not perfect, beings.   But over all a
Divine providence reigns, and nothing is exempt from
its operation.   Instead of simply dismissing phenomena
to which we seem to have grown superior, it is better
to ask ourselves the question, what was God's purpose
in permitting them; what place did they bear in the
whole economy of things?   There is a truth in the
assumption that exceptional lives must have begun in
an exceptional way.   And if this truth has sometimes
been expressed in forms very different from the Christian,
we must take the world-process as a whole; and we
must judge it by its end and not by its beginnings.   We
must look not so much at its rudiments as at its
culmination; or, rather, we should look at its rudiments in the light of its culmination.   History derives
a new meaning when we think of it as issuing in the
Incarnation.

I prefer to rest—and I believe that we may well rest
—in general considerations such as these.   There is
a point beyond which curiosity cannot profitably be
carried.   More tangible results are to be obtained from
an examination of the main narrative of the Gospels
and Acts.   This is the proper field of historical criticism.
And in this field it must be acknowledged that much
has been gained.   Here, too, as well as in the field of
literary criticism, there has been a very real reaction.
The wholesale scepticism of the times of Strauss and
Baur has come to an end.   The study of the New

Testament has shared in the improved knowledge of antiquity in general. The actors in the history are treated more as living men and living women. The surroundings among which they moved are more fully understood. A sustained endeavour has been made to follow sympathetically the processes of their thought. On all hands there has been an effort to penetrate through *formulæ* learnt by rote to inner realities. The note of a higher sincerity runs through the teaching of our time. The broad basis, so to speak, of early Christian history is being more securely laid; extravagances are being pruned away, and erratic experiments dropped.

It is really in regard to what I have called ultimate problems, the highest questions arising out of the history, that the stress is being felt at present. It is being felt in England. There has been a good deal of discussion amongst us about the real significance, more particularly of two clauses of the Apostles' Creed. But what with us has been desultory, on the Continent—and especially in Germany—has been more systematic. And it is to this movement of criticism in Germany that I consider it my duty to direct your attention.

Perhaps some surprise may be felt that I should give precedence to this over the French movement, associated with the name of the Abbé Loisy. The knowledge of French is more widespread in this country than the knowledge of German, and it is probable that M. Loisy's books have been read by many of the clergy, and have made some impression. For the internal history of the Church of Rome his work is no doubt of great significance. Also on the theory of development and the

course of Church history there is much to be learnt
from him. But his Biblical criticism overshoots the
mark too far to be really important. Besides, difficult
as it would be for most of us to combine his critical
views with his views on doctrine, we must recognize
the fact that in doctrine he is not an innovator.

Really the German factor is the most important.
What Germany is saying to-day, many circles in Europe
and America will be saying to-morrow. And there are
special features to attract our attention in what is going
on in Germany at the present time.

We might say that since the beginning of the new
century a change has come over the method of German
theology. It had been prepared for before that date,
but in these recent years it has become more pronounced.

The leading characteristic is that, instead of being
highly technical and elaborate, as we had been accustomed to see it, it has of late become much more
popular. It has definitely laid itself out to appeal to
the people. And it has acquired in a marked degree
the popular qualities of directness, force, and vividness
of presentation.

Another comparatively new characteristic is the tendency to combined enterprises. The German professor
of the past, as a rule, stood by himself and played for
his own hand; but we now see strong groups, especially of the younger professors, uniting together in
popular publications. I do not refer only to the
increase in the number of excellently organized
magazines, such as the *Theologische Rundschau*, but I
have in mind more particularly—(1) A series of popular

tracts known as the *Religions-geschichtliche Volksbücher*, or 'Tracts on Religious History,' edited by Schiele of Marburg; and (2) a new translation, with introductions and commentaries, also addressed to the general public, of the books of the New Testament, under the editorship of Johannes Weiss, the son of the well-known Professor Bernhard Weiss of Berlin. Both these series must be described as very good in their kind. Johannes Weiss is one of the ablest of the rising young professors. He has among his colleagues Jülicher, whose *Introduction to the New Testament* has been translated into English by Miss Janet Ward, and Bousset, editor of the *Rundschau*, who takes the tract on 'Jesus' in the other series; that on the 'Sources for the Life of Jesus' is by Professor Paul Wernle of Basel, whose *Beginnings of Christianity* has also been translated into English among the publications of the Theological Translation Fund (Williams & Norgate). Not mixed up in these joint undertakings is Professor Freiherr Hermann von Soden of Berlin, who has lately brought out two considerable pamphlets—one on the *Writings of the New Testament*, and the other on the *Leading Problems of the Life of Christ*. These pamphlets are very similar in character to the works of which I have just been speaking, and have the same general object. Along with them may be mentioned the three Lives of Christ, by O. Holtzmann (translated), P. W. Schmidt and Rudolf Otto.[1]

Now there are two common properties to be noticed in all this literature. The first is its moderation, from

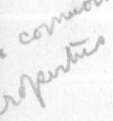

---

[1] I should like also to refer to a valuable constructive essay by Deissman in *Beiträge zur Weiterentwicklung der christl. Religion*.

the point of view of literary criticism.   It may be said
generally to represent the standpoint taken up by
Harnack in his preface, to which I have referred—that is
to say, it (or, rather, much of it) treats all the Pauline
Epistles as genuine except the Pastorals, and these it
regards as worked up from Pauline materials.   The
other fact to be noticed is that on the most important
and central points of all—the Divine Person of our Lord
—the writers cut themselves adrift from the universal
verdict of the Church and from traditional Christianity.
They make no attack upon the Creeds, but they deliberately ignore them, and in one or two places where this
most important question would naturally come up, they
in set terms deny what the Creeds affirm.   As a rule,
the central doctrine of all is not so much contested as
quietly put aside.   The constructive view of primitive
Christianity is built up without it.

It is difficult to describe the attitude of these writers
with perfect justice.   In the main it is not aggressive.
Where it is aggressive—as, no doubt, it is strongly in
the case of Wernle—the attack is aimed not against the
Gospels or their contents, but against the formulation
of Church doctrine.   There is much impatience of this
all round, but in regard to our Lord Himself the attitude
is wholly reverent.   Indeed, I began by asking myself
whether it was not possible that the negative expressions that are occasionally met with might not be,
perhaps, only a strong assertion of our Lord's complete
humanity.   I am afraid that in the instances that I
have in mind there is something more than this.   Still,
even in the writers in whom they occur they are not at
all prominent, and there are some writers in whom they

do not occur at all.   It is common to the whole school
to reject the ideas of a miraculous Birth or a miraculous
Resurrection.   But, apart from this, there is in greater
or less degree what we may call, perhaps, an open side
in the conception of the Person of our Lord; a side, I
mean, that is not bounded by a hard-and-fast line of
negation, but that does lie open in the direction of the
Divine.   One of the best points is, that the sense of
wonder is still retained.   There is the feeling that there
is something—the writers do not attempt to say what
—that cannot be measured by ordinary standards.   It
might perhaps be said that the general position is like
that which we associate with the better Unitarianism.

It will be understood that the negative result, as far
as it goes, could only be obtained by throwing over not
merely the unanimous judgment of the Catholic Church,
but all real authority of such Apostles as St. Paul and
St. John.   For the writers of whom I am speaking it
may be said that practically there is no such thing as
authority of any kind.   There may be, and there is, a
great deal of very genuine admiration, but this does
not necessarily imply belief.   We may say briefly that
the data worked up in a constructive sense are derived
entirely from the synoptical portions of the first three
Gospels (of course, excluding the first two chapters
of St. Matthew and St. Luke) and from the ideas as
to what is historically probable current now in the
twentieth century.

It will be seen that this position is really an extension
of that taken up in Harnack's famous lectures.   It is
the views there expressed pushed to their logical
conclusion, with the negatives in some cases inserted

which Harnack did not insert. Harnack, you will remember, professed to take in St. Paul and St. John in his estimate of what was really essential in Christianity; but, as a matter of fact, he never did so, or did not do so at all adequately.

This alone must surely be regarded as a serious defect. An adequate estimate of Christianity cannot be formed in this way, just from the common material of the Synoptic Gospels. To suppose that it is possible to leave out St. Paul and St. John is in itself an immense assumption. It is an assumption so immense that I only do not like to lay stress upon it still more, because it seems to me that the writers of whom I have been speaking have not themselves arrived at clear ideas about it. They must realize that this is, on the very threshold, a difficulty with which they will have to reckon. And then, it is only the first of their difficulties, just as St. Paul and St. John are the first links in the chain of Christian thought and Christian history. That which purports to be in any sense an estimate of Christianity must deal with it as a whole, and cannot be allowed to stop short at what is really only, as it were, its alphabet.

Apart from this, when we come to close quarters with the theory, we see that even if we could grant the data on which it rests, those data would not be satisfied. I will return to this point before I have done.

I have no doubt you will think that from a theory such as I have described, it cannot be possible for you to draw for yourselves much in the way of encouragement or reassurance. You will think that it belongs to the general pessimism in which the present outlook may seem to be involved. I suppose that we most of us in this country have our moments of pessimism; the Americans are the only confirmed optimists with whom I am acquainted, and that is one of the reasons why it is good for us to come in contact with them. And yet I cannot but think that the pessimistic inference would be wrong, and that we shall see it to be wrong when we recover our balance. I believe that after all there is a hopeful side to the state of things that we are contemplating.

In the first place, you will think it a small mercy and little enough to be thankful for; and yet I confess that I am thankful when I call to mind the fact that this latest phase of criticism—the last stage of a process that has been going on for nearly one hundred and fifty years—should leave us so much as it does. The furnace has certainly been heated seven times over, and yet this group of facts, the common matter of the Synoptic Gospels, remains substantially unscathed. Of course it too has been questioned, and it is being questioned still in some quarters, but not by a sane criticism or a criticism really founded upon knowledge. The criticism of which I have been speaking—that of von Soden and Johannes Weiss and Bousset—is sane, and it is founded upon knowledge. It seems to be safe to say that what these men do not question will never be questioned with success. Doubts may be raised, but they will never permanently hold their ground. We have, then, I cannot but think, in the criticism of these men an irreducible minimum. And that minimum, I must needs think, is an Archimedean point; grant us so much, and we shall recover what ought to be recovered in time.

That is what I conceive to be the first hopeful sign; and the second is another aspect, or particular illustration, of the first. What is now left us, we may be sure is built upon the solid rock; the gates of Hades itself will not prevail against it. But what does this rescued matter contain? It contains two things which I believe will be found to be the key to all the rest. The scholars to whom I have been referring are agreed—or, if they are not yet all quite agreed, they are bound to become so in the long-run—(1) That our Lord really believed Himself to be the Messiah, and (2) that He also believed Himself to be in a unique sense Son of God. There may be dispute over what we mean by 'unique sense.' It is allowed that our Lord Jesus Christ drew a clear distinction between Himself and all the children of men. That is the foundation-stone of the Creeds. Grant us that, and the rest will follow.

These two concessions are my second ground of hope. They are axioms which I conceive bar the way against any further fall. The Christian faith can, I believe, be reconstructed out of them. My third ground of hope is one that will perhaps surprise you. I have had so much to criticise in the writers I have mentioned by name that you will hardly expect me to end by pronouncing a eulogy upon them. But it would not be candid in me not to do so. For one thing, the writings of these men in Germany mark a reaction in favour of religion. The position there is distinctly better than it was some fifteen years ago. For another thing, it is true the three writers, von Soden, Bousset, and

Johannes Weiss, have all in the course of their papers
said things that I regard as nothing less than admirable. I very much doubt whether we have anything so admirable in English. Occasional passages
may, perhaps, be found in Newman which cover some
of the points to which I am about to refer, but I greatly
doubt if he or any other English writer has collected them
altogether in such a well-balanced whole. I have in
view the portraiture—the human portraiture of our
Lord Jesus Christ. All three writers have said excellent
things about this. I will only quote from one, Baron
von Soden. I will venture to quote from him at some
length, because it seems to me that to do full justice he
should be quoted at some length; and you shall judge
for yourselves.

He is arguing against the view of Bernhard Weiss,
to which I believe that there is something parallel in
Bishop Gore's *Bampton Lectures* (see pp. 168-171), that
the personality of our Lord is so universal that we are
not to look for individual traits in it. Von Soden calls
this Docetism; and he asserts that, on the contrary,
the portrait of Christ has marked individual features.
I am not sure that the two views are really so opposed
as they may seem; but we will hear what von Soden
has to say first. We must make allowance for the
point of view; if we were writing ourselves, our
language would not be quite the same; and yet it need
not be very different, because we too believe that our
Lord was very Man :—

'Jesus is of a fiery temperament, which is yet at
the same time gentle, which can be patient and wait
but at the decisive moment strikes and does not spare.

He sees things just as they are.   In His clear eye are
reflected the quiet pictures of nature with all their
charms as clearly as the many-coloured life of men, as
the inexorable relations of fact with all their consequences.   And yet with this eye of the realist, He can
also see with deep insight below the surface of things ;
every passing show becomes to Him parable (*Alles
Vergängliche wird ihm zum Gleichnis*).   And through
all that men do or leave undone He reads into their
hearts.   He loves contemplation ; quiet is the home of
the soul to which He constantly resorts ; but along
with this there goes a force of energy that cannot rest,
but as constantly drives Him into the life of men.   His
was a nature essentially practical.   He saw all things
in concrete reality.   Every kind of theorizing, abstrac-
tion, speculation, and philosophy lay far from Him.
And yet He always saw the particular in its connection
with the whole.   He never lost Himself in casuistry.
Jesus is an individualist.   His concern is with the
single human soul.   And yet He is not an individualist.
For every human soul is to Him of equal value.   He
always has in view the whole world of men and its
needs.   The leading idea of His preaching, the kingdom
of God, is a social factor.   Jesus was a poet.   With
the eye of a poet He looked upon nature, and observed
the ways of men.   He had the plastic skill to describe
the intricate life in nature, the manifold shapings of
destiny in the life of men.   And yet He wrote no
poetry; His mission was to act and to create.   The
nature of Jesus was not unsocial.   He does not with-
draw from active intercourse ; He rather courts it
But He never loses Himself among men.   He is never
merged in society.   He is constantly drawn towards
the loneliness of the mountain, of the desert, of night.

The nature of Jesus was peaceful, and yet He does not
shrink from conflict.   Indeed, one has the impression
that His spirits rose when the swords crossed and
flashed in the play of battle.   He seeks out His
opponent, and compels him to stand.   It is the Prince
of Peace who says, "I am not come to bring peace,
but a sword."   Jesus was very tolerant towards men.
He could understand every failing.   And yet He was
inexorably strict in His moral judgment.   To the man
who thought himself right when he was really wrong
He showed no mercy.

   ' He shapes His own world spontaneously, altogether
from within outwards, in a way that is in the highest
sense original.   In the strength of this world He
ignores as of no account the ideas and customs of His
countrymen that do not agree with it ; the very thought
of compromise does not enter His mind ; and yet, in
spite of all this, He is full of piety towards all that has
come down from the past.   He is no critic.   Whatever
is worthless or untenable drops away from Him, as it
were of itself.   This is His attitude towards the sacred
Scriptures of His people.   Whatever in them is transitory is as though He did not notice it, so little does it
affect Him or engage His attention.   He is no revolutionary, not even a reformer.   He left the world just
as it was, and built up another of His own by its side,
or on the top of it.

   ' And this nature of His is sound to the core.   In
spite of all its inwardness, there is not a trace of
emotional excess.   In spite of all the intensity of
devotion, there is nothing of ecstasy or visions.
Apocalyptic dreams take no hold on His soul.   What
He says is, as it were, all of a piece—it comes up
spontaneously, clear as crystal, out of His soul.   For

Him there are no "ifs" and "buts."   He finds at once
the decisive point.   In His mind the most intricate
questions resolve themselves as if by magic.

'All His ideas take their bearing from those of His
people, from their customs, from their laws.   The conceptions that He finds in existence, as the product
of their development, He utilizes and makes them the
vehicles for His own ideas.   For all the piety with
which Jesus clings to tradition, for all the sureness
with which He discerns the voice of God in the sacred
Scriptures of His people, He is not bound down by any
authority, not even that of Moses, though He is glad
to appeal to it, and that perhaps not only for the sake
of His opponents.

'We may see from many of these traits that in the
nature of Jesus there was no lack of contrasts.   But
they are always resolved in the wonderful completeness
and harmony of His being.   The opposites are always
in equilibrium.   Therefore His personality, many-sided
as it is, is not complicated.   In the last resort they are
not indeed so many independent qualities ; but, strictly
speaking, under the action of His human nature and
its surroundings, they are just so many prismatic rays
in the diamond of His soul' (*Die wichtigsten Fragen
im Leben Jesu*, pp. 85–88).

I must not quote any more, though I find it hard to
break off—and the more so because the next paragraph
deals with the love of Jesus for mankind, which compelled Him, 'instead of living in blissful content in
Himself and in His God, to devote Himself to the
service of men and on the altar of that service to offer
up His own soul, His own peace, His own heaven.'
And the next topic is His consciousness as Son.   You

will understand the temptation to reproduce more of these paragraphs. But really the passage that I have quoted is complete in itself. You will have observed that there is a single idea underlying it all—and it is this idea which seems to me to make it so valuable— viz. the idea of the apparent contrasts that are fused and harmonized in the human character of Christ. As the writer truly says, they are not really contrasts, but rather 'prismatic rays' in a single gem. And I am a little surprised that he does not seem to see that this is a sufficient answer to his criticism of Bernhard Weiss. After all, the unity transcends the differences. And what a transcendent unity it is! How does it take us up to the very heart and centre of all that we call human! What in another would have been so many idiosyncrasies, in Him are sublimely universal. Are we not carried down to the very bases of being? We most of us live, as it were, in compartments; and our vision is bounded by these compartments; but the truths that lay open to our Lord are elemental and eternal. May we not say that, if there was to be an incarnation of the Divine in human form, this and nothing else would be the form that it would assume?

And then I will also ask you to recall what was said about the sense of Messiahship and the filial relation to God. It is allowed that these are distinct and deeply rooted features in the consciousness of Christ. When we give due weight to this fact, does it not carry us a long way on the road towards the Christianity of the Creeds? And is not the portrait that results as a whole marked by a singular coherence and consistency? The coherence and consistency hold good so long as we think of the sense of Messiahship and Sonship as real: they are dissipated and lost if we permit ourselves to think of them as a delusion.

The last remark, with which I will bring this lengthy paper to a close, has reference to the author of the quotation. Can we afford to think of one who writes with so much insight, and who, if I am not mistaken, helps us so much with our own questionings, as an enemy? I hardly think we can, in spite of the divergence which separates his opinions from ours. Rather, it seems to me that the problem, the very grave problem, which lies before the Church of England at this moment is how to appropriate and assimilate the really valuable material in the writings of this author and his allies without relaxing our grasp upon our own fundamental beliefs.

18

Printed by
MORRISON & GIBB LIMITED
Edinburgh

SOME WORKS REFERRED TO IN THIS BOOK

AND

PUBLISHED BY MESSRS. T. & T. CLARK.

————◆————

HASTINGS' DICTIONARY OF THE BIBLE:

Dealing with its Language, Literature, and Contents, including the Biblical Theology. With Maps and Illustrations. Now complete, in Five Volumes (including the *Extra* Volume), with full Indexes. Price per Volume, in cloth, 28s. ; in half-morocco, from 34s.

This great work has taken its place, as ' The Times ' says, as ' the standard authority for biblical students of the present generation.' In this country and America, in the Colonies, and even among people of other languages and of various creeds, it is in constant and increasing demand.

The *Guardian* says : 'We have no hesitation in recommending Hastings' Dictionary to students of the Bible as the best work of its kind which exists in English.'

The *Methodist Recorder* says : 'It is far away in advance of any other Bible Dictionary that has ever been published, in real usefulness for preachers, Bible students, and teachers.'

The *Bookman* says : 'This Dictionary sprang into fame with its first volume, and its reputation has been growing ever since. For scholarship, temper, and judgment combined, we have nothing else equal to it in English.'

————

THE WORDS OF JESUS:

Considered in the Light of Post-Biblical Jewish Writings and the Aramaic Language. By Prof. G. DALMAN, Leipzig. *Authorised English Translation* by Prof. D. M. KAY, St. Andrews. Post 8vo, 7s. 6d. net.

' The most critical and scientific examination of the leading conceptions of the Gospels that has yet appeared.'—Prof. W. SANDAY, LL.D.

THE LIFE OF OUR LORD UPON THE EARTH:

Considered in its Historical, Chronological, and Geographical Relations. By the Rev. SAMUEL J. ANDREWS. A New and Revised Edition (the only Authorised Edition in this Country). Demy 8vo, 9s.

** This book has long been an acknowledged authority with scholars and with the general public. In order to retain for it the rank it has gained, the author has undertaken a complete revision, having almost entirely rewritten the work in the light of recent researches.

'As a teacher's apparatus, I would recommend—(1) *Andrews' Life of Our Lord*, an unpretentious but excellent book, in which the apologetic difficulties in the details of the life are treated with much candour and success.'— Professor J. STALKER, D.D.

THE LIFE OF CHRIST.

By Dr. BERNHARD WEISS, Professor of Theology, Berlin. Three Vols. 8vo, 18s. net.

'The authority of John's Gospel is vindicated with great fulness and success. Altogether the book seems destined to hold a very distinguished, if not absolutely unique, place in the criticism of the New Testament. Its fearless search after truth, its independence of spirit, its extent of research, its thoughtful and discriminating tone, must secure for it a very high reputation.' —*Congregationalist.*

THE JEWISH AND THE CHRISTIAN MESSIAH:

A Study in the Earliest History of Christianity. By Prof. VINCENT HENRY STANTON, M.A., D.D., Trinity College, Cambridge. Demy 8vo, 10s. 6d.

'Dr. Stanton's book answers a real want, and will be indispensable to students of the origin of Christianity.'—*Guardian.*

and Published by Messrs. T. and T. Clark.

ROMANS.

By the Rev. WILLIAM SANDAY, D.D., LL.D., Litt.D., Lady Margaret Professor of Divinity and Canon of Christ Church, Oxford, and the Rev. ARTHUR C. HEADLAM, D.D., Principal of King's College, London. In post 8vo, Fifth Edition (562 pp.), 12s.

Principal F. H. CHASE, D.D., Cambridge, says: 'We welcome it as an epoch-making contribution to the study of St. Paul.'

'This is an excellent commentary, scholarly, clear, doctrinal, reverent, and learned. . . . It is a volume which will bring credit to English scholarship, and while it is the crown of much good work on the part of the elder editor, it gives promise of equally good work in the future from both.'—*Guardian.*

'A most valuable gift to the student of Romans. . . . It is the fullest and freshest in learning, the most patient, the most willing to be intelligible, and to make the Apostle so ; and it need not be added, in any work of Dr. Sanday, that in textual criticism it will be a standard authority.'—*British Weekly.*

'Will at once take its place in the front rank of similar works. Its rich fulness of learning, its careful and dispassionate statement of difficulties, and its candour, which will not affect an undue positiveness, call upon us to give it a very hearty welcome.'—*Record.*

'It stands easily at the head of English commentaries. It has qualities, especially in what concerns the text, in which it is superior to the best works of Continental scholars.'—*Critical Review.*

GREEK - ENGLISH LEXICON OF THE NEW TESTAMENT,

Being Grimm's Wilke's Clavis Novi Testamenti. Translated, Revised, and Enlarged by Prof. JOSEPH HENRY THAYER, D.D., Harvard University. Fourth Edition, demy 4to, price 36s.

'The best New Testament Greek Lexicon. . . . It is a treasury of the results of exact scholarship.'—BISHOP WESTCOTT.

'An excellent book, the value of which for English students will, I feel sure, be best appreciated by those who use it most carefully.'—Professor F. J. A. HORT, D.D.

'This work has been eagerly looked for. . . . The result is an excellent book, which I do not doubt will be the best in the field for many years to come.'—Professor W. SANDAY, D.D., in the *Academy.*

'Undoubtedly the best of its kind. Beautifully printed and well translated, . . . it will be prized by students of the Christian Scriptures.'—*Athenæum.*

The International Critical Commentary

ON THE HOLY SCRIPTURES OF THE OLD AND NEW TESTAMENTS.

UNDER THE EDITORSHIP OF

The Rev. S. R. DRIVER, D.D., Oxford; the Rev. A. PLUMMER, M.A., D.D., Durham; and the Rev. C. A. BRIGGS, D.D., New York.

'The publication of this series marks an epoch in English exegesis.'—*British Weekly*.

The First Twelve Volumes are now ready, viz.:—

In post 8vo (540 pp.), price 12s.,

Numbers. By Professor G. BUCHANAN GRAY, D.D, Oxford.

Church Bells says: 'Dr. Gray's commentary will be indispensable to every English student.'

In post 8vo, Third Edition (530 pp.), price 12s.,

Deuteronomy. By Professor S. R. DRIVER, D.D., Oxford.

Prof. G. A. SMITH says: 'The series could have had no better introduction than this volume from its Old Testament editor. . . . Dr. Driver has achieved a commentary of rare learning and still more rare candour and sobriety of judgment.'

In post 8vo, Second Edition (526 pp.), price 12s.,

Judges. By Professor GEORGE F. MOORE, D.D., Harvard University.

BISHOP H. E. RYLE, D.D., says: 'I think it may safely be averred that so full and scientific a commentary upon the text and subject-matter of the Book of Judges has never been produced in the English language.'

In post 8vo (460 pp.), price 12s.,

The Books of Samuel. By Professor HENRY P. SMITH, D.D., Amherst College.

Literature says: 'The most complete and minute commentary hitherto published.'

In post 8vo (590 pp.), price 12s.,

The Book of Proverbs. By Professor C. H. TOY, D.D., Harvard University.

The *Bookman* says: 'The commentary is full, though scholarly and business like, and must at once take its place as the authority on "Proverbs."'

Volumes now ready (continued)—

In post 8vo (600 pp.), price 12s.,

Amos and Hosea. By President W. R. HARPER, Ph.D., Chicago University.

The *Methodist Recorder* says: 'For thoroughness and excellence of workmanship, for clearness of arrangement and exposition, and for comprehensiveness and accuracy in the handling of textual, grammatical, and exegetical questions, this work should rank among the foremost.'

In post 8vo (375 pp.), price 10s. 6d.,

St. Mark's Gospel. By Professor EZRA P. GOULD, D.D., Philadelphia.

The *Baptist Magazine* says: 'As luminously suggestive as it is concise and sober. The commentary proper is thoughtful, judicious, and erudite—the work of a master in hermeneutics.'

In post 8vo, Fourth Edition (678 pp.), price 12s.,

St. Luke's Gospel. By Rev. ALFRED PLUMMER, D.D.

The *Guardian* says: 'We feel heartily that the book will bring credit to English scholarship, and that in its carefulness, its sobriety of tone, its thoughtfulness, its reverence, it will contribute to a stronger faith in the essential trustworthiness of the gospel record.'

In post 8vo, Fifth Edition (562 pp.), price 12s.,

Romans. By Professor WILLIAM SANDAY, D.D., LL.D., Oxford, and Principal A. C. HEADLAM, D.D., London.

The BISHOP OF ELY says: 'We welcome it as an epoch-making contribution to the study of St. Paul.'

In post 8vo (368 pp.), price 10s. 6d.,

Ephesians and Colossians. By Professor T. K. ABBOTT, D.Lit., Dublin.

The *Expository Times* says: 'There is no work in all the "International" series that is more faithful or more felicitous. . . . Dr. Abbott understands these Epistles —we had almost said as if he had written them.'

In post 8vo (240 pp.), price 8s. 6d.,

Philippians and Philemon. By Professor MARVIN R. VINCENT, D.D., New York.

The *Scotsman* says: 'In every way worthy of the series which was so well commenced [in the New Testament] with the admirable commentary on the Romans by Dr. Sanday and Dr. Headlam.'

In post 8vo, Second Edition (370 pp.), price 10s. 6d.,

St. Peter and St. Jude. By Professor CHARLES BIGG, D.D., Oxford.

The *Guardian* says: 'A first-rate critical edition of these Epistles has been for a long time a felt want in English theological literature . . . this has been at last supplied by the labours of Canon Bigg. . . . His notes are full of interest and suggestiveness.'

** *A Prospectus, giving full details of the Series, with list of Contributors, post free on application.*

Eras of the Christian Church.

EDITED BY JOHN FULTON, D.D., LL.D.

In Ten Volumes, price 6s. each.

The *Guardian* says: 'These volumes certainly must be said to answer their descriptions admirably. The reader will find in them studies in the history of the Church in a series of short chapters which are always interesting and often very picturesque.'

THE AGE OF HILDEBRAND.
By Professor M. R. VINCENT, D.D.

THE GREAT WESTERN SCHISM.
By CLINTON LOCKE, D.D.

THE AGE OF THE CRUSADES.
By JAMES M. LUDLOW, D.D.

THE ECUMENICAL COUNCILS.
By Professor W. P. DU BOSE, D.D,

THE AGE OF THE RENASCENCE.
By HENRY VAN DYKE, D.D., and PAUL VAN DYKE.

THE ANGLICAN REFORMATION.
By Professor W. R. CLARK, LL.D., D.C.L., Trinity College, Toronto.   (Editor and Translator of Bishop Hefele's *Councils of the Church.*)

THE AGE OF CHARLEMAGNE.
By Professor CHARLES L. WELLS.

THE POST-APOSTOLIC AGE.
By LUCIUS WATERMAN, D.D., with Introduction by the Right Rev. H. C. POTTER, D.D., LL.D., Bishop of New York.

THE APOSTOLIC AGE.
By J. VERNON BARTLET, M.A., Oxford.

THE PROTESTANT REFORMATION.
By Professor W. WALKER, Ph.D., D.D., Hartford.

'These "ERAS" are histories that will be enjoyably read and easily remembered. . . . Professor Vincent had a great subject allotted to him, and "The Age of Hildebrand" is an altogether worthy treatment of it. . . . In "The Age of the Crusades" we have the prose version of a story familiar to most of us in the trappings of romance.   Dr. Ludlow holds the attention of his readers. . . . "The Great Western Schism" is a bright and popular résumé.'—*Literary World.*

THE TEACHING OF JESUS.

By Prof. HANS HINRICH WENDT, D.D., Jena.   Two Vols.
8vo, 21s.

'Dr. Wendt has produced a remarkably fresh and suggestive work, deserving
to be ranked among the most important contributions to biblical theology.
. . . There is hardly a page which is not suggestive ; and, apart from the
general value of its conclusions, there are numerous specimens of ingenious
exegesis thrown out with more or less confidence as to particular passages.'
—*Critical Review.*

THE KINGDOM OF GOD;

Or, Christ's Teaching according to the Synoptical Gospels.   By the
late Prof. A. B. BRUCE, D.D.   Post 8vo, Sixth Edition, 7s. 6d.

'To Dr. Bruce belongs the honour of giving to English-speaking Christians
the first really scientific treatment of this transcendent theme . . . his book
is the best monograph on the subject in existence.'—Prof. JAMES STALKER,
D.D., in the *British Weekly.*

HISTORY OF THE JEWISH PEOPLE IN THE TIME OF JESUS CHRIST.

By Prof. E. SCHÜRER, D.D., University of Göttingen.   Complete
in Five Vols. 8vo, 26s. 3d.   INDEX VOL. (100 pp. 8vo), 2s. 6d.
net.

'Every English commentary has for some years contained references to
"Schürer" as the great authority upon such matters. . . .   There is no guide
to these intricate and difficult times which even approaches him.'—*Record.*

BIBLICAL THEOLOGY OF THE NEW TESTAMENT.

By Prof. BERNHARD WEISS, Berlin.   Two Vols. 8vo, 12s. net.

'Written throughout with freshness, vigour, and perfect command of the
material. . . . This is a field which Weiss has made his own.   His work far
excels the numerous works of his predecessors in thoroughness and completeness.'—*Methodist Recorder.*

✳

NEW TESTAMENT THEOLOGY;

Or, Historical Account of the Teaching of Jesus and of Primitive
Christianity according to the New Testament Sources. By Prof.
Dr. WILLIBALD BEYSCHLAG, Halle. Two Vols. 8vo, Second
Edition, 18s. net.

'It is not only very able, but it is a truly valuable contribution to its
subject, and no one who takes upon himself to expound the deep things of
God as set forth by the New Testament writers should neglect to make an
earnest study of it, and thus enrich his ministration of the word.'—Professor
A. S. PEAKE, M.A.

A SYSTEM OF CHRISTIAN DOCTRINE.

By Prof. I. A. DORNER, D.D., Berlin. Four Vols. 8vo, 21s. net.

'Had it been the work of an entire lifetime, it would have been a monument
of marvellous industry and rare scholarship. It is a tribute alike to the
genius, the learning, and the untiring perseverance of its author.'—*Baptist
Magazine*.

JUSTIFICATION AND RECONCILIATION.

By ALBRECHT RITSCHL. Edited by Prof. H. R. MACKINTOSH,
D.Phil., and A. B. MACAULAY, M.A. Second Edition. One
large Vol. 8vo, 14s.

'At last there is provided what has been a desideratum for years—a really
reliable translation of the great dogmatic work on "Justification," by which
the most noted of modern theologians chiefly made his mark on the thinking
of his age.'—*Critical Review*.

THE PROPHECIES OF JESUS CHRIST,

relating to His Death, Resurrection, and Second Coming, and
their Fulfilment. By Dr. P. SCHWARTZKOPFF. *Authorised
Translation*. Crown 8vo, 5s.

'Deserves ample recognition as an honest, reverential, and able attempt to
solve one of the most difficult problems connected with the Person and Work
of Christ. . . . He has produced a book blossoming on every page with
suggestions, and worthy of the most serious study of theologians.'—Professor
MARCUS DODS, in the *Critical Review*.

and Published by Messrs. T. and T. Clark.

THE INTERNATIONAL CRITICAL COMMENTARY.

ST. LUKE'S GOSPEL.

By the Rev. ALFRED PLUMMER, M.A., D.D., Master of University College, Durham, formerly Fellow and Senior Tutor of Trinity College, Oxford. In post 8vo, Fourth Edition (678 pp.), 12s.

'It is distinguished throughout by learning, sobriety of judgment, and sound exegesis. It is a weighty contribution to the interpretation of the Third Gospel, and will take an honourable place in the series of which it forms a part.'—*Critical Review.*

'The best commentary on St. Luke yet published. Dr. Plummer's gifts for the work were already well known and appreciated, and he has not disappointed us in this his latest work.'—*Church Bells.*

'Marked by great learning and extreme common sense. . . . Altogether the book is far and away the best commentary on Luke we yet have in English.'—*Biblical World.*

' We feel heartily that the book will bring credit to English scholarship, and that in its carefulness, its sobriety of tone, its thoughtfulness, its reverence, it will contribute to a stronger faith in the essential trustworthiness of the gospel record.'—*Guardian.*

THE WRITINGS OF TERTULLIAN. To the NATIONS; APOLOGY; To the MARTYRS, ETC.
Three Vols.

TERTULLIAN AGAINST MARCION. One Vol.

THE WRITINGS OF IRENÆUS. Vol. I.

THE WRITINGS OF HIPPOLYTUS. Vol. I.

THE WRITINGS OF IRENÆUS (Completion) AND HIPPOLYTUS (Completion). One Vol.

The above Works are included in 'The Ante-Nicene Christian Library'; a Collection of all the Works of the Fathers of the Christian Church prior to the Council of Nicæa. Single Volumes, price 10s. 6d.; any Four Volumes, or more, at the Subscription rate of 5s. 3d. per Volume.